Lecture Notes in Computer Science 10546

Commenced Publication in 1973
Founding and Former Series Editors:
Gerhard Goos, Juris Hartmanis, and Jan van Leeuwen

More information about this series at http://www.springer.com/series/7409

Julian Szymański · Yannis Velegrakis (Eds.)

Semantic Keyword-Based Search on Structured Data Sources

Third International KEYSTONE Conference, IKC 2017
Gdańsk, Poland, September 11–12, 2017
Revised Selected Papers and COST Action IC1302 Reports

 Springer

Editors
Julian Szymański 🆔
Gdańsk University of Technology
Gdańsk
Poland

Yannis Velegrakis 🆔
Università degli Studi di Trento
Trento
Italy

ISSN 0302-9743   ISSN 1611-3349 (electronic)
Lecture Notes in Computer Science
ISBN 978-3-319-74496-4   ISBN 978-3-319-74497-1 (eBook)
https://doi.org/10.1007/978-3-319-74497-1

Library of Congress Control Number: 2018931879

LNCS Sublibrary: SL3 – Information Systems and Applications, incl. Internet/Web, and HCI

Printed on acid-free paper

This Springer imprint is published by the registered company Springer International Publishing AG
part of Springer Nature
The registered company address is: Gewerbestrasse 11, 6330 Cham, Switzerland

Preface

This book constitutes the last publication of the KEYSTONE cost action IC1302 (semantic KEYword-based Search on sTructured data sOurcEs).[1] The aim of the action was to promote scientific cooperation in the area of keyword search by combining expertise from many different related fields. As such, it involved researchers from information retrieval, natural language processing, ontology management, indexing, Semantic Web and Linked Data.

The book is divided into two parts. The first contains the papers presented at the Third International KEYSTONE Conference (IKC 2017), which was held in Gdansk, Poland, on September 11 and 12, 2017, while the second part contains a number of reports that summarize the major activities and achievements that have taken place in the context of the action.

For IKC 2017, 18 papers were accepted, of which 13 as full length, and five as short. The papers went through a reviewing process by three independent reviewers. The names of the reviewers were known to the program chairs but were kept from the authors. The conference featured two keynote talks. The first was research-oriented on the topic of "Data Cleaning in the Big Data Era." It was delivered by Paolo Papotti, an assistant professor at Eurecom—Data Science, France. The second was industry-oriented on the challenges of a data Entrepreneurs in commercial machine-learning projects. It was delivered by Jacek Kawalec from Voicelab, Poland. The conference concluded with a brainstorming panel session on ideas of how a COST action can be further improved.

Regarding the KEYSTONE activities, the current text book includes a description of the topics of the short-term scientific missions, the outcomes of the summer schools, and the results achieved within the various Work Packages. There have been four such Work Packages: (1) Representation of Structured Data Sources, (2) Keyword Search, (3) User Interaction and Keyword Query Interpretation, and (4) Research Integration, Showcases, Benchmarks, and Evaluations. Furthermore, there is a short report by the chair of the action (Francesco Guerra, University of Modena and Reggio Emilia), the vice chair, Jorge Cardoso (Huawei), the scientific coordinator, Yannis Velegrakis (University of Trento), and the dissemination coordinator, John G. Breslin (NUI Galway).

We would like to kindly thank all the reviewers and the participants for making IKC 2017 and the action in general a success. Special thanks to Francesco Guerra for the excellent coordination of the action, the WP leaders, and the Management Committee in general. We also thank Tomasz Boiński for his support and the truly professional local organization of the conference.

January 2018

Julian Szymański
Yannis Velegrakis

---

[1] http://www.keystone-cost.eu.

Organization

General and Program Committee Chairs

Julian Szymański   Gdańsk University of Technology, Poland
Yannis Velegrakis   University of Trento, Italy

Local Organization Chairs

Julian Szymański   Gdańsk University of Technology, Poland
Tomasz Boiński   Gdańsk University of Technology, Poland

Program Committee

Charlie Abela   University of Malta, Malta
Khalid Belhajjame   PSL, Université Paris-Dauphine, LAMSADE, France
Maria Bielikova   Slovak University of Technology in Bratislava, Slovakia
Tomasz Boiński   Gdańsk University of Technology, Poland
Omar Boucelma   LSIS, Aix-Marseille University, France
Peter Butka   Technical University Kosice, Slovakia
Jorge Cardoso   University of Coimbra, Portugal
Elena Demidova   L3S Research Center, Germany
Dorian Gorgan   Technical University of Cluj-Napoca Cluj-Napoca,
                        Romania
Francesco Guerra   University of Modena and Reggio Emilia, Italy
Marko Horvat   Polytechnic of Zagreb, Croatia
Dragan Ivanović   University of Novi Sad, Serbia
Georgia Kapitsaki   University of Cyprus, Cyprus
Mihai Lupu   Vienna University of Technology, Austria
Gjorgji Madjarov   Ss. Cyril and Methodius University,
                        Republic of Macedonia
Sanda Martinčić-Ipšić   University of Rijeka, Croatia
Ana Mestrović   University of Rijeka, Croatia
Paolo Missier   Newcastle University, UK
Jelena Mitrović   University of Passau, Germany
Vesna Pajić   University of Belgrade, Serbia
Alexandre Miguel   Pinto Universidade de Lisboa, Portugal
Laura Po   Universita di Modena e Reggio Emilia, Italy
Florin Pop   University Politehnica of Bucharest, Romania
Gianmaria Silvello   University of Padova, Italy
Andrzej Sobecki   Gdansk University of Technology, Poland
Raquel Trillo-Lado   Universidad de Zaragoza, Spain
Genoveva Vargas   Solar CNRS-LIG-LAFMIA, France

José R. R. Viqueira   University of Santiago de Compostela, Spain
Manolis Wallace   University of the Peloponnese, Greece

Action Organization

Coordinator and Management Committee Chair

Francesco Guerra   Università di Modena e Reggio Emilia, Italy

Vice Chair

Jorge Cardoso   Huawei Research Center, Germany

Scientific Coordinator

Yannis Velegrakis   University of Trento, Italy

Communications Coordinator

John Breslin   Insight Centre for Data Analytics, NUI Galway, Ireland

Working Group Coordinators

WG1

Stefan Dietze   L3S Research Center, Germany
Raquel Trillo Lado   Universidad de Zaragoza, Spain

WG2

Elena Demidova   L3S Research Center, Germany
Julian Szymański   Gdańsk University of Technology, Poland

WG3

Omar Boucelma   Aix-Marseille University, France
Bogdan Cautis   University of Paris-Sud, France

WG4

Paulo Rupino Cunha   University of Coimbra, Portugal
Ngoc-Thanh Nguyen   Wroclaw University of Science and Technology, Poland

Short-Term Scientific Missions Coordinators

Abdulhussain E. Mahdi   University of Limerick, Ireland

Education Activities Coordinator

Charlie Abela   University of Malta, Malta

Management Committee

Charlie Abela
Burak Acar
Vladimir Alexiev
Joel Azzopardi
Krisztian Balog
Omar Boucelma
John Breslin
Peter Butka
Andrea Calì
Jorge Cardoso
Marjan Ceh
Fabio Crestani
Tomche Delev
Elena Demidova
Gilles Falquet
Antonio Fariña Martínez
Dorian Gorgan
Yaakov HaCohen-Kerner
Preben Hansen
Yigal Hoffner
Marko Horvat
Geert-Jan Houben
Dragab Ivanovic

Georgia Kapitsaki
Innar Liiv
Gjorgji Madjarov
Abdulhussain Mahdi
Ioana Manolescu
Sanda Martincic Ipsic
Sergio Matos
Loizos Michael
Paolo Missier
Ngoc Thanh Nguyen
Kjetil Norvag
Andreas Nürnberger
Florin Pop
Michail Salampasis
Peter Schalk
Ranka Stankovic
Yannis Stavrakas
Henrik Strindberg
Julian Szymanski
Vagan Terziyan
Martin Theobald
Raquel Trillo Lado
Yannis Velegrakis

Regular Members

Miguel A. Martínez-Prieto, Spain - WG1, WG2, WG4
Wouter Addink, The Netherlands - WG1, WG2, WG3, WG4
Muhammad Ajmal, Portugal - WG1, WG3
Mocanu Alexandra, Romania - WG1, WG2, WG3, WG4
Zakariae Aloulen, France - WG1, WG2, WG3, WG4
Raquel Amaro, Portugal - WG3
Ioannis Anagnostopoulos, Greece - WG1, WG2, WG3, WG4
Petre Andreea-Cristina, Romania - WG1, WG3, WG4
José Antonio Cotelo Lema, Spain - WG1, WG2, WG4
Elena Apostol, Romania - WG1, WG2, WG4
Ghislain Atemezing, France - WG1, WG2, WG4
Gabriela Avram, Ireland - WG3
Neda B. Marvasti, Turkey - WG3
Dariusz Barbucha, Poland - WG4
Ilaria Bartolini, Italy - WG1, WG2

Besnik Fetahu, Germany - WG1, WG2, WG4
George Fletcher, The Netherlands - WG1, WG2
Andre Freitas, Ireland - WG1, WG2, WG3
Giovanni Fulantelli, Italy - WG1
Pedro Furtado, Portugal - WG1, WG2, WG3, WG4
Ujwal Gadiraju, Germany - WG1, WG4
Mehmet Gencer, Turkey - WG1, WG2, WG4
Parisa Ghodous, France - WG1, WG4
Adam Harasimowicz, Poland - WG2
Claudia Hauff, The Netherlands - WG2, WG3
Ramon Hermoso, Spain - WG1, WG2, WG3
Jan Hidders, The Netherlands - WG1, WG2, WG4
Djoerd Hiemstra, The Netherlands - WG2, WG3
Helge Holzmann, Germany - WG1, WG2, WG3
Jun Hong, UK - WG2
Atanas Hristov, Republic of Macedonia - WG1, WG4
Sergio Ilarri, Spain - WG1
Ekaterini Ioannou, Greece - WG1, WG2, WG4
Marina Ivasic-Kos, Croatia - WG1, WG2
Tomislav Jagušt, Croatia - WG1, WG2
Cheikh Kacfach Emani, France - WG3, WG4
Nattiya Kanhabua, Germany - WG2, WG3
Kristina Kapanova, Bulgaria - WG1, WG2
Olivera Kitanović, Russia - WG1, WG2, WG3
Adebayo Kolawole John, Italy - WG1, WG2, WG3, WG4
Xenia Koulouri, Greece - WG4
Aleksandar Kovacevic, Russia - WG2, WG3
Łukasz Kucharczyk, Poland - WG2
Javier Lacasta, Spain - WG1, WG2
Susana Ladra González, Spain - WG1, WG2
Colin Layfield, Malta - WG1, WG2, WG3, WG4
Chaya Liebeskind, Israel - WG1, WG2, WG3, WG4
Pedro Lopes, Portugal - WG1, WG3, WG4
Diego López-de-Ipiña, Spain - WG1, WG3
Martin Lopez-Nores, Spain - WG1, WG4
Mayte Lozano, Spain - WG1
Philipp Ludwig, Germany - WG1, WG2, WG3, WG4
Angel Luis, Spain - WG1, WG2, WG3, WG4
Mihai Lupu, Austria - WG3, WG4
Jacek M. Czerniak, Poland - WG2, WG3, WG4
Peter Macko, Slovenia - WG1, WG2, WG3, WG4
Nicholas Mamo, Malta - WG1, WG2, WG3, WG4
Federica Mandreoli, Italy - WG2
Vasile Manta, Romania - WG1, WG2
Stephane Marchand-Maillet, Switzerland - WG1, WG2, WG3, WG4
Ivana Marenzi, Germany - WG2, WG3, WG4

Teodor Stefanut, Romania - WG1, WG2, WG3, WG4
Velislava Stoykova, Bulgaria - WG1, WG2, WG3, WG4
Henrik Strindberg, Sweden - WG1, WG2, WG3, WG4
Sara Suárez Gonzalo, Spain - WG1, WG2, WG3, WG4
Rados Sumrada, Slovenia - WG2
Davide Taibi, Italy - WG1
Thanassis Tiropanis, UK - WG2, WG3
Konstantin Todorov, France - WG1, WG2, WG3
Sergio Toral Marin, Spain - WG1
Riccardo Torlone, Italy - WG1, WG2, WG3
Ciprian-Octavian Truică, Romania - WG1, WG2, WG3, WG4
Martín Ugarte, Belgium - WG1, WG3, WG4
Ricardo Usbeck, Germany - WG1, WG2, WG3, WG4
Suzan Uskudarli, Turkey - WG3
Lucia Vacariu, Romania - WG1, WG2, WG4
Stijn Vansummeren, Belgium - WG1, WG2, WG4
Genoveva Vargas-Solar, France - WG1, WG3
Iraklis Varlamis, Greece - WG2, WG3, WG4
Michalis Vazirgiannis, Greece - WG1, WG4
Athanasios Velios, UK - WG1
Bacu Victor, Romania - WG1, WG2
Lucian Vintan, Romania - WG1, WG2, WG3, WG4
Stasa Vujicic Stankovic, Russia - WG1, WG2, WG3, WG4
Nikola Vulović, Russia - WG1, WG2, WG3, WG4
Manolis Wallace, Greece- WG1, WG2, WG3, WG4
Adam Wyner, UK - WG1, WG2
Wang Xinyu, France - WG1, WG2, WG3, WG4
Pinar Yolum, Turkey - WG1, WG2, WG3, WG4
Ran Yu, Germany - WG1, WG3, WG4
Hubert Zarzycki, Poland - WG1, WG2, WG3, WG4
Sergej Zerr, Germany - WG1, WG2
Yiwei Zhou, UK - WG4
Slavko Zitnik, Slovenia - WG1, WG2, WG3, WG4

Contents

The KEYSTONE COST Action

Proceedings of the KEYSTONE Conference 2017

Formalization and Visualization of the Narrative for Museum Guides

Ioannis Bourlakos[1], Manolis Wallace[1](✉), Angeliki Antoniou[2],
Costas Vassilakis[2], George Lepouras[2], and Anna Vassiliki Karapanagiotou[3]

[1] Knowledge and Uncertainty Research Laboratory,
Department of Informatics and Telecommunications,
University of the Peloponnese, 22 131 Tripolis, Greece
{jbourlak,wallace}@uop.gr
[2] Department of Informatics and Telecommunications,
University of the Peloponnese, 221 31 Tripolis, Greece
{angelant,costas,gl}@uop.gr
[3] Ephorate of Antiquities of Arcadia,
Hellenic Ministry of Culture and Athletics,
221 31 Tripolis, Greece
akarapanagiotou@culture.gr
http://gav.uop.gr, http://dit.uop.gr, http://www.yppo.gr/

Abstract. There is a wide range of meta-data standards for the documentation of museum related information, such as CIDOC-CRM; these standards focus on the description of distinct exhibits. In contrast, there is a lack of standards for the digitization and documentation of the routes followed and information provided by museum guides. In this work we propose the notion of the *narrative*, which can be used to model a guided museum visit. We provide a formalization for the narrative so that it can be digitally encoded, and thus preserved, shared, re-used, further developed and exploited, and also propose an intuitive visualization approach.

Keywords: Narrative · Narrative segment · Guided tour
Documentation · UML · Constraints · External media · Visualization
Museum guide

1 Introduction

There are currently more than 19000 museums in Europe and even more archaeological sites [13]. And given that the preservation of cultural heritage is at the very core of the foundations of the European Union – the Lisbon treaty, a constitutional basis of the European Union, states that the Union "shall respect its rich cultural and linguistic diversity, and shall ensure that Europe's cultural heritage is safeguarded and enhanced" [14] – it should come as no surprise that in the period 2007–2013 alone the EU invested a whooping 4.5 billion EUR in cultural heritage and related research.

© Springer International Publishing AG, part of Springer Nature 2018
J. Szymański and Y. Velegrakis (Eds.): IKC 2017, LNCS 10546, pp. 3–13, 2018.
https://doi.org/10.1007/978-3-319-74497-1_1

Much of that has been directed towards digitization, producing a vast amount of digital documents. Tellingly, Europeana connects more than 50 million objects from over 3 thousand institutions, a number that continues to rise as more institutions become involved and more collections are included [15,16].

So far we have achieved maturity in documentation standards for museum content [2], with CIDOC-CRM standing out [1]. We also have at our disposal a wide range of supporting end user environments and data storage systems. As such, most museums currently possess standardized digital documentations for their collections; these documentations are often interconnected at the regional, national, or even pan-European level via Europeana.

However, there is an important aspect of museum related information that is still being overlooked by documentation standards: the design and delivery of the overall museum visit experience. This refers to the type of information that museum guides use to serve their visitors, and that makes the best museum guides stand out from the rest. As we will explain, this information, that we will call herein *narrative* is valuable, expensive, endangered and unexploited. With this in mind, in this work we shall propose a formalization for this type of information, allowing for museum guided visit plans to be documented, stored, shared and re-used. In order to maximize the utility of our proposal, we look at the narrative from the perspective of the expert that designs and delivers it, rather than the perspective of the system that stores and handles it.

The remaining of this paper is structured as follows: In Sect. 2 we explain why we examine the value of the information regarding the museum guided visit. Continuing, in Sect. 3 we follow a museum guide's approach to the design of a visit, which leads us to the specification of a typology of museum visit segments in Sect. 4. Of course, this is not the end. It is just the beginning; in Sect. 6 we discuss what we have learned from the early experience with the application of our approach, how we plan to move forward and what the future entails. Section 7 lists our concluding remarks.

2   The Value of the Narration

Museum exhibitions are, more often than not, masterful works of art and study. Archaeologists study the collections of the museum producing vast amounts of scientific documentation. They also work hard to identify and select the most important, most telling and most complementary items to put on display. Then museologists study the selected items and their documentation, take into consideration the architecture of the space as well as the characteristics of the expected audience, and design the exhibition. Everything, from the placement of each exhibit, to the accompanying short text, and from the direction of the light to the most probably route a visitor will follow, are carefully thought out in order to provide the best possible museum visit experience.

All this is included in the price of the entrance ticket, and everyone who has entered the museum can enjoy it at no additional cost. Still, visitors find it reasonable to pay additional amounts for the services of a museum guide; clearly, these visitors acknowledge that the guided tour, with all the carefully selected bits and pieces of stimulating information, and the guide's captive performance, adds **value** to their overall experience.

But how does the guided tour come to be? Its basis is information that is already publicly available, most commonly in books, some times also in on-line sources. A museum guide will go through vast amounts of information about the items on display and will make a selection of what to present. This selection will typically consist of fine a balance of "important" archaeological and historical facts, entry level archaeological observations to facilitate involvement, anecdotes and even jokes to break the flow of scientific information and avoid mental overload and links to the audience's background, profession, age group etc. to stimulate engagement and reflection. And then, after every distinct delivery of the content, the museum guide uses the direct or indirect feedback of what worked well with the audience and what did not, in order to further enhance the guided tour for the next group. Overall, a museum guide's plan for a visit is something that starts with many hours of study and planning and is further developed over a longer period of time. It is therefore an **expensive** good, the creation and refinement of which require considerable resources.

Most guides start with a core text of their narration, in the form of a typed document. This document is printed out, and although not always visible to the audience is typically readily available to the guide. At the end of guided tours, particularly after the first times that a narration is used, guides will add handwritten notes about possible enhancements to the content itself or even the way it is delivered. Over time, these notes become the guides' most cherished and valuable professional property, as it is these notes that allow them to delivery their guided tours, serving as the script of a performance that is planned to the detail. But this script, in its refined form, is typically available in a single printed copy with additional handwritten notes. And thus, it runs the **danger** of being destroyed, stolen or lost. And even if the script is not lost before that, it is certainly lost when a museum guide retires.

The information documenting each exhibit separately, or a collection as a whole, is typically stored in a standardized, digital form. Thus, it can be searched, shared, reused and/or combined with other sources. It would be very interesting to be able to perform similar actions based on the narratives. For example, it would be interesting to be able to search for exhibits that are chosen for tours of specific topics, or to automatically identify the most popular items. As long as the narrative is not standardize and non digital, this information cannot be harvested and further **exploited**.

In summary, the way things stand now, the narrative of guided tours has a great value and is expensive to develop, but it runs the danger of perishing and it is not being fully exploited.

Related works in the field focus more in aspects such as (a) content editing and resource management for narratives (e.g. the Storyspace platform [7]), (b) digital and informational enhancement of narratives (e.g. [8]), and (c) educational goals and performance (e.g. [9,10]). These aspects related to the notion of the narrative are nonetheless rather important. However, we notice the lack of focus on a documentation format for the representation, preservability and interchange of narratives.

Motivated by these observations, in this work we set out to specify an extensible documentation format that will allow narratives to be digitally encoded, and, thus, preserved, shared, re-used, further developed and exploited, while they retain their original structure, their educational goals, their various constraints, and their relevance to external resources.

3   The Narrative

A good museum guide is a combination of many things. An educator, that educates the audience about the content and value of the observed exhibitions; a performer, that delivers a presentation in a lively and captivating manner; a psychologist, that is able to detect and adopt to the moods of the audience. And, most importantly, a museum guide is a contractor, that provides guided tours under a strict and unforgiving constraint: time.

Any other deviation may be forgiven, or even go unnoticed; but regardless of what happens between the beginning and the end of a guided tour, the overall duration of the tour must always be exactly what was agreed and what the audience - who are also the paying visitors - have purchased.

Thus, when setting out to design a new museum tour, the guide starts by developing different segments, such as specific exhibits of interest. The narration of the respective presentation is written to every detail, tested and timed, so that the guide knows the exact duration each segment requires.

Finally, the guide strings together the different segments in a convenient sequence, for example taking into consideration the physical location of the

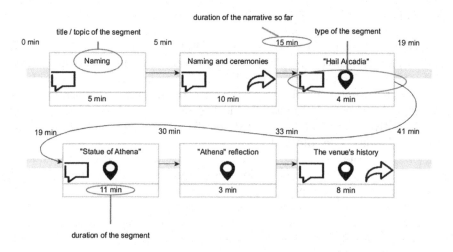

Fig. 1. The general structure of a museum visit guide's notes

exhibits. Depending on whether the overall duration is too long or too short, the guide may edit the narrations or even add or remove segments altogether.

The final design of the tour is a well scripted scenario of a sequence of steps. An intuitive way to visualize the narrative is shown in Fig. 1. Here the narrative is depicted as a sequence of boxes, corresponding to segments, each one readily displaying the most important information about it: the type, topic and duration. The cumulative duration up to each segment is also displayed, as this is the most important information for the museum guide at the time of the delivery of the guided tour.

The full description of the narrative also includes the goals or learning objectives, in the case of education oriented tours, the constraints, such as not suitable for rainy days if it is for an outdoors venue, the audience characteristics, such as maximum size of group, typical ages, countries of origin, cultural background etc., and the bibliographic sources the narrative is based on.

In the following section we examine in more detail the different types of segments that a museum guide may consider, their characteristics, and the way to visualize them.

4   Segment Typology and Visualization

A segment is a part of the narrative which accomplishes a certain sub-goal (i.e. *title*) of the narrative, in a given time frame (i.e. *duration*); it is performed under certain conditions and it can be characterized essentially by three main attributes:

- the rendition of a self-contained narration fragment (hereafter *narration*),
- the presence of a certain exhibit or point-of-interest (hereafter *exhibit*), and
- the requirement for the participants to physically move in order to proceed with the itinerary (hereafter *movement*).

The *narration*, *exhibit*, and *movement* attributes are essentially orthogonal. Their presence or absence can vary independently and their combinations represent respectively varying situations during a narrative. Thus, we have the following eight possible types of segments:

- Narration and exhibit. This is the most commonly used segment. It corresponds to the narration delivered while observing an exhibit.
- Only narration. This is a typical segment for the beginning of the narrative, where an overall introduction is given before the actual tour of the exhibits starts.
- Narration, exhibit and movement. When presenting considerably larger objects, as for example the outside of a temple, the guide may talk to the audience while walking with them so that they can see it from different sides.
- Narration and movement. Guides will sometimes talk to their audience while moving between sections. This is more common in outdoor tours where distances between different points of interest are bigger.

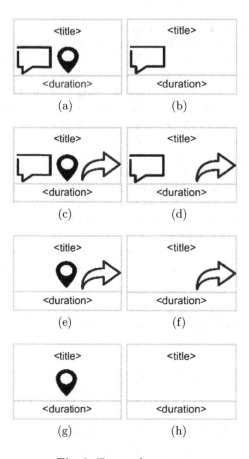

Fig. 2. Types of segments

- Exhibit and movement. Similar to the narration, exhibit and movement combination, this type of segment is typically used in outdoor setting, when the guide moves the group so that they can observe a larger object from different points of view.
- Only movement. The most common way to move between different sections is by having the audience follow the guide. Moving in this manner is considerably faster than, for example, the combination of movement and narration.
- Only exhibit. This is when the guide gives the audience some time to observe an exhibit.
- None of the three attributes. This is a valid segment that is used in guided tours of considerably longer duration. It corresponds to a break.

These combinations can offer valuable information at a high-level design of a narrative. We utilize the expressiveness of the three attributes to visualize a segment and, by extension, a narrative.

We visualize a segment using a rectangle box. If the given segment involves narration, we add a chat-bubble shape at the bottom-left side of the box; see Fig. 2(b). If the segment should be performed at a certain exhibit, we add a point-marker shape at the bottom-center part of the box; see Fig. 2(g). And, if the segment requires movement, we add an arrow shape at the bottom-right side of the box; see Fig. 2(f).

We have chosen three visually discrete portions of the segment box (i.e. bottom-left, bottom-center, and bottom-right) as placeholders for the respective attribute glyphs in order to emphasize on their orthogonality and to facilitate the visual existence or absence of each attribute.

As we saw in the previous section, the top of the rectangle is used to depict the title/topic of the segment and just below the rectangle we depict the expected duration. In addition to these, the full description of a segment may also include the text of the narration, supplementary visual aids that may be used and their timing in the narration, constraints and, optionally, the goals or learning objectives. The bibliography upon which the narration has been based may also be noted.

5   UML Representation and XML Specification

Following the description of our core concepts of *narrative, segment, narration* and *narration part*, we have designed a UML class diagram that illustrates their relationships and includes the mandatory information for their definition.

A narrative is initially defined by a title, educational goals, a description, the language of its content and the venue at which it may take place. Additionally, it may contain descriptions of its accompanying bibliography and a set of constraints.

A narrative must include an ordered collection of narrative segments. A *segment* is a partially autonomous part of the narrative that it may represent various types of steps in a narrative trail, the way we presented in Sect. 3. As such, it may be defined primarily by a combination of an exhibit, a narration performance and/or a movement requirement. Additionally, it should have a certain duration and it might be marked as optional (i.e. it may be skipped in certain performances). A segment may also include its own specific bibliography. A segment may define its own set of constraints or constraint overrides to the overall narrative (e.g. inaccessible exhibits due to restoration processes, or due to weather conditions in semi-open venues).

In our proposed formalization of narrative, the narration that may be performed during a segment is composed by certain *narration parts*. A *narration part*, in its simplest form, may contain a certain part of the text that a narrator would perform. The whole text of the narration may be divided in more than one parts in order to be precisely related to external *media* (e.g. images, audio, maps, web-pages etc.), that may frame it.

What follows naturally is the specification of a structure or format for the encoding of the narrative. The UML class design of the narrative has been the

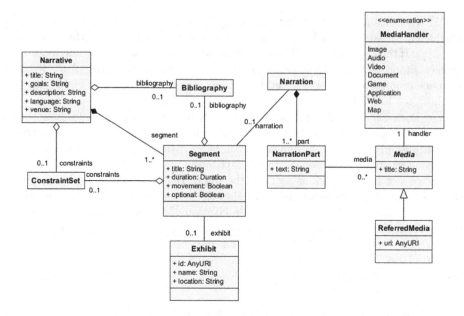

Fig. 3. UML class diagram representation of narrative's core concepts

guide for the specification of the respective XML schema. We have actually already developed an XML based syntax, described in XML Schema Definition (XSD).

The XSD schema comprises three files,

- `narrative.xsd` which contains the definitions for `Narrative`, `Segment`, `Narration` and `NarrationPart` elements,
- `types.xsd` which contains the definitions for general types such as `Bibliography`, `Media`, `Exhibit`, `Author`, etc., and,
- `constraints.xsd` which contains the extensible definition for `Constraint` elements, and utility types such as `ConstraintSet` that represents a certain collection of constraints, and `ConstraintDomain` that acts as a semantical package and namespace of constraints (e.g. physical environment constraints, audience constraints etc.).

We do not include the detailed schema here because (a) it is rather trivial and uninteresting given the detail of the description of the structure and contents given in Sects. 3 and 4 and (b) the size of the schema file makes it impossible to include it in this paper. The interested reader can refer to the file on our site: http://gav.uop.gr/docs/ikc2017files/.

6   Lessons Learned and the Way Forward

Although we sincerely believe there is a utility in the visualization approach described in the previous sections, especially in narrative flow and time management, we do not see it as the core contribution of this work. What we feel brings the most potential is the structuring and formalization of the narrative.

We have been applying our approach in a real life setting in the context of the CrossCult project [3]. The CrossCult project aims to help European citizens understand and perceive their common past and present in an holistic manner, while fostering retention and promoting reflection. To this end, the CrossCult project adopts guidelines formulated in recent research [5,6] regarding the design of the interactive experiences and their narratives. With narratives being such a central part of the project, we were in need of a way to describe narratives, as well as of a way to quickly review and compare large numbers of them; hence the motivation for this work.

A standardized, simple and structured formulation of the narrative makes it easier to share but also to co-develop narratives. The digital format also allows for searches that were not possible before, such as "which exhibits are visited when discussing ancient medical practices?" or "which exhibits are shared between most guided tours?".

When it comes to the visualization, we notice that, simply by observing the visualization of the narrative, it is quite easy to identify the route that the group will follow. Thus, by quickly reviewing the visualizations of all the active narratives at a given time, one can easily identify (a) points where congestion might occur and (b) parts of the museum that are less visited; this last part can be used to select areas to use for additional activities or to specify which other narratives could be activated without a problem.

What is perhaps more telling of the potential, is the fact that the digital storage of the narrative has permitted us to use the same narrative, unaltered, in three different contexts:

- In the project's native tablet application.
- Delivery by a human guide (Fig. 4(b))
- In an experimental setting using Google Cardboards (Fig. 4(a) and [4])

And any feedback received from either of these application settings is used to update the joint narrative, thus also reflecting upon the other application settings as well.

(a)   (b)

Fig. 4. Different modes of delivery of the same narrative

Moving forward, our first plan is to develop a graphical user interface, based on the visualization approach presented herein, to enable the documentation of narratives from the guides themselves, without the need for technical support. Based on that, we may see larger numbers of documented and digitized narratives, a trend we hope will one day lead to open source narratives.

7 Conclusions

In this paper we focused on the valuable, expensive, endangered and vastly unexploited treasures of the narratives of guided museum tours. We proposed a formalization for the narrative, that directly leads to its digitization, and an intuitive visualization.

Both have opened new ways: the visualization in the direction of understanding how the narrative works in the space of the museum and co-exists with other narratives and the formalization in the direction of storing, searching, sharing, co-editing and re-using the different settings and contexts.

Closing, we should mention that term "narrative" have been used before, in the setting of games and storytelling [11,12], but with a different meaning than the one considered in this work.

Acknowledgments. We gratefully acknowledge support from the following projects:

This work has been partially supported by COST Action IC1302: Semantic keyword-based search on structured data sources (KEYSTONE).

This work has been partially funded by the project CrossCult: "Empowering reuse of digital cultural heritage in context-aware crosscuts of European history", funded by the European Union's Horizon 2020 research and innovation program, Grant#693150.

References

1. Doerr, M.: The CIDOC conceptual reference module: an ontological approach to semantic interoperability of metadata. AI Mag. **24**(3), 75–92 (2003)
2. Cataloguing Cultural Objects Commons: What Is CCO? (2017). http://cco.vrafoundation.org/index.php/aboutindex/. Accessed 10 June 2017
3. Vassilakis, C., Antoniou, A., Lepouras, G., Wallace, M., Lykourentzou, I., Naudet, Y.: Interconnecting objects, visitors, sites and (hi)stories across cultural and historical concepts: the CrossCult project. In: Ioannides, M., Fink, E., Moropoulou, A., Hagedorn-Saupe, M., Fresa, A., Liestøl, G., Rajcic, V., Grussenmeyer, P. (eds.) EuroMed 2016. LNCS, vol. 10058, pp. 501–510. Springer, Cham (2016). https://doi.org/10.1007/978-3-319-48496-9_39
4. Theodorakopoulos, M., Papageorgopoulos, N., Mourti, A., Antoniou, A., Wallace, M., Lepouras, G., Vassilakis, C., Platis, N.: Personalized augmented reality experiences in museums using Google cardboards. In: 12th International Workshop on Semantic and Social Media Adaptation and Personalization (SMAP 2017), Bratislava, Slovakia, 9–10 July 2017
5. Berglund, S., Ekman, J., Deegan-Krause, K., Knuten, T. (eds.): The Handbook of Political Change in Eastern Europe. Edward Elgar Publishing, Cheltenham (2013)

6. Burton, A.: A Primer for Teaching World History: Ten Design Principles, p. 2011. Duke University Press, Durham (2011)
7. Wolff, A., Mulholland, P., Collins, T.: Storyspace: a story-driven approach for creating museum narratives. In: Proceedings of the 23rd ACM Conference on Hypertext and Social Media (HT 2012), pp. 89–98. ACM, New York (2012)
8. Ross, C., Hudson-Smith, A., Warwick, C., Terras, M., Gray, S.: Enhancing museum narratives: tales of things and UCL's grant museum. In: The Mobile Story: Narrative Practices with Locative Technologies, pp. 276–289, September 2013. https://doi.org/10.4324/9780203080788
9. Garoian, C.R.: Performing the museum. Stud. Art Educ. **42**(3), 234–248 (2001). https://doi.org/10.1080/00393541.2001.11651700
10. Callaway, C., Stock, O., Dekoven, E., Noy, K., Citron, Y., Dobrin, Y.: Mobile drama in an instrumented museum: inducing group conversation via coordinated narratives. New Rev. Hypermedia Multimedia **18**(1–2), 37–61 (2012). https://doi.org/10.1080/13614568.2012.617844
11. Charles, F., Lozano, M., Mead, S.J., Bisquerra, A.F., Cavazza, M.: Planning formalisms and authoring in interactive storytelling. In: Proceedings of TIDSE (2003)
12. Kybartas, B., Bidarra, R.: A semantic foundation for mixed-initiative computational storytelling. In: Schoenau-Fog, H., Bruni, L.E., Louchart, S., Baceviciute, S. (eds.) ICIDS 2015. LNCS, vol. 9445, pp. 162–169. Springer, Cham (2015). https://doi.org/10.1007/978-3-319-27036-4_15
13. EGMUS: European Group on Museum Statistics. http://www.egmus.eu/. Accessed 10 June 2017
14. Treaty of Lisbon amending the Treaty on European Union and the Treaty establishing the European Community, Official Journal of the European Union, vol. 50, notice no. 2007/C 306/01 (2007)
15. Purday, J.: Think culture: Europeana.eu from concept to construction. Electron. Libr. **27**(6), 919–937 (2009)
16. Europeana Collections. http://www.europeana.eu/portal/en. Accessed 10 June 2017

Data Reduction Techniques Applied on Automatic Identification System Data

Claudia Ifrim[1], Iulian Iuga[2], Florin Pop[1], Manolis Wallace[3]([⊠]),
and Vassilis Poulopoulos[3]

[1] Faculty of Automatic Control and Computers Computer Science Department,
University Politehnica of Bucharest, Bucharest 060042, Romania
claudia.ifrim@hpc.pub.ro, florin.pop@cs.pub.ro
[2] Bucharest, Romania
[3] Knowledge and Uncertainty Research Laboratory
Department of Informatics and Telecommunications,
University of the Peloponnese,
22 131 Tripolis, Greece
{wallace,vacilos}@uop.gr
http://acs.pub.ro/
http://gav.uop.gr

Abstract. In recent years, the constant increase of waterway traffic generates a high volume of Automatic Identification System data that require a big effort to be processed and analyzed in near real-time. In this paper, we analyze an Automatic Identification System data set and we propose a data reduction technique that can be applied on Automatic Identification System data without losing any important information in order to reduce it to a manageable size data set that can be further used for analysis or can be easily used for Automatic Identification System data visualization applications.

Keywords: AIS data · Data reduction techniques · Data analysis
AIS data visualization · Intelligent transport systems

1 Introduction

The Automatic Identification System (AIS) is an automated tracking system used on ships and by vessel traffic services (VTS) for identifying and locating vessels by digitally broadcasting information such as unique identification of the ship, position, course, speed or navigation status in an interval of seconds to other nearby ships, AIS base stations and satellites [1].

AIS is intended to assist a vessel's watch-standing officers and allows maritime authorities to track and monitor vessel movements. On board, it is integrated with other navigation aids, such as: Global Positioning System (GPS),

---

I. Iuga—Independent Researcher.

© Springer International Publishing AG, part of Springer Nature 2018
J. Szymański and Y. Velegrakis (Eds.): IKC 2017, LNCS 10546, pp. 14–19, 2018.
https://doi.org/10.1007/978-3-319-74497-1_2

Radio Detection And Ranging (RADAR), Electronic Chart Display Information System (ECDIS), Voyage Data Recorder (VDR), Automatic Radar Plotting Aid (ARPA) and other electronic navigation sensors.

Despite the constant increase of waterway traffic, we still don't have a global integrated monitoring and surveillance policy (or a unique standard) for sea traffic. This policy could offer us a solution for an efficient management of the increasing traffic and a better planning of resources. Tracking and monitoring commercial and recreation vessels (that requires to have an AIS equipment on board) on waterways represents an important issue for national security, economic and environmental sectors.

AIS data retrieved by AIS base stations or satellites is stored in data stations for current and future use. The massive amount of AIS data can easily overload a database and the storage system in a short period of time, leading to an increase of the processing and querying time.

In our paper we propose a reduction technique that can be applied on AIS data sets in order to reduce its size without compromising important information about the monitored vessels on waterways. Using a manageable sized AIS data set, applications that use historic and real-time AIS data can improve their performances by decreasing their response time to queries by processing fewer records that provide the same quality for their responses.

The rest of the paper is organized as follows: Sect. 2 describes what types of errors can be detected on AIS data and how can we treat or correct them; Sect. 3 presents a technique to reduce the amount of data without loosing important informations regarding our monitored vessels; in Sect. 4 we present our obtained results using the proposed reduction technique on our AIS data set and Sect. 5 discusses the main conclusions obtained and planned future work.

2   AIS Data Pre-processing

AIS data is reported as ASCII data packets as a byte stream using the NMEA 0183 or NMEA 2000 data formats. AIS packets have the introducer "!AIVDM" (reports from other ships) or "!AIVDO" (reports from the "own" ship). A standard about the AIVDM/AIVDO messages is [9]. This was expanded and clarified by [10]. The ASCII format for AIVDM/AIVDO representations of AIS radio messages have been set by [11]. An example of a typical AIVDM data packet is:

!AIVDM,1,1,,B,177KQJ5000G?tO'K¿RA1wUbN0TKH,0*5C

The meaning of each field is:

- Field 1, !AIVDM, identifies this as an AIVDM packet.
- Field 2 (1 in this example) is the count of fragments in the message.
- Field 3 (1 in this example) is the fragment number of this sentence, one based.
- Field 4 (empty in this example) is a sequential message ID for multi-sentence messages.

- Field 5 (B in this example) is a radio channel code. AIS uses the high side of the duplex from two VHF radio channels: AIS Channel A is 161.975 Mhz (87B); AIS Channel B is 162.025 Mhz (88B). Codes 1 and 2 may also be encountered instead of A or B.
- Field 6 (177KQJ5000G?tO'K¿RA1wUbN0TKH in this example) is the data payload.
- Field 7 (0) is the number of fill bits requires to pad the data payload to a 6 bit boundary, ranging from 0 to 5.
- The *-separated suffix (*5C) is the NMEA 0183 checksum for the sentence, preceded by "*".

There are 27 AIS messages types, but the most used in the wild are the position reports. By regulations the frequency of messages vary and can be analyzed at http://www.itu.int/rec/R-REC-M.1371/en.

In our data reduction technique we will consider the messages 1, 2, 3 (Position Reports), 18 (Standard Class B equipment position report)and their extended data 5 (Ship static and voyage related data), 19 (Extended class B equipment position report), 24 (Static data report). Message 4 (Base Station Report) will be treated just to display the general geographic distribution of Base Stations.

The following library was used for decoding AIS stream, see https://github.com/schwehr/libais/tree/master/src/libais mC++ decoder for Automatic Identification System for tracking ships and decoding maritime information. Some extensions have been added to deploy the data in a convenient structure for this task.

Some information was eliminated as an initial cleanup:

- Coordinates greater that 180, −180 latitude and 90, −90 longitude
- The 0,0 location. As it is a real possibility that a ship can be in the 0,0 lat long spot it can be there for a specific amount of time. Usually the 0,0 messages are generated by instrumentations errors (eg. lost GPS connections).

3   AIS Data Reduction

Analyzing our AIS data set we observe that the records number can reach more than 2 million per month. Considering the increased number of vessels that install AIS devices on board, the number of records that will be stored can only increase and the only solution that we have is it to propose a reduction technique that could be applied on AIS data records in order to reduce its size without loosing any valuable informations and to be able to optimally store and query historic AIS data.

We know that all AIS broad-casted messages transmit three basic elements of information: MMSI number, message type, a repeat indicator designed for repeating messages over obstacles by relay devices.

We also know that AIS Message 1, 2, 3 (Position Report Class A) reports navigational information (longitude and latitude, time, heading, speed, ships navigation status) and AIS Message 5 contains static and voyage related data of the ship (entered by hand).

The first step is to identify the attributes within the data that can be used to reduce the number of AIS data records.

Analyzing the messages transmitted by a single vessel on a specific voyage, we can observe that the only attributes that are constantly changing are the ship location and the timestamp. We also observe that after a period on time attributes like speed and heading are also changing. Based on our observations on the AIS data set we conclude that the attributes location, speed, heading and timestamp can be used to develop our reduction algorithm. The attributes location, speed (if < 0.1 knots) and timestamp bring us informations regarding vessel's stops on it's route and their duration. The attributes location and heading let us discover if a vessel is traveling in a straight line or if it is changing it's direction and give us enough information in order to recreate the vessel's path from the starting point to the destination.

The proposed reduction technique compares all the records from the AIS data set. In this stage, we will mark redundant records as unimportant. We will set some tolerance values for our attributes and we will test the results obtain in order to better adjust them to our data set.

In the first step we will extract all the unique MMSI values. For every unique MMSI value we will extract all it's records in chronological order. The first record is considered a relevant record and it's values for attributes like long, lat, speed, heading and timestamp are used as base values for further comparisons.

Iterating through all the records of the MMSI we will compare the selected attributes values. If the values of lat, long and timestamp are equal the record is considered duplicate and is marked as unimportant. If the values are different we will compare the speed and heading. If those values are higher than our tolerance values compared to the base attribute values, then the record will be considered important and marked accordingly. The values used for further comparisons will be updated with the ones of the latest record marked as important. The process will continue until all the records are compared and marked accordingly.

4   Results

The AIS data set that we used for our experiments contains informations gathered from Black Sea area and contains 136 008 000 records - no preprocessing applied on the initial data set. In order to store the data we used a PostgreSQL database with PostGIS extension.

In the following subsections we will present the results obtained after we detect and correct the errors on our AIS data set and applied the reduction technique presented in Sect. 3 and finally we will compare the data visualization of our data set before (Fig. 1(a)) and after the reduction was applied (Fig. 1(b) and (c)).

4.1   Data Reduction Applied on AIS Data Set

Our initial dataset contained 136 008 000 records (area Constanta port, Romania) and some informations were excluded as an initial cleanup (mentioned in Sect. 2), and after this correction we reduced the amount of records with 20%.

For this set we followed the algorithm described in Sect. 3 using different parameters for speed and heading of the vessels. The results obtained are presented in Table 1.

Table 1. Initial records vs. reduced records

Initial number of records	Unique MMSI	Speed difference param	No. of records after reduction
752 552	458	Less than 0.1	248 743
752 552	458	Less than 0.15	204 338
752 552	458	Less than 0.2	202 248
752 552	458	Less than 0.5	187 881
752 552	458	Less than 1	177 845

In the following section we will show some visualization of our dataset on the map, in order to easily compare the results obtained after applying our data reduction algorithm.

We observed that the reduced data still preserve unaltered information about the position, speed, heading and path of a vessel and the number of records are substantial reduced.

4.2   Data Visualization

In this section we present the visualization of the initial dataset, the visualization of the reduced dataset using different parameters for the speed difference and in the last image we will have a representation of the initial dataset compared with the reduced dataset resulted after we applied our reduction algorithm.

(a) Initial dataset - density map   (b) Speed difference less than 0.2   (c) Speed difference less than 0.5

Fig. 1. Visualization of the reduced dataset

5 Conclusions

As a conclusion for our experiment we consider that our reduction algorithm can be successfully used on AIS datasets (we preserve unaltered information for speed, heading, position and path of vessels) and the reduced information can be easily managed by applications that can be used in ports for the organization and planning of maritime traffic especially within ports or other dense traffic areas.

We also plan to improve our reduction algorithm by reducing data based on timestamp differences and we also want adapt it for real-time data streams.

Acknowledgments. This work has been partially supported by COST Action IC1302: Semantic keyword-based search on structured data sources (KEYSTONE); we particularly acknowledge the support of the grant COST-STSM-IC1302-36978: "Curating Data Analysis Workflows for Better Workflow Discovery".

References

1. What is the Automatic Identification System (AIS)? https://help.marinetraffic. com/hc/en-us/articles/204581828-What-is-the-Automatic-Identification-System-AIS-
2. Lanitis, A., Taylor, C.J., Cootes, T.F.: Automatic face identification system using flexible appearance models. Image Vision Comput. **13**(5), 393–401 (1995)
3. Harati-Mokhtari, A., et al.: Automatic Identification System (AIS): data reliability and human error implications. J. Navig. **60**(3), 373–389 (2007)
4. Automatic identification system. https://en.wikipedia.org/wiki/Automatic_identification_system
5. Wang, J., et al.: A new automatic identification system of insect images at the order level. Knowl.-Based Syst. **33**, 102–110 (2012)
6. http://www.navcen.uscg.gov/
7. Greene, M.: Radio frequency automatic identification system. U.S. Patent No. 5,204,681, 20 April 1993
8. https://github.com/trendmicro/ais
9. ITU Recommendation M.1371, Technical Characteristics for a Universal Shipborne Automatic Identification System Using Time Division Multiple Access [ITU1371]
10. IALA Technical Clarifications on Recommendation ITU-R M.1371-1
11. IEC-PAS 61162–100, "Maritime navigation and radiocommunication equipment and systems" [IEC-PAS]

FIRE: Finding Important News REports

Nicholas Mamo$^{(\boxtimes)}$ and Joel Azzopardi

University of Malta, Msida MSD 2080, Malta
{nicholas.mamo.14,joel.azzopardi}@um.edu.mt

Abstract. Every day, an immeasurable number of news items are published. Social media greatly contributes to the dissemination of information, making it difficult to stay on top of what is happening. Twitter stands out among popular social networks due to its large user base and the immediateness with which news is spread.

In this paper, we present a solution named Finding Important News REports (FIRE) that exploits the information available on Twitter to identify and track breaking news, and the defining articles that discuss them. The methods used in FIRE present context-specific problems when dealing with the micro-messages of Twitter, and thus they are the subject of research.

FIRE demonstrates how Twitter's conversation habits do nothing to shackle the detection of important news. To the contrary, the developed system is able to extract newsworthy stories that are important to the general population, and do so before Twitter itself. Moreover, the results emphasize the need for reliable and efficient spam and noise filtering tools.

Keywords: Twitter · Emerging topic detection and tracking
Spam filtering

1 Introduction

As technology becomes more widespread, and we embrace the information age, the content that is available and published at any point in time becomes decreasingly consumable. News items are covered multiple times, from different facets, and with varying degrees of biases. However, all items contribute something to a story. This makes it all the more difficult for netizens to stay on top of the news that is developing around them. In addition, readers are buried under piles of information, most of which is irrelevant to their interests.

Extracting important news items is thus a vital step in deciding what drives conversations, and doing this in a timely manner is critical in identifying news stories as they break. At the end of the day, it is up to the consumers themselves to filter this data, identifying what they deem to be important from an overwhelming number of articles published at all times of the day. This calls for an automated system that achieves this objective automatically and using the means and networks at its disposal.

© Springer International Publishing AG, part of Springer Nature 2018
J. Szymański and Y. Velegrakis (Eds.): IKC 2017, LNCS 10546, pp. 20–31, 2018.
https://doi.org/10.1007/978-3-319-74497-1_3

All of this information exists in a world that is more connected than ever before, with more than 2.7 billion people present on at least one social network by January 2017[1]. Of these, a few networks stand out, including Facebook and Twitter. Our project, *Finding Important News REports* (FIRE), uses the Twitter stream to identify interesting and newsworthy stories in a timely manner, allowing users to stay on top of emerging news. In doing so, the tedious filtering task is eliminated for its users.

The proposed system's overall goal is thus to isolate the most important breaking news and events from an inundating stream of tweets, and unearth informative news reports. This is achieved through clustering, topic detection and tracking, and spam and noise removal methods.

The paper is organized as follows. Section 2 outlines relevant research. Subsequently, Sect. 3 examines the design of FIRE, and Sect. 4 goes into more detail about the implementation of the developed system. Section 5 evaluates FIRE and presents its results, before Sect. 6 draws the main conclusions.

2   Related Work

Twitter stands out among social networks thanks to a variety of characteristics - most notably its conversations consist of 140-character messages. In fact, although Twitter's user base is much smaller than Facebook's, hundreds of thousands of tweets are published every minute. Twitter's brevity means that messages can be published quickly, making the network an ideal tool to disseminate news as it unfolds. Thus, Twitter is an excellent resource to discover emerging topics. Naturally, a key distinction in topic detection is what constitutes a topic.

[1] defines a topic as a "coherent set of semantically related terms that express a single argument," emphasizing the underlying meaning of topics. More specifically, [1,2] exploit sudden peaks in keyword interests to detect breaking topics. Furthermore, the consensus is that trending news is one whose existence is longer than some expectation, and a breaking news item is recent. The concept of timing is also important in topic tracking [3].

The idea of what is important to Twitter users is also of significance. [4] models it on the subject's popularity seeing as "content that attracts large audiences can be easily propagated even if its author is not popular." FIRE adopts a definition of importance that is in line with that of interestingness, reflecting content that is being discussed by large sections of the Twitter population.

TwitterStand is one system that exploits Twitter to detect breaking news around the world similarly to FIRE [5]. [1,6] too use Twitter to detect emerging terms in real-time, but their approach limits the number of topics that they can detect, and do not track events. Moreover, these systems take too long to update, with [6] spending half an hour sampling before processing the resulting tweets. Twitter itself detects some popular topics, but this includes trends that have no news value, such as *#MyNextCarWill*.

---

[1] http://www.smartinsights.com/social-media-marketing/social-media-strategy/new-global-social-media-research/. Last accessed on April 4, 2017.

In such systems, the basic building blocks are individual tweets, but clustering is one approach that can be used to group together syntactically-similar documents to form a number of clusters [7,8]. These groups revolve around the same concepts, which is why clustering has been used to collect and detect topics in real-time [5]. However, a drawback of clustering approaches is that they usually focus on syntax, disregarding semantics. Thus, topic modelling approaches, such as LSA, have been used to extract the latent themes behind documents [9].

One popular approach is the K-Means algorithm, which splits the documents into k clusters, but this necessitates prior knowledge on the number of groups. Incremental approaches, such as the No-K-Means algorithm, work around this problem by processing documents only once, assigning them to the closest cluster as they arrive [10]. Notwithstanding this advantage, such methods still necessitate a threshold heuristic for comparisons, and due to memory requirements, a ceiling may have to be put on the number of documents or their ages [7,10].

An additional problem that comes with Twitter is spam and noise. Given the richness of Twitter, content and author features have been exploited to classify and remove noise [11]. Whereas [11] uses SVM, other classifiers exist. For example, artificial neural networks (ANN) are supervised systems comprising a set of connected nodes. They are initially trained on a set of vectors, represented by their features, and when fed new instances, deliver a classification [12].

Studies have also made use of keyword lists to filter out tweets, but spam evolves rapidly, rendering such techniques invalid quickly [13]. Thus, other studies focus on users' behaviour and social relationships to predict a user's classification [13]. Nonetheless, their large, graph-like structure renders them impractical for real-time systems built atop a constantly-evolving social network like Twitter.

Ultimately, the core of finding breaking news stories is often topic detection. [6] describes one such method that uses a term aging model to limit the amount of content in storage. The method considers breaking topics as those that are significantly more popular at present compared to the past. [1] represents this popularity by two concepts; nutrition is the keyword's quality, based on the user's authority, whereas energy is a measure of the term's emergence.

Finally, topic tracking on Twitter seems to be the least-explored category. Most applications, such as TweetDeck and Twitter, achieve this through the use of manual searches, giving users the responsibility of defining searches. However, systems that detect emerging news and track it for the duration of its existence do not seem to exist to the best of our knowledge.

3   Design

3.1   Overall System Design

The endgoal of FIRE is to determine how Twitter's potential in news dissemination can be exploited to detect and track emerging news, thus finding reports that discuss them. This system achieves this goal from a sample of tweets, and works its way towards retrieving news reports and other information relevant to the topics that are found. The process is outlined in Fig. 1.

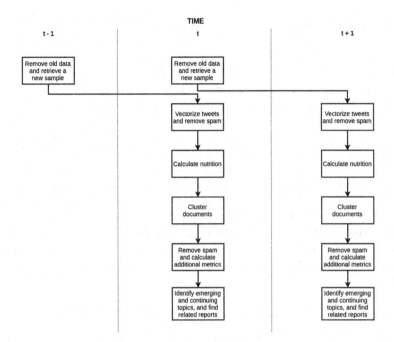

Fig. 1. FIRE's overall workflow

The process starts by removing old data, making space for a new sample to be collected from the public Twitter stream. The tweets in this new sample are then converted into vectors, and spam is removed, before nutrition is calculated for each term. Subsequently, the vectors are clustered together, and noisy clusters are removed. Finally, FIRE identifies emerging topics and performs topic tracking. The ensuing subsections will examine each component in more detail.

3.2 Sampling and Vectorization

FIRE's cycle starts off by removing old data in order to make space for the new sample. Sampling lasts five minutes, but it is not computationally intensive, allowing tweets collected in the previous time window to be processed simultaneously. During sampling, FIRE also collects features that describe tweets and their authors. The user features collected include the account age and handle, and the number of followers, followees, statuses and favorites. Metrics related to each tweet are also saved, including the tweet's ID, its text, and the lists of hashtags and mentions.

Tweets are then converted into vectors - a representation that is common in Information Retrieval (IR), and which allows comparisons using techniques like cosine similarity [10]. Thus, tweets are converted into tokens, removing stopwords and stemming words using a Porter Stemmer [14]. The user and content metrics are then stored as vector attributes using arrays, as described in Sect. 4.

FIRE also updates the document frequency table for the day. This table records the number of times each term appears across documents, and is used to calculate the Term Frequency-Inverse Document Frequency (TF-IDF). FIRE uses one such table for each of the preceding six days, which when combined serve as a background corpus, penalizing words that appear frequently. Therefore the final step is to normalize the vectors based on this combined table [9,10].

One pitfall of user-created content is spam. Therefore at this stage, the spam and noise in the sample has to be curbed to avoid spam clusters. This accelerates clustering and post-processing. Preprocessing is split into two stages.

First of all, some of the collected metrics are converted into ratios, some of which have been shown to be useful in differentiating between spam and informative content [11]. These ratios include the author's ratio of followers to followees, the author's ratio of followers to statuses, the author's average number of tweet favourites per day, and a tweet quality metric based on the rationale that the longer and more diverse a tweet is, the more expressive and descriptive it is, computed as follows:

$$quality_t = log(|tokens_t|) \cdot \frac{|unique\ tokens_t|}{|tokens_t|}, \tag{1}$$

where t is the tweet in question. Secondly, FIRE uses a set of static rules, developed through experimentation in the lack of a tagged spam corpus, to remove tweets if they are highly likely to be spam, or their authors are probably career spammers. Thus tweets are removed if they have more than two hashtags, a low quality score, or if the author has never favourited a tweet or if they have less than one follower for every thousand tweets that they published.

3.3   Nutrition and Clustering

The topic detection approach is based on the algorithm outlined in [6], and thus term nutrition is calculated next. Unlike this algorithm, FIRE's nutrition is proportional to term frequency, or the content's popularity, ignoring the author's reputation. Nutrition is defined as:

$$nutrition_k^t = \sum_{tw_j \in TW_k^t} w_{k,j}, \tag{2}$$

where $w_{k,j}$ is the TF-IDF weight of term k at time window t in the vector representation of tweet tw_j in the set of tweets TW_k^t. Nutrition is later used to detect bursts. For example Fig. 2 clearly indicates spikes in interest in South Korea and its president's impeachment, and in Düsseldorf. Having calculated the nutrition, the system proceeds to cluster the documents. Due to the real-time nature of FIRE, an adaptation of the No-K-Means algorithm detailed in [9] and explained in more detail in Sect. 4 was used to cluster tweets.

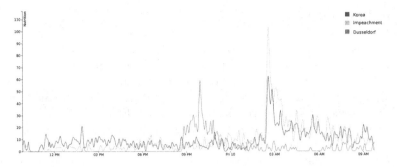

Fig. 2. The nutrition change of keywords related to the Düsseldorf axe attack and the impeachment of South Korea's President on March 9 and March 10, 2017

3.4 Spam Removal and Topic Detection

The final stage in the cycle is the choice of which clusters could harbour newsworthy topics. Topic detection is based on 'burst', which is used in [6] and related works, and which represents a measure of a keyword's importance relative to the past. In FIRE, the burst is computed over the 25 most representative vectors within each cluster, or on all vectors if the cluster is smaller, as follows:

$$burst_k^t = \sum_{x=t-s}^{t-1} ((nutr_k^t)^2 - (nutr_k^x)^2) \cdot \frac{1}{log(t-x+1)}, \tag{3}$$

where $nutr_k^t$ is the nutrition of keyword k at time window t [6]. The next step is to discard low-quality clusters to accelerate the time-consuming NLP process tasked with identifying named entities in cluster labels.

Clusters are removed if they have less than three documents or if they have high intra-similarity, if they revolve around a hashtag, the identified emerging keywords are not important within the cluster, or the average author favourites few tweets and has few followers for every status posted. A representative tweet is then selected from each remaining cluster as a label. This selection is based on a scoring mechanism that also considers the vector's similarity with the centroid since the label should be representative of its cluster:

$$q_{t,c} = log(|tok_t|) \cdot \frac{|unique\ tok_t|}{|tok_t|} \cdot sim(t, centroid_c), \tag{4}$$

where t is the tweet in question, c is the cluster that it pertains to, and $sim(t, centroid_c)$ is the cosine similarity between tweet t and the centroid of cluster c. This tweet is thus used to extract named entities, serving to explain the trend in more detail.

A neural network then uses 14 inputs split into three groups - the user metrics, the content features, and other attributes related with the topic's quality. As a result, the output is a judgement on the newsworthiness of each candidate topic. Accepted trends are cross-checked with topics that had been found to be emerging earlier to determine whether they are a continuation of an older event or new topics. Finally, reports and other information are fetched for new stories.

4   Implementation

The developed system is split into a backend that detects emerging topics, and a frontend that serves as a portal to users, ensuring that the performance is optimized on both ends. In the backend, the process starts by collecting a sample, and concludes by saving topic information, facilitating retrieval by the frontend.

Twitter provides its own developer facilities; the REST API allows developers to download tweets, whereas the Streaming API allows developers to collect tweets in real-time. It should be noted that the Streaming API's main drawback is that it only makes available a small sample of the tweets published at any given moment[2]. FIRE uses the Phirehose library[3], built atop Twitter's Streaming API to collect tweets and related metrics. Subsequently, the vectorization process derives vectors, described in Sect. 3.2, in an optimized manner.

At the vectorization stage, only non-zero components are stored using PHP arrays, based on an ordered map data structure, and the metrics described in Sect. 3.2 are saved similarly as attributes. Subsequently, the document frequency tables from the previous six days are combined and used to normalize the vectors using TF-IDF. These tables are based on a hash table and only contain the term frequencies across all documents and the number of documents included, thus avoiding having to calculate frequencies upon each request. To conclude preprocessing, noise and spam messages are removed, freeing up their space.

After calculating nutrition for each term as described in Sect. 3.3, FIRE proceeds to clustering. Tweets are grouped together using a variant of the No-K-Means algorithm described in [10]; tweet vectors are received sequentially and assigned to the closest cluster provided that similarity is over a predefined threshold. Otherwise, a new cluster is created. The algorithm also uses a freeze period to disable comparisons with inactive clusters. FIRE's only adaptation affects the freeze period, which grows proportionally with cluster sizes, allowing clusters to accrue more information. Thus, the freeze period is calculated as:

$$age_c = freeze \cdot (log(|c| + 1) + 1 - log(2))^l, \tag{5}$$

where age_c is the maximum age of cluster c, $freeze$ is the base freeze period, $|c|$ is the size of the cluster, and l is the extension coefficient. Clusters themselves are made up of the member vectors and the centroid. For optimization purposes, this centroid is also calculated incrementally:

$$centroid_{c,n} = \frac{centroid_{c,n-1} \cdot (|c| - 1) + v}{|c|}, \tag{6}$$

where $centroid_{c,n}$ is the cluster's centroid c at time period n, v is the vector being added, and $|c|$ represents the number of vectors in the cluster, including the new vector. These clusters are thus candidate emerging topics; FIRE visits

---

[2] https://dev.twitter.com/streaming/reference/get/status-es/sample. Last accessed on April 4, 2017.

[3] https://github.com/fennb/phirehose/. Last accessed on April 9, 2017.

them and calculates the burst values on the 25 most representative vectors, or on all vectors if the cluster is smaller.

An important cluster metric is the similarity score between the bursty keywords and the most important terms in the documents. This can be used to eliminate clusters whose bursty keywords are trivial. In order to achieve this, the most important terms in the cluster, equivalent to the number of bursty terms, are retrieved and compared:

$$similarity = \frac{\sum_{k \in b} |pos_{k,c} - pos_{k,b}|}{|c|^2}, \tag{7}$$

where $pos_{k,c}$ is the position of keyword k in the list of the most significant components c, or $|c|$ if it is not in this list, and $pos_{k,b}$ is the position of keyword k in the list of bursty keywords b. The system then computes additional metrics about the cluster's content authors, and discards noisy clusters. Thus, the process starts to deal with candidate topics, rather than just clusters. These topics are supplemented with additional information, such as named entities extracted from the cluster labels, before they are judged by an ANN on their newsworthiness.

The ANN adopted is a multi-layer perceptron (MLP) with 14 inputs relating to tweet, user and topic features. The MLP also contains one hidden layer with seven units, and one output. The fast computation makes MLPs suitable for the scope of FIRE. Finally, detected topics are compared to older topics found in the previous 12 hours using cosine similarity. If the new topic is deemed similar to an older story, then it is said to be a continuation of it.

In conclusion, media and news reports related to the event are retrieved using Twitter's REST API based on keyword searches, and entity information is fetched from Wikipedia to supplement the news. This information is saved as a JSON file that is available to the frontend.

5   Results and Evaluation

The modules in FIRE work together to detect emerging news. Therefore in this section, the clustering, topic detection and judgement components are evaluated.

5.1   Evaluation of the Clustering Component

The first experiments, presented in Table 1, evaluate the clustering algorithms on the corpus of tweets from [15], which revolves around events and covers a number of news categories. It should be noted that Twitter only allows developers to "distribute or allow download of Tweet IDs and/or User IDs."[4] As a result, corpora have to be downloaded anew via the REST API, but deleted tweets are irretrievable. This means that the results of other studies may not be directly comparable to FIRE's own evaluations, even if they use the same data

---

[4] https://dev.twitter.com/overview/terms/agreement-and-policy#f-be-a-good-partner-to-twitter. Last accessed on April 4, 2017.

Table 1. Comparison of results using different clustering approaches

	Precision	Recall	F1	Time (s)
K-Means	0.78	**0.51**	0.52	58127
K-Means (LSA)	0.54	0.23	0.25	77330
No-K-Means	**0.99**	0.25	0.3	57
No-K-Means (LSA)	0.8	0.47	0.45	23
No-K-Means variant	0.98	0.26	0.31	80
No-K-Means variant (LSA)	0.74	0.46	0.41	32
DBSCAN	0.99	0.33	0.4	**15**
MajorClust	0.97	0.43	**0.56**	5382

set. In this case, the corpus created in [15] contains around 79,000 tweets. The *irlba* library[5] for R was used to compute LSA on the tweets before they were clustered [16].

The K-Means algorithm was observed to perform well, perhaps because the number of events are known, which is not the case in reality. Moreover, the LSA version of the algorithm suffered the effect of having fewer dimensions, with a particularly low F1 value. DBSCAN and MajorClust - the two graph-based solutions - too achieved high precision scores, greatly contributing to high F1 scores. However, the construction of large graphs was observed to take a long time, rendering both methods unsuitable for real-time settings. Due to the memory requirements related to the construction of a graph based on the LSA documents, experimentation did not tackle these variations.

The best versions of No-K-Means, with a threshold of 0.3, took considerably less time than the alternatives, but still obtained low recall values. This arises because the process yielded many small clusters - an observation that could be a result of the absence of retweets, which make up 30% of the corpus [15] and which would be clustered together easily. LSA leads to a notable improvement; fewer dimensions coalesced tweets with similar topics, but sacrificed precision.

5.2 Evaluation of the Topic Detection Component

In the first topic detection experiment, the system collected Twitter trends in real-time between Sunday 16th April 2017 and Saturday 22nd April 2017 using the REST API. As was the case in [2], FIRE coalesces Twitter trends relating to the same event, but retains sub-topics that are picked by FIRE as well. Trends that are not newsworthy were removed. Just like in [2], the comparison is based on the precision, recall and F1 measures. The top keywords during each time window are used as a baseline. Similarly to [6], the second experiment evaluates the newsworthiness of topics by comparing results with news portals, but multiple sources are used since FIRE can detect news from all over the world.

---

[5] https://cran.r-project.org/web/packages/irlba/index.html. Last accessed on April 9, 2017.

Table 2. Comparison of topic detection results

		Precision	Recall	F1	Time (m)
US	**FIRE**	0.28	**0.45**	**0.35**	−25.1
	Cataldi	**0.47**	0.17	0.18	25.6
	Baseline	0.01	0.11	0.03	5.6
UK	**FIRE**	0.22	0.38	0.27	−**38.7**
	Cataldi	0.4	0.12	0.16	17.4
	Baseline	0.01	0.09	0.02	8.7

The precision and recall values in Table 2 indicate that FIRE and Twitter detect different topics due to various factors. For example, fewer tweets are published at night, allowing Twitter to pick up small topics that cannot be detected with the small sample available to FIRE.

The low precision values are explained by the fact that FIRE processes English tweets, capturing emerging topics from all over the world. Naturally, Twitter trends in the USA and in the UK differ, negatively affecting the results for both countries. Table 2 also displays worse performances in the UK than in the US, arising from two factors.

Firstly, Twitter collects smaller trends in the UK since there are fewer users. Secondly, primetime in the UK coincides with early afternoon in the USA, which enjoys a larger audience. On the other hand, while it is morning in the UK, Asia is in its primetime. Although not predominantly English-speaking, many English tweets still originate from Asia, making it more difficult to capture UK trends.

The results also show that FIRE is capable of detecting many trends much earlier than Twitter. In the UK, trends are detected even earlier than in the US. In fact, it is common for US trends to be picked up by UK users, but only after they appear in the USA. This time delay favours FIRE's results in the UK.

Nonetheless, the low precision values beg the question of whether the news that FIRE reports is actually newsworthy or not. The second experiment yielded an average precision of 0.87, indicating that the captured topics are newsworthy.

5.3 Evaluation of the Topic Judgement Component

Determining whether a candidate topic is spam or not is an important stage in FIRE. The evaluation compares a rule-based system and artificial neural networks, determining whether machine learning techniques are better suited at the task than rules written by a human judge.

Since the nature of this system is unique, training and test data sets comprising 1000 instances each were labelled manually using real examples. Four different ANNs were trained on these training sets - one for each group of attributes described in Sect. 3.4, and another one that used all groups. In all cases, the base structure is an MLP with one hidden layer containing half the number of inputs as hidden neurons.

Table 3. Comparison of judgement method results

	Type 1	Type 2	Correct
Rule	0.276	0.229	75%
Simple	**0.212**	0.088	**86.2%**
User	0.983	**0.007**	59.7%
Cluster	0.83	0.12	59.2%
Combined	0.281	0.066	84.7%

The results of Table 3 show how ANNs can out-perform the rule-based system. An interesting observation is that the user-based ANN returns few false positives, indicating that users offer clear indications of whether a topic is newsworthy or spam. On the other hand, both the user- and cluster-based ANNs reject many valid topics, rendering them ineffectual to decide the newsworthiness of clusters. Indeed, all approaches reject many valid topics. Different factors affect this result. For instance, as news gets shared around more, the most important keywords do not change. However, the list of emerging keywords shifts as these important terms lose burstiness. Ultimately, this leads to systems interpreting stories as being dissemination of topics that broke earlier.

6   Conclusions and Future Work

FIRE demonstrates how even a small sample of tweets and limited resources can unearth breaking news, helping individuals to identify what the world is talking about from an inundating and disorganized stream of content. In fact, the evaluation in Sect. 5.1 indicates that rather than shackling the initial process, the succinct nature of tweets helps to cluster messages that discuss the same topics. Furthermore, the evaluation in Sect. 5.2 indicates that FIRE is capable of detecting news stories before Twitter itself. Finally, Sect. 5.3 indicates the potential of the feature-rich nature of tweets in differentiating between what is truly newsworthy, and what is spam.

Nonetheless, the results obtained by FIRE call for a closer look at certain areas that hold promise to exploit all of Twitter's potential. More experimentation should be carried out with larger samples to examine how the structure performs with more content. Similarly, more experiments with additional user and content features are required to investigate further the relationship between these metrics and noisy content. Personalization can also be added to the system by processing tweets from particular countries, leading to an assessment of FIRE's potential to extract news items that are important within a country.

Notwithstanding the potential that can still be exploited by future work, the developed system is robust enough to be taken into a real-time setting. This would help identify weaknesses in the system, and thus optimize it further.

References

1. Cataldi, M., Di Caro, L., Schifanella, C.: Emerging topic detection on Twitter based on temporal and social terms evaluation. In: Proceedings of the Tenth International Workshop on Multimedia Data Mining, MDMKDD 2010, pp. 4:1–4:10. ACM, New York (2010)
2. Madani, A., Boussaid, O., Zegour, D.E.: Real-time trending topics detection and description from Twitter content. Soc. Netw. Anal. Min. **5**(1), 1–13 (2015)
3. Vosecky, J., Jiang, D., Leung, K.W.-T., Ng, W.: Dynamic multi-faceted topic discovery in Twitter. In: Proceedings of the 22nd ACM International Conference on Information & Knowledge Management, CIKM 2013, pp. 879–884. ACM, New York (2013)
4. Yang, M.-C., Rim, H.-C.: Identifying interesting Twitter contents using topical analysis. Expert Syst. Appl. **41**(9), 4330–4336 (2014)
5. Sankaranarayanan, J., Samet, H., Teitler, B.E., Lieberman, M.D., Sperling, J.: Twitterstand: news in tweets. In: Proceedings of the 17th ACM SIGSPATIAL International Conference on Advances in Geographic Information Systems, GIS 2009, pp. 42–51. ACM, New York (2009)
6. Cataldi, M., Caro, L.D., Schifanella, C.: Personalized emerging topic detection based on a term aging model. ACM Trans. Intell. Syst. Technol. **5**(1), 7:1–7:27 (2014)
7. Vadrevu, S., Teo, C.H., Rajan, S., Punera, K., Dom, B., Smola, A.J., Chang, Y., Zheng, Z.: Scalable clustering of news search results. In: Proceedings of the Fourth ACM International Conference on Web Search and Data Mining, WSDM 2011, pp. 675–684. ACM, New York (2011)
8. Legány, C., Juhász, S., Babos, A.: Cluster validity measurement techniques. In: Proceedings of the 5th WSEAS International Conference on Artificial Intelligence, Knowledge Engineering and Data Bases, AIKED 2006, pp. 388–393. World Scientific and Engineering Academy and Society (WSEAS), Stevens Point (2006)
9. Staff, C., Azzopardi, J., Layfield, C., Mercieca, D.: Search results clustering without external resources. In: 2015 26th International Workshop on Database and Expert Systems Applications (DEXA), pp. 276–280, September 2015
10. Azzopardi, J., Staff, C.: Incremental clustering of news reports. Algorithms **5**(3), 364 (2012)
11. Benevenuto, F., Magno, G., Rodrigues, T., Almeida, V.: Detecting spammers on Twitter. In: Collaboration, Electronic Messaging, Anti-Abuse and Spam Conference (CEAS) (2010)
12. Gardner, M.W., Dorling, S.R.: Artificial neural networks (the multilayer perceptron)—a review of applications in the atmospheric sciences. Atmos. Environ. **32**(14), 2627–2636 (1998)
13. Shen, H., Liu, X.: Detecting spammers on Twitter based on content and social interaction. In: 2015 International Conference on Network and Information Systems for Computers, pp. 413–417, January 2015
14. Porter, M.F.: An algorithm for suffix stripping. Program **14**(3), 130–137 (1980)
15. McMinn, A.J., Moshfeghi, Y., Jose, J.M.: Building a large-scale corpus for evaluating event detection on Twitter. In: Proceedings of the 22nd ACM International Conference on Information & Knowledge Management, CIKM 2013, pp. 409–418. ACM, New York (2013)
16. Ştefănescu, D., Banjade, R., Rus, V.: Latent semantic analysis models on Wikipedia and TASA. In: Language Resources Evaluation Conference (LREC) (2014)

Analysing and Visualising Parliamentary Questions: A Linked Data Approach

Charlie Abela$^{(\boxtimes)}$ and Joel Azzopardi

Department of Artificial Intelligence, University of Malta, Msida, Malta
{charlie.abela,joel.azzopardi}@um.edu.mt

Abstract. In many national parliaments, Members can exercise a basic Parliamentary function of holding the Executive to account by submitting Questions to Government Ministers. In certain parliaments, Members also have the faculty of either requesting a written answer or an oral one. Parliamentary Questions (PQs) often generate significant media attention and public interest, and are considered to be a very useful tool for parliamentarians to scrutinise the Government's operative and financial administration. Interesting insights about individual Members of Parliament (MPs) as well as about the Parliament as a collective institution can be gleaned by analysing PQs. In this paper we present a linked data approach to PQs that is complemented with visualisations intended to increase the accessibility, by citizens, to this rich repository of parliamentary data. We use PQ data from the Maltese Parliament ranging over the last four legislatures and present an application called *PQViz* that exploits graph analytics to expose interesting insights from this data.

Keywords: Linked data · Graph analytics · Visualisations
Parliamentary data

1 Introduction

Many national legislatures provide tools like Parliamentary Questions (PQs) intended to scrutinise the respective governments and keep them accountable [15]. Through PQs, individual Members of Parliament (MPs) table questions to the executive members of Government to scrutinise the Government's operative and financial administration. Over time, the number of questions tabled in parliament can become staggeringly high and keeping track of all the information that is found within these PQs becomes challenging. This is especially true for media in general that tend to pay considerable attention to the PQ sessions because the nature of PQs appear to generate increased level of citizens' engagement with the political process [16].

Although PQs are very central to the parliament's procedure, the content and nature of questions asked, vary considerably. It is in fact very common to find PQs related to issues specific to a particular locality that is part of the

© Springer International Publishing AG, part of Springer Nature 2018
J. Szymański and Y. Velegrakis (Eds.): IKC 2017, LNCS 10546, pp. 32–43, 2018.
https://doi.org/10.1007/978-3-319-74497-1_4

asking MP's constituency, as well as PQs that are related to issues of national importance. This leaves the specifics of the questions asked and the reasons behind them open to conjecture [14].

Yet finding information about specific topics mentioned in PQs as well as who enquired about such topics and when, is no simple feat given that the number of PQs grows with every parliamentary sitting. In the last four years of the 12th legislature, parliamentarians from the Maltese Parliament made over 31K PQs in almost 500 parliamentary sessions. This data is made accessible through a web portal[1]. Through the available interface, it is possible to apply filters over the PQ data, some of which are only useful if the user knows what to look for and/or is familiar with the whole PQ process. One such filter, filters PQs by sitting, which results in a list of parliamentary sittings that can then be expanded to display all the PQs that were asked during that sitting. Another tool available on this portal is a form-based search which requires that the user enters specific information about PQs and/or sittings, such as the PQ or sitting number, the date that a PQ was raised and who was the Minister to whom the PQ was asked. A keyword search is also available, however the result is a list of PQs that need to be expanded individually.

In this paper we report about research being conducted in the *apps4Parliament* project. This project is being done in collaboration with the Office of the Speaker (OS) within the Parliament of Malta who is the principal office holder of the House of Representatives. Through this research we intend to address some of the challenges mentioned in the previous paragraph, which are synonymous to archived data repositories. More specifically we want to provide a suite of tools to make parliamentary data more accessible and searchable for the common citizen. In this research we primarily focus on the PQ dataset and present the application entitled *PQViz*[2]. In this application:

i. PQ data is linked to MPs' profile data so that it is possible to more comprehensively display information about the MPs that asked questions and the Ministers that answered them;

ii. graph analytics and visualisations are used to leverage on the interaction between MPs from the different parties and presents an interesting, interactive visualisation through which common citizens can more intuitively understand questions like: who asked whom about what, who asked the most PQs, and who answered them.

The rest of the paper is structured as follows. In Sect. 2 we present research which is closely related to our own and in Sect. 3 we provide information about PQs from the Maltese Parliament. This is followed with a detailed description in Sect. 4, of the linked data approach adopted to link PQ data. In Sect. 5 we describe how graph analytics and visualisations are used to make PQ data more easily accessible through the *PQViz* tool. Finally, in Sect. 6 we discuss how we intend to extend this tool to cater also for topic analysis over PQ data.

---

[1] http://pq.gov.mt/.

[2] https://parlament.opendatamalta.com/pqs_V2/.

2   Related Work

Government organisations publish different kinds of data to enable transparency and satisfy their legal obligations. Through portals like that of the UK government[3], numerous datasets are being published to promote openness. This in turn has fostered the interest of the Web community which has over time became more and more intrigued with the idea of Open Government Data (OGD).

[1] states that it is important to open government data for three main reasons which include transparency, but also to release social and commercial value and to increase participatory governance. Initiatives like *Apps for Democracy*[4] and *Show Us a Better Way*[5] that promoted open data technologies have shown that OGD can be useful for different stake holders including citizens, businesses and government agencies.

There are however different challenges when opening up government data. Data content, format, structure and quality tend to vary considerably [2]. Exploring OGD is not trivial since it is imperative that the right sources are found to address the task at hand. The provision of OGD portals as reported by [1] is a step which many governments have undertaken. Such portals are intended to act as a one-stop shop to facilitate consumer's access to government data. The Global Open Data Index[6] tracks whether published data is accessible to all stakeholders and measures a global level of openness. For the local Maltese sphere the Global Open Data Index of 2013, ranked Malta 21st with a score of 52%, however the National Data Strategy for Data-Driven Public Administration that deals with the opening up of Public Sector Information (PSI) is currently still being drafted[7]. One of the first challenges that we had to obtain Parliamentary data to reuse was precisely the lack of effective open data. The PQ data available on the Maltese Parliament's portal cannot be considered to be Open Data since it is not covered by an Open Data commons licence. It is possible to reproduce without charge or further permissions from the Maltese Government and/or the Maltese House of Representatives (MHoR) provided that the reproduced material is a true copy of the original data and that MHoR are identified as being the source. Other parliaments such as the UK Parliament provide an Open Parliament licence[8] which allows for more flexibility in the way that parliamentary data can be used, reused and distributed.

Another important aspect highlighted by [5,7] is the availability of datasets that are effectively linked along the Linked Open Data (LOD)[9] principals defined by Tim Berners-Lee. The variety of data formats is however a bottleneck that needs to be addressed before interlinking the data. The most common nonproprietary formats include XML, CSV and JSON. For effective linking however,

---

[3] http://data.gov.uk.

[4] http://www.appsfordemocracy.org/.

[5] http://www.showusabetterway.co.uk/.

[6] http://index.okfn.org.

[7] https://mita.gov.mt/en/nationaldatastrategy/Documents/Data-DrivenPublic Administration(Malta).pdf.

[8] http://www.parliament.uk/site-information/copyright/open-parliament-licence/.

[9] https://www.w3.org/DesignIssues/LinkedData.html.

an ontology based approach coupled with RDF serialisation is the most popular approach [2,5,7,9]. Translation between these formats (and other related ones) and RDF was the focus of several research including [8,17,18].

Another aspect that has been found to be challenging for non-tech savvy web users is the lack of technical knowledge and understanding of the intricacies of LOD technologies. In research conducted by [4,11] the main focus was on the need for suitable visualisation tools for Linked Data (LD). The former presents a comprehensive survey discussing efforts in the Semantic Web community to visualise LD and identifies how visual tool support can lead to more effective and intuitive user interaction with LD. The latter, on the other hand, presents visual tools developed as part of the LinDA project[10], aimed at allowing SMEs to explore, visualise and analyse LOD for their daily tasks. In [13] the focus is on providing a tool called WebVOWL to visualise OWL ontologies using a force-directed graph layout. Through WebVOWL ontologies can be explored and optimised using various techniques.

OGD data related to the UK's general election was analysed in [10]. The authors used the RDF Open Cube vocabulary [3] to model multi-dimensional statistical data as RDF.

3   PQs in the Maltese Parliament

The first half hour of every parliamentary sitting of the Maltese Parliament are dedicated for questions. There are on average 65 MPs in the Maltese Parliament, however only MPs from the opposing benches and MPs from the Government's back-bench can pose questions to the cabinet[11]. Every MP is entitled to put not more than six questions for oral answers for one sitting, provided that at least three days' notice is given. A MP may also submit questions for written answers.

Answered PQs are uploaded to the PQ portal via a system that is currently based on proprietary software. A document, with amongst other things, a copy of all the PQs answered during a particular sitting is also made available on the Parliaments' website[12].

The structure of every PQ consists primarily of a PQ ID, the date when the question was made, the sitting number, the title of the question, the name of the MP that asked the question and that of the Minister that answered, the question itself and the answer given. It is not uncommon for a PQ to also have attached to it, documents that the Minister presents to Parliament to comprehensively answer the question. Listing 1.1 is an XML representation of a particular PQ with number 27059, that was asked on 29th July 2016 during sitting number 446 of the current (XII) legislature. Note that both question and answer in this example are being reproduced in English, nevertheless, Maltese PQs are saved in the native language.

---

[10] http://linda-project.eu/.

[11] Cabinet includes the Prim Minister and Ministers.

[12] A copy of the PQs asked during the sitting held on 8th March 2017 is found here: http://parlament.mt/sittingdetails?sid=5764&l=1&legcat=13&forcat=12.

```
 1  <pq>
 2  <id>C1257D2E0046DFA1C125805E00275E7E</id>
 3  <pq_written_reply>N</pq_written_reply>
 4  <reply_category_id>FINAL</reply_category_id>
 5  <pq_no>27059</pq_no>
 6  <pq_sitting_date>02/11/2016 09:00</pq_sitting_date>
 7  <pq_sitting>446</pq_sitting>
 8  <pq_raised_by_gender>M</pq_raised_by_gender>
 9  <pq_raised_by_name>ANTHONY</pq_raised_by_name>
10  <pq_raised_by_surname>AGIUS DECELIS</pq_raised_by_surname>
11  <pq_min_name>Ministy for Economy, Investment and Small Enterprises</pq_min_name>
12  <pq_minister_name>CHRIS CARDONA</pq_minister_name>
13  <pq_category_id>ORAL</pq_category_id>
14  <pq_date_raised>29/07/2016</pq_date_raised>
15  <pq_raisedby_mp_id>AGDA</pq_raisedby_mp_id>
16  <pq_addressed_to_ministry_id>EIIZ</pq_addressed_to_ministry_id>
17  <pq_heading>Commerce Licences</pq_heading>
18  <pq_legis_no>XII</pq_legis_no>
19  <pq_text>Can the Minister say how many commercial licences were issued from the year 2013
            till this date?</pq_text>
20  <reply_text> I inform the Honory Gentleman that I am placing this information on the Table
            of the House.</reply_text>
21  </pq>
```

Listing 1.1: PQ structured data

4   PQViz: Linking Parliamentary Questions

A PQ by itself is as important as the content that it includes, and even then, it is
not easy to appreciate how important is the topic, who are the players involved
(who's asking and who is answering), how many other PQs deal with the same
topic, whether other MPs have asked questions about this same topic to this
Minister or to other Ministers. For this reason tools need to be made available
so that this information can be extracted.

As pointed out in Sect. 1, the existing PQ portal does provide tools through
which this information can be extracted, yet they are not intended for the common citizen and are time consuming to use. One way that information about
PQs can be given more context and made more comprehensive is by adopting
a linked data approach [1]. This is the approach that we have adopted in the
PQViz application. The architecture of the application is depicted in Fig. 1 and
in the following sections we will discuss the challenges that we had to address,
and the solutions that we adopted to transform and link PQ data.

4.1   Harvesting Parliamentary Data

Through the collaboration with the OS we have been given access to the PQ
web service. A batch process is executed on the server side at weekly intervals
so that the system is always updated with the latest list of PQs. The format of
the PQ data is XML and is similar to the excerpt shown in Listing 1.1.

The XML of new PQs is preprocessed and cleaned to make sure that any formatting issues are resolved. The main issues that needed to be tackled included
the following:

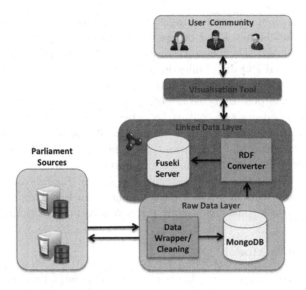

Fig. 1. PQViz architecture

- Whilst the PQ data provides an MP ID uniquely made up of the name and surname of the MP who raised the question, it did not provide a similar ID for the minister who answered the question. Only the minister's name is provided and although a ministry ID is provided, it is not uncommon that this changes when there is a change in the portfolio name, for instance after there is a cabinet reshuffle;
- There was a degree of inconsistency on the usage of MP IDs, names and ministry descriptions used. Apparently the initial data entry interface used by parliamentary staff did not enforce the use of certain specified vocabularies when inserting such data. This resulted in multiple variations of the same name/description, for example: Anġelo Farruġia and Anġlu Farruġia. There were also cases of errors in the IDs used which resulted in multiple IDs being associated to the same MP.
- No details were provided on the party membership of the MPs submitting the PQs and the ministers answering the PQs.

To address these issues, and also to simplify the querying mechanism, a separate collection was created to hold the details of every MP (including cabinet members) within each legislature. The profile data for each MP was extracted using dedicated wrappers from the relevant pages on Parliament's web portal. The pages that were scraped were those that included profile details for each MP in the current legislature, as well as pages that included details of MPs that formed part of past legislatures. The collected details included also party details, professional titles, email addresses, personal websites (when available) and contact phone numbers. Of particular interest was the information about the roles that MPs occupied, that is whether they were Ministers or Junior Ministers, when they were appointed and when they ceased to occupy those roles.

Each MP was then assigned a single unique ID that was taken from the PQ collection when available and/or otherwise generated using the templates used from the provided MP IDs. These IDs were then checked for uniqueness.

Both the MP and PQ data collections are stored in a MongoDB[13] database. We have adopted this approach primarily to have a backup of the clean data, but also to have the possibility to try out different options. In MongoDB data stored as a JSON objects and converting between XML and JSON is a straight forward process that is handled by a simple transformation class that we have implemented. Once the MPs collections are generated, the PQs collection was cleaned from errors and inconsistencies and harmonised with the details in the MPs collections. This process was performed by submitting relevant "Aggregate" queries to MongoDB on the PQs collection, and then updating the MongoDB collection to remove inconsistencies and erroneous variations in names and IDs.

4.2   Linked Data Model

The RDF Converter component shown in Fig. 1 automatically extracts the MP objects and the latest set of PQs from the MongoDB database and transforms every JSON object to RDF.

MP profile data does not usually change that often, thus this transformation process is only performed whenever some parliamentary reshuffle occurs. During the 12th legislature for example, this happened a number of times, whereby a Minister's portfolio was changed, or a Junior Minister was demoted and/or promoted.

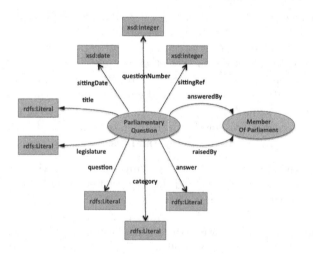

Fig. 2. PQ model

---

[13] https://www.mongodb.com/.

```
1  <rdf:Description rdf:about="&mp;mp00000">
2    <rdf:type rdf:resource="&dbo;MemberOfParliament"/>
3    <foaf:name>Jesmond Mugliett</foaf:name>
4    <foaf:title>Mr</foaf:title>
5    <foaf:firstName>Jesmond</foaf:firstName>
6    <foaf:surname>Mugliett</foaf:surname>
7    <mp:party rdf:resource="&dbr;Nationalist_Party_(Malta)"/>
8    <mp:elected>
9      <rdf:Description>
10       <mp:legislature>VIII</mp:legislature>
11       <mp:electedDate>29-10-96</mp:electedDate>
12       <mp:oathofAllegiance>05-12-96</mp:oathofAllegiance>
13       <mp:dissolution>03-08-98</mp:dissolution>
14     </rdf:Description>
15   </mp:elected>
16   <mp:elected>
17     <rdf:Description>
18       <mp:legislature>IX</mp:legislature>
19       <mp:electedDate>08-09-1998</mp:electedDate>
20       <mp:oathofAllegiance>24-10-1998</mp:oathofAllegiance>
21       <mp:dissolution>15-04-2003</mp:dissolution>
22       <mp:ministerRole>
23         <rdf:Description>
24           <mp:appointedRole>24-09-1998</mp:appointedRole>
25           <mp:roleTitle>Parliamentary Secretary in the Ministry of Education</mp:roleTitle>
26         </rdf:Description>
27       </mp:ministerRole>
28     </rdf:Description>
29   </mp:elected>
30   <mp:elected>
31     <rdf:Description>
32       <mp:legislature>X</mp:legislature>
33       <mp:electedDate>14-04-2003</mp:electedDate>
34       <mp:oathofAllegiance>24-05-2003</mp:oathofAllegiance>
35       <mp:dissolution>09-03-2008</mp:dissolution>
36       <mp:ministerRole>
37         <rdf:Description>
38           <mp:appointed>15-04-2003</mp:appointed>
39           <mp:roleTitle>Parliamentary Secretary in the Ministry of
                  Education</mp:roleTitle>
40         </rdf:Description>
41       </mp:ministerRole>
42       <mp:ministerRole>
43         <rdf:Description>
44           <mp:appointedRole>20-03-2004</mp:appointedRole>
45           <mp:roleTitle>Minister for Youth and the Arts</mp:roleTitle>
46         </rdf:Description>
47       </mp:ministerRole>
48     </rdf:Description>
49   </mp:elected>
50   <mp:elected>
51     <rdf:Description>
52       <mp:legislature>XI</mp:legislature>
53       <mp:electedDate>12-03-2008</mp:electedDate>
54       <mp:oathofAllegiance>10-05-2008</mp:oathofAllegiance>
55       <mp:dissolution>07-01-2013</mp:dissolution>
56     </rdf:Description>
57   </mp:elected>
58 </rdf:Description>
```

Listing 1.2: MP RDF profile

To perform the translation from JSON to RDF we considered different research solutions [2,12,17,18]. We decided to use the RDF Translator[14] discussed in [17] that is based on a Python library through which it is possible to translate between different serialisations including JSON and RDF/XML.

---

[14] http://rdf-translator.appspot.com/.

The model depicted in Fig. 2 represents the PQ model used to generated an RDF version of a PQ. Every PQ is associated with the *ParliamentaryQuestion* type and assigned a unique ID based on the legislature and the PQ number assigned to it by Parliament. The PQ number is reset with every new legislature. A PQ is *raisedBy* and *answeredBy* by a *dbo:MemberOfParliament* (refer to the MP profile model discussed below). Other properties of interest include the actual *question* and *answer* which are currently considered to be Literals. Nevertheless, it is not uncommon for PQ answers to include information in a tabular format as well as attached documentation. We intend to cater for such data in a future release of the application.

As stated in Sect. 4.1, the MP profile is composed of data extracted from different parliamentary sources. The MP profile Listing 1.2 refers to a MP that belongs to the Nationalist party, linked to *dbr:Nationalist_Party_(Malta)* and has been elected in four legislatures. For every legislature the profile includes information about the date that the MP was elected, the date that he/she took the oath and the date when his term ended. The profile also includes information about the roles, apart from that of an MP, that the MP occupied during each legislature. In some cases such as during the 10th legislature, the MP in question occupied two different roles, that of a Parliamentary Secretary (i.e. a Junior Minister) and that of a Minister. In the near future we plan to introduce other personal information about every MP such as email, phone number and personal website.

The RDFied, PQ and MP data is then persisted in an Apache Fuseki server[15] and is queried by the visualisation layer through SPARQL.

5   PQViz: Interaction Graph

PQViz exploits PQ and MP data to construct a graph that represents the interactions between the MPs. Every node in the graph represents an MP and the edge represents the interaction, based on PQs asked and answered.

The graph structure is complimented with a visualisation layer that is currently based on D3[16]. This popular Javascript library accepts a JSON representation of a graph and renders the structure using a variety of possible layouts.

In *PQViz* we use bubbles and a force-directed graph layout to make the graph interactive. Currently we are considering PQs from the 9th up till the 12th legislature[17]. The user can immediately view the topmost 15 MPs that have either asked or answered the most PQs during a particular legislature (Fig. 3). The force-directed layout can however be used to drill down to specific MP interactions to visualise which MPs asked questions to whom as can be seen in Fig. 4.

The application uses a number of visualisation cues to display the information. The size of the bubble depends on a computed value that takes into consideration

---

[15] https://jena.apache.org/.

[16] https://d3js.org/.

[17] We will soon be considering the 13th legislature which has just started.

the number of questions asked and/or answered, while the colour of the bubble is the same as that of the MP's party. When the user clicks on the interaction between two specific MPs, the application displays the profiles of both MPs and the actual PQs that were asked. The user can scroll through this list and go through the details of each PQ.

From the interaction graph, it is possible to extract a number of statistics that are currently not being displayed, but which can be of interest to the users. Apart from the total number of questions asked and/or answered over each legislature by individual MPs, it is possible to compute the number of questions asked by (and answered by) one particular MP to another. This information, complimented with information about the topics discussed in the PQs (we refer

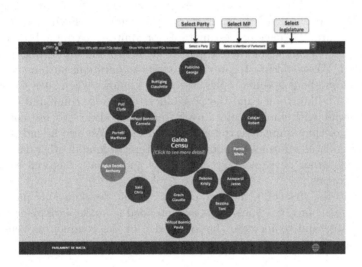

Fig. 3. Topmost MPs that asked the most PQs

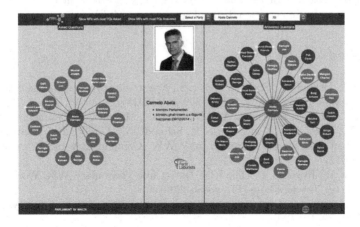

Fig. 4. Interaction graphs for a particular MP

the reader to Sect. 6), is useful to understand better the individual MPs' interests and how these interests potentially changed over time.

6 Future Work

PQViz exists both as a web-based application, however it can be downloaded as a mobile app from both Google's Play Store and Apple Store. We are furthermore continuing our efforts to extend *PQViz* with a set of new features to make it more useful and interesting. One such feature will take into consideration the topics of the PQs. This is somewhat of a challenge because PQs are in Maltese and unfortunately there aren't many tools available to work with the language. We intend to leverage on existing tools found on the Maltese Language Resources server (MLRS)[18] which is an ongoing effort intended to increase the number of natural language processing tools for Maltese. We intend to introduce a search facility to allow for these topics to be found and interesting results to be generated. We would like to provide answers to questions such as which MP asked the most about specific topics, the time windows when such topics were considered to be hot topics and the possibility to identify communities of MPs that have dealt with similar topics over time. The idea is to use community detection algorithms similar to those discussed in [6]. We also intend to exploit relevant and related information about specific topics found in other data sources which include other parliamentary documents and debates, as well as articles from news portals.

PQViz is the first of a number of apps being developed as part of the *apps4Parliament* project. These apps are intended to make parliamentary data more accessible and to increase the knowledge of the common citizens about parliamentary governance.

Acknowledgments. This work is part of the *apps4Parliament* project and is being done in collaboration with the Office of the Speaker (Parliament of Malta) and co-funded by the Malta Information Technology Agency (MITA).

References

1. Attard, J., Orlandi, F., Scerri, S., Auer, S.: A systematic review of open government data initiatives. Gov. Inf. Q. **32**(4), 399–418 (2015)
2. Böhm, C., Freitag, M., Heise, A., Lehmann, C., Mascher, A., Naumann, F., Ercegovac, V., Hernández, M.A., Haase, P., Schmidt, M.: GovWILD: integrating open government data for transparency. In: WWW (Companion Volume), pp. 321–324. ACM (2012)
3. Cyganiak, R., Reynold, D.: The RDF Data Cube Vocabulary. W3C Working Draft (2014). http://www.w3.org/TR/vocab-data-cube/
4. Dadzie, A., Rowe, M.: Approaches to visualising linked data: a survey. Semant. Web **2**(2), 89–124 (2011)

---

[18] http://mlrs.research.um.edu.mt/.

5. Ding, L., DiFranzo, D., Graves, A., Michaelis, J., Li, X., McGuinness, D., Hendler, J.: Data-gov Wiki: Towards linking government data. In: Proceedings of AAAI Spring Symposium on Linked Data Meets Artificial Intelligence (2010)
6. Fortunato, S.: Community detection in graphs. Phys. Rep. **486**(3–5), 75–174 (2010). ISSN 0370–1573
7. Hall, W., Schraefel, M.C., Gibbins, N., Berners-Lee, T., Glaser, H., Shadbolt, N., O'Hara, K.: Linked open government data: lessons from Data.gov.uk. IEEE Intell. Syst. **27**(3), 16–24 (2012)
8. Hasapis, P., Fotopoulou, E., Zafeiropoulos, A., Mouzakitis, S., Koussouris, S., Petychakis, M., Kapourani, B., Zanetti, N., Molinari, F., Virtuoso, S., Rubattino, C.: Business value creation from linked data analytics: The LinDA approach. In: eChallenges e-2014 Conference, Belfast, Northern Ireland, 29–31 October 2014
9. Hoxha, J., Brahaj, A.: Open government data on the web: a semantic approach. In: Proceedings of the 2011 International Conference on Emerging Intelligent Data and Web Technologies (EIDWT 2011), pp. 107–113. IEEE Computer Society, Washington, DC (2011)
10. Kalampokis, E., Tambouris, E., Tarabanis, K.: Linked open government data analytics. In: Wimmer, M.A., Janssen, M., Scholl, H.J. (eds.) EGOV 2013. LNCS, vol. 8074, pp. 99–110. Springer, Heidelberg (2013). https://doi.org/10.1007/978-3-642-40358-3_9
11. Thellmann, K., Orlandi, F., Auer, S.: LinDA - visualising and exploring linked data. In: Proceedings of the Posters and Demos Track of 10th International Conference on Semantic Systems - SEMANTiCS 2014. CEUR-WS, vol. 1224, pp. 39-42 (2014)
12. Lanthaler, M., Gütl, C.: On using JSON-LD to create evolvable restful services. In: Proceedings of the 3rd International Workshop RESTful Design, pp. 25–32 (2012)
13. Lohmann, S., Link, V., Marbach, E., Negru, S.: WebVOWL: Web-based visualization of ontologies. In: Lambrix, P., Hyvönen, E., Blomqvist, E., Presutti, V., Qi, G., Sattler, U., Ding, Y., Ghidini, C. (eds.) EKAW 2014. LNCS (LNAI), vol. 8982, pp. 154–158. Springer, Cham (2015). https://doi.org/10.1007/978-3-319-17966-7_21
14. Martin, S.: Parliamentary questions, the behaviour of legislators, and the function of legislatures: an introduction. J. Legislative Stud. **17**(3), 259–270 (2011)
15. Norton, P.: Introduction: Parliament since 1960. In: Franklin, M., Norton, P. (eds.) Parliamentary Questions. Clarendon Press, Oxford (1993)
16. Salmond, R.: Parliamentary Question Times: How Legislative Accountability Mechanisms Affect Mass Political Engagement. Unpublished paper, University of Michigan (2010)
17. Stolz, A., Rodriguez-Castro, B., Hepp, M.: RDF Translator: A RESTful Multi-Format Data Converter for the Semantic Web. Technical report, E-Business and Web Science Research Group (2013)
18. Weaver, J., Tarjan, P.: Facebook linked data via the graph API. Semant. Web **4**(3), 245–250 (2013)

Keyword Extraction from Parallel Abstracts of Scientific Publications

Slobodan Beliga[1(✉)], Olivera Kitanović[2], Ranka Stanković[2], and Sanda Martinčić-Ipšić[1]

[1] Department of Informatics, University of Rijeka,
Radmile Matejčić 2, 51 000 Rijeka, Croatia
{sbeliga,smarti}@inf.uniri.hr
[2] Faculty of Mining and Geology, University of Belgrade,
Đušina 7, 11 000 Belgrade, Serbia
{olivera.kitanovic,ranka.stankovic}@rgf.bg.ac.rs

Abstract. In this paper, we study the keyword extraction from parallel abstracts of scientific publication in the Serbian and English languages. The keywords are extracted by a selectivity-based keyword extraction method. The method is based on the structural and statistical properties of text represented as a complex network. The constructed parallel corpus of scientific abstracts with annotated keywords allows a better comparison of the performance of the method across languages since we have the controlled experimental environment and data. The achieved keyword extraction results measured with an F1 score are 49.57% for English and 46.73% for the Serbian language, if we disregard keywords that are not present in the abstracts. In case that we evaluate against the whole keyword set, the F1 scores are 40.08% and 45.71% respectively. This work shows that SBKE can be easily ported to new a language, domain and type of text in the sense of its structure. Still, there are drawbacks – the method can extract only the words that appear in the text.

Keywords: Graph-based keyword extraction
Bilingual keyword extraction · SBKE method · Parallel abstracts

1 Introduction

The task of keyword extraction is to automatically identify a set of terms that best describes the document [1,2]. Keyword extraction can be a demanding task, especially when the aim is keyword extraction from bilingual or multilingual textual sources. In such a case, a keyword extraction method should be insensitive to natural language or appropriate for extraction in different natural languages at the same time.

One of the open research questions in the keyword extraction task is to develop a method that is general enough for keyword extraction in several languages simultaneously. Therefore, we focus on a method that can be easily ported to a new language. The prerequisites needed for this desirable characteristic are

© Springer International Publishing AG, part of Springer Nature 2018
J. Szymański and Y. Velegrakis (Eds.): IKC 2017, LNCS 10546, pp. 44–55, 2018.
https://doi.org/10.1007/978-3-319-74497-1_5

that the method does not require deeper linguistic preprocessing. We believe that this is especially important for extraction tasks in low-resourced languages that have less developed language tools [10]. In other words, more sophisticated keyword extraction methods in the text preprocessing step usually use some heuristics to gain in performance by using semantic or syntactic knowledge. As the source of syntactic knowledge, methods usually use part-of-speech tags (POS) in order to restrict access to certain types of words (e.g. nouns, verbs or adjectives) [14,19,20] or suffix sequences which denote the sequence of morphological suffixes of its words [27,29].

Wikipedia is one of the most commonly used semantic sources: using n-grams that appear in Wikipedia article titles as candidates for keywords [22], utilizing Wikipedia as a thesaurus for candidate selection from documents' content [21], exploiting links on Wikipedia to detect keywords candidates [24] or using terminological databases to encode the salience of candidate keyphrases [28]. The methods can be also based on extracted noun-phrase chunks that satisfy predefined lexico-semantic patterns [23]. These different approaches for keyword extraction are effective on various textual sources, such as scientific articles [26], news articles [8,9], blogs [22], meeting transcripts [20], emails [25], web pages [27], etc. However, if such a keyword extraction method needs to be applicable in a bilingual or multilingual environment then the module which incorporates semantic or linguistic knowledge needs to be developed for each language separately.

In this paper, we test the applicability of a graph-enabled method called the selectivity-based keyword extraction method (SBKE) proposed in [8] for the bilingual keyword extraction task. The dataset consists of parallel Serbian-English abstracts from scientific articles from the domain of geology and mining including annotated keywords by the authors of articles. In the scientific literature, methods were studied and compared in different languages: besides the most studied – English language [2,8,13,19,21,22,25,26] are Portuguese [3], Polish [7], Croatian [8], French and Spanish [4–6]. However, no studies report the extraction from parallel texts of different languages with bilingual keyword annotations. To the best of our knowledge, this will present a graph-based keyword extraction for parallel abstracts in scientific articles for the first time, as well as a new bilingual keyword extraction dataset. The main contributions of this paper are:

(1) the development of bilingual (Serbian-English) keyword extraction dataset, and
(2) the comparative study of the effectiveness of the SBKE method for keyword extraction on parallel texts written in two languages.

In addition, in this work we test whether the SBKE method is portable to a new language, in this research Serbian (in addition to Croatian and English [8]), to a new domain of geology and mining (in addition to domains of news and technical reports from Wikipedia [8]) and finally, that SBKE can be applicable to short texts, hence abstracts from scientific articles.

In Sect. 2, we provide a description of the methodology. First, we briefly explain the SBKE keyword extraction method (Subsect. 2.1), then we provide a brief overview of the used NLP tools for Serbian and English (Subsect. 2.2) and used evaluation methodology (Subsect. 2.3). The description of the used parallel dataset for English and Serbian languages is in Sect. 3. Section 4 presents the results, while the concluding remarks and future plans are in Sect. 5.

2   Methodology

A detailed description of the selectivity-based keyword extraction method (SBKE) is available in [8]. However, in the following section we will explain the basic characteristics of the method to ensure the readability and completeness of the manuscript.

2.1   The SBKE Method

The network or graph-based approach, where a network (or graph) of words is used for the representation of texts, enables the exploration of the relationships and structural information incorporated in a text very efficiently. Although, there are variations, the usual way of representing documents as a graph models words as vertices (nodes) and their relations as edges (links). The weight of the link is proportional to the overall co-ccurrence frequencies of the corresponding word pairs within a corpus. We will focus on the network construction around co-occurrence relations of adjacent words within sentences, since it requires no semantic or syntactic preprocessing of the input text. Network enabled keyword extraction methods exploit various structural properties (usually centrality measures) of the nodes in a network for the extracting and ranking of keyword candidates [1].

The selectivity-based keyword extraction method is a network-enabled method for keyword extraction which consists of two phases: **(1) keyword extraction** and **(2) keyword expansion**. The node selectivity value is calculated from the weighted network as the average weight distributed on the links of a single node and is then used in the procedure of keyword candidate ranking and extraction [8,9]. The node in/outselectivity and generalized in/outselectivity values are calculated from a directed weighted network as the average weight distributed on the ingoing/outgoing links of the single node and used in the procedure of keyword candidate ranking and extraction. This method does not require linguistic knowledge (apart from stemming or lemmatization) as it is derived purely from the statistical and structural information of the network [10].

In this study, we use the SBKE method on a directed and weighted network. An individual network is constructed separately for each Serbian and for each English text. More preciously, from all the constructed networks, we rank the nodes according to the highest in/out-selectivity values above a threshold greater than 1, as proposed in [8]. Therefore, we obtain two sets of extracted keywords, one for the Serbian, and one for the English version of the text. Preserving the same threshold value in all documents resulted in a different number of extracted nodes (one-word long keyword candidates) from each network, which is the union of the highly-ranked nodes according to the in/out-selectivity values for the particular language.

2.2 Text Preprocessing Tools

Serbian is a highly inflectional Slavic language. Although we use the keyword extraction method designed with light or no linguistic knowledge, some text preprocessing is needed and includes the conversion of the input text to lowercase, the removal of misspelled symbols and lemmatization. In a similar way, we preprocessed the English text: converted to lowercase and stemmed using the Porter stemmer. Stemming and lemmatization are also needed for a better matching of the extracted and annotated keywords during evaluation to overcome differences between the inflected forms in the text and the lemmatized keyword forms of the same word.

In the text preprocessing stage for the English language we use:

(1) Stop-word list - extracted from the Natural Language Toolkit (NLTK) for Python [11], and
(2) the Porter stemmer [11] for stemming as a procedure to map all words with the same stem to a common form (stem). Its main use is as part of the term normalization process (removing the inflectional suffixes from words).

For preprocessing of texts in the Serbian language we use:

(1) Stop-word list - prepared at the Human Language Technology Group at the University of Belgrade [30], and
(2) a Serbian lemmatizer. For lemmatization, we use Serbian morphological electronic dictionaries and grammars developed within the University of Belgrade Human Language Technology Group [17]. Morphological electronic dictionaries of Serbian for NLP have been developing for many years now. In the dictionary of lemmas (DELAS) each lemma is described in full detail so that the dictionary of forms containing all the necessary grammatical information (DELAF) can be generated from it, and subsequently used for various NLP tasks. Serbian e-dictionaries of simple forms have reached a considerable size: they have more than 140,000 lemmas generating more than 5 million forms and 18,000 multi-word lemmas [18].

Different approaches (stemming and lemmatization) were caused by the differences in morphological feature of these two languages. The goal of both stemming and lemmatization is to reduce inflectional forms and sometimes derivationally related forms of a word to a common base form. Lemmatization is the process of grouping together the inflected forms of a word so they can be analyzed as a single item, identified by the word's lemma, or a dictionary form. Stemming usually refers to a process that chops off the ends of words in the hope of achieving this goal correctly most of the time. Serbian, like other Slavic languages, is a highly-inflected language, with complex grammatical rules that cannot be adequately expressed by stemming rules. However, for highly-inflected languages, lemmatization can hardly be avoided as each keyword can have many inflected forms (for multiword units from five to ten or even more). On the other hand, for English several efficient and accurate stemmers are available and we used the Porter stemmer, as one of the widely-used stemmers for the text preprocessing of the English language.

Both stemming and lemmatization play very important roles when it comes to increasing the relevance and recall capabilities of a retrieval system. When these techniques are used, the number of indexes used is reduced because the system is using one index to present several similar words that have the same root or stem [12].

2.3 Evaluation Methodology

The dataset used in this experiment contains only one set of annotated keywords – provided by the author(s) of each abstract (scientific paper). In the case when only one set of annotated keywords is available, the evaluation of the keyword extraction is performed as in the standard information retrieval tasks. Hence, precision (P), recall (R) and the $F1$ score are used for the evaluation. When comparing the performance of an automatic method (algorithm) with a human annotation, precision is calculated as the number of keywords in the intersection of a set of keywords annotated by a human (A) and a set of keywords annotated using algorithm (B) divided by the number of keywords annotated using the algorithm:

$$P = \frac{A \cap B}{B}. \tag{1}$$

The recall is calculated as the number of keywords in the intersection of a set of keywords annotated by a human and a set of keywords annotated using the algorithm divided by the number of keywords annotated by a human:

$$R = \frac{A \cap B}{A}. \tag{2}$$

The $F1$ score is the harmonic mean of precision and recall, calculated as:

$$F1 = \frac{2PR}{P + R}. \tag{3}$$

3 Textual Resources

In this experiment, we have used abstracts from the scientific journal "Underground Mining Engineering" published by the University of Belgrade, Faculty of Mining and Geology. Apart from technical underground mining related topics, the journal publishes papers from other fields of mining, geology, and geosciences, as well as from other scientific and technical disciplines having a direct or indirect application in mining. During the period of 2004–2012, the journal published 55 papers bilingually, in Serbian and in English. These papers are available online as aligned parallel text in the Biblisha[1] digital library, as well as separate documents. The Biblisha digital library contains scientific publications from other journals

---

[1] http://jerteh.rs/biblisha/ListaDokumenata.aspx?JCID=2&lng=en.

and also contains project reports that are published in two languages – Serbian and English. All the documents are provided with the usual metadata (article's author(s), publication date, title, keywords, abstract etc.) and are aligned at the sentence level [15, 16].

For the research presented in this paper, we used a collection of 50 bilingual documents with approximately 4,800 aligned sentences. Since papers were published bilingually, they were already available both in Serbian and English, where most of the papers were originally written in Serbian and then translated into English by professional translators. Texts have various lengths, in Serbian the texts contain from 34 to 259 words (on average 100) and in English from 44 to 286 words (on average 110). The statistics of the used English and Serbian parallel abstract are presented in Table 1.

All the documents are supplied with metadata and keywords, annotated by human experts – the authors of the articles. The number of annotated keywords ranges from 3 to 18 in the Serbian and from 3 to 15 in the English texts (the average in both is 7). Scientists usually define keywords in their lemmatized form, while in the Serbian texts (and rarely in English) they appear in many inflected forms, which are different from lemma. Bilingual Serbian-English KE dataset introduced in this paper is publicly available from http://langnet.uniri.hr/resources.html.

The previous research [14] for terminology extraction in the Serbian language used the rule-based method for multi-word term extraction that relies on lexical resources for modeling various syntactic structures of multi-word terms. It is applied in several domains, also among them is the corpus of Serbian texts from the geology and mining domain containing more than 600,000 simple word forms. Part of this approach was the automatic elimination of less probable candidates: extracted and lemmatized multiword terms are filtered to reject falsely offered lemmas and then they are ranked by introducing measures that combine the linguistic and statistical information (C-Value, T-Score, LLR, and Keyness). In previous research, all the texts were joined and the entire collection was treated as a single text, while for the research presented in this paper, the text processing and analysis is performed per each text document in the collection. SBKE method does not include calculation of C-Value, T-Score, LLR, and Keyness, it follows the procedure described in Subsect. 2.1.

Table 1 presents the descriptive statistics for 50 parallel abstracts in the Serbian and English language including the average value, the minimal and maximal number of words in rows for each category presented by columns. The first column is related to the numbers of words in the text, the KW count lists the number of keywords given by an author, while KW in the text shows how many keywords given by an author are actually present in the abstract. The difference between the KW count and KW in text values depicts the number of OOV (out-of-vocabulary) annotated keywords.

Table 1. The statistics for 50 parallel abstracts in Serbian and English language.

	Serbian			English		
	#words	#KW	#KWinText	#words	#KW	#KWinText
Average	100.6	6.64	5.38	110.48	6.72	5.5
Min	34	3	2	44	3	2
Max	259	18	13	286	15	12

4   Results

The results of the experiments are presented in terms of R, P and the $F1$ score in Table 2. The left part of Table 2 presents the evaluation performance of the SBKE method according to the set of annotated keywords – provided by the author(s) of the abstracts. The right part of the table presents the evaluation according to the set of annotated keywords without out-of-vocabulary (OOV) words. All OOV words are removed from the set of keywords for the evaluation. The results are shown for one-word long keywords even though the SBKE can extract keywords that contain two or three words.

When analyzing the results, it is important to consider the fact that the keywords are specified by domain scientists and this can be highly subjective, comprising of a lot of background knowledge on the topic. Sometimes their approach to keywords selection is oriented on the overall meaning and essence. Thereafter, in several cases the given keywords are not present in the text as the same term, in those cases, the concept is replaced with a synonym or hypernym.

For Serbian as well as for English languages, recall achieves higher values than precision (from 3% to 17%). This also holds for the Croatian and English languages as elaborated in our previous work [8] regardless of the inclusion or removal of OOV keywords, reflecting the greediness of the SBKE method. Note that the SBKE method is designed as "greedy" and extracts as much candidates as possible, which can cause the over-generation problem. Still, the SBKE method can circumvent the overgeneration problem by simple tuning of the filter applied to the weights during the expansion steps of setting the appropriate cut-off threshold during the extraction phase.

Note that the results in this study are better for the Serbian than for the English language (see Table 2). This is in line with our previous findings for the Croatian language [8]. Both, Serbian and Croatian language are morphologically rich, and closely related languages from South Slavic language family. Unlike English, which is inflectional language and has a strict word ordering in a sentence.

Next, in the right part of Table 2 (without OOV keywords) the evaluation results show that the SBKE method for Serbian achieves an F1 score of 49.57%, and for English an $F1$ score of 46.73%. The results of all measures (R, P, and $F1$) are generally higher when they are measured for keywords without OOV words. This is expected because people tagged ~18% of the keywords in English, and ~19% in Serbian that did not appear in the original texts.

So far, the SBKE method has been tested on longer English Wikipedia texts (with an average length of 5,919 words per text) and Croatian newspaper articles (with an average length of 335 words per text), where SBKE achieved F1 scores of 24.8% and 34.21% for Croatian and English respectively [8]. In the present study, the method is tested on abstracts of scientific articles with an average length of 100 words per abstract in Serbian and 110 per abstract in English – shorter texts. This is the reason why we stopped after the first phase (called keyword extraction in the SBKE method). Usually, SBKE performs better on longer texts (containing more information on the structural properties of the input text), but here we can explore the performance on the shorter texts [8]. The achieved results suggest that SBKE can be applied to shorter documents as well. Since SBKE is grounded in a structural and statistical information incorporated into the network structure the expected outcome is to achieve better performance on larger texts and on the whole document collection. In this case, SBKE proved correctly also on shorter texts. This outcome requires deeper further investigation which we plan to address in the future.

Moreover, the benefit of this work could be considered in future research, as the initial step in extracting concepts for the construction of the ontology for the domain of geology and mining in the Serbian language.

Finally, it is worth mentioning that the different structure and syntax of the Serbian and English languages are reflected in the results. By combining (translating) Serbian and English keywords, a larger set of keywords can be obtained. This is the advantage of bilingual keyword extraction, which standard methods for keyword extraction cannot reach, and remains an open question for future work.

Table 3 represents two different examples of abstracts in the test dataset in a form of a preprocessed texts. On the left side is an example where the SBKE method returned a larger set of keywords where the broader concept "method" is added to "analytic hierarchy processes (AHP)". On the right side of the table is an example where the word "speed" is listed as a keyword specified by a human, but in the text the author used a synonym term "velocity" (stemmed to: veloc). Since the word "speed" is not present in the original text, the method will never extract it as a keyword. Similar examples adversely affect the success of extraction and reduce the efficiency of the SBKE method in terms of $F1$ score. These examples

Table 2. Results of keyword extraction for parallel (Serbian-English) abstracts in scientific articles expressed in terms of R, P and an $F1$ score for all keywords defined by an author (in the left part) and for keywords without out-of-vocabulary (OOV) words (in the right part).

	All keywords			Without OOV		
	R [%]	P [%]	$F1$ [%]	R [%]	P [%]	$F1$ [%]
Serbian	54.32	45.96	45.71	63.38	45.96	49.57
English	44.62	41.20	40.08	55.58	44.48	46.73

Table 3. Two examples for extracted keywords compared to pre-assigned keywords on parallel Serbian-English abstracts. The keywords discussed in the example are underlined or written in *italic*.

Serbian	English
Author: analitički hijerarhijski proces (AHP)	**Author:** concret qualiti *speed* wave ultrasound
SBKE Method: *izbor* hijerarhijski analitički ahp proces *metod*	**SBKE Method:** concret qualiti wave ultrasound
Text: primena *metod* analitički hijerarhijski proces ahp kod *izbor* utovarni-transportni mašina. u ovaj rad prezentovan ona *metod* analitički hijerarhijski proces ahp i njen primena kod proces odlučivanje u rudarski inženjerstvo. konkretan u ovaj rad dat ona primena ahp *metod* kod *izbor* model utovarni-transportni mahati ne sa električni pogon na osnov utvrđen kriterijum odlučivanje kao i dodeljivanje težinski koeficijenata pojedin kriterijum, koji uticati na proces donošienje konačan odluka	**Text:** estim of the qualiti of built-in concret by the ultrasound observ. thi paper present result of the propag *veloc* investig of ultrasound wave in the concret construct so call non-destruct method in situ due to inspect of concret qualiti that is inbuilt into the bodi of the durutovici dam built for the pljevlja coal mine. by the *veloc* of ultrasound wave measur the follow paramet will be concret homogen presenc of gap crack and other defect in concret as well as concret qualiti relat to it strength

imply the possibility for the introduction of semantical knowledge into the further stages of the presented keyword extraction method. Namely, the list of extracted keyword candidates in the next stage can be expanded/corrected with semantic knowledge, with expansion to synonyms, hypernyms and/or hyponyms, which can be of high importance for application recall improvement.

5   Conclusion

In this work, we explored the keyword extraction from parallel abstracts of scientific papers from the domain of geology and mining in the Serbian and English languages. We show that the selectivity-based keyword extraction (SBKE) method is general enough to be easily ported to another language – Serbian, because it requires only shallow linguistic preprocessing. Then we tested the applicability of the SBKE method in a new and highly specialized scientific domain – a text collection from the geology and mining domain. Finally, the scientific abstract is limited to the number of characters, therefore we also test the applicability of SBKE on short texts.

The experimental part of the paper is focused on the performance of the SBKE method on parallel texts from the Serbian and English languages[2].

---

[2] Bilingual Serbian-English KE dataset is publicly available from http://langnet.uniri.hr/resources.html.

The new set-up of parallel texts enabled better insights into the performance across different languages simultaneously preserving the nature, size, and content of the texts. Usually, we compare unrelated datasets across languages. This set-up provides a controlled and fair environment for the evaluation.

We can conclude that SBKE can be easily ported to a different language, domain and type of text in the sense of its structure. Still, there are drawbacks, the method can extract only the words that appear in the text. However, we performed the evaluation with and without the out-of-vocabulary (OOV) keywords, showing that the results are promising even for the included OOV keywords.

In future work, we are planning to expand the keyword extraction from abstracts to whole scientific articles from the domain of mining and geology which are available in complete written form in both Serbian and English languages. It is important to compare keyword extraction results from whole papers with those extracted solely from short abstracts. Besides that, extracted keywords from whole papers can serve as a basis for the first approximation of a geological ontology construction. In addition, we will explore, if we can gain by translating the set of annotated keywords from the source to the target language and obtain larger sets of annotated keywords.

Acknowledgments. The authors would like to acknowledge networking support by the ICT COST Action IC1302 KEYSTONE – Semantic keyword-based search on structured data sources (www.keystone-cost.eu). The authors would also like to thank the University of Rijeka for the support under the LangNet project (13.13.2.2.07).

References

1. Beliga, S., Meštrović, A., Martinčić-Ipšić, S.: An overview of graph-based keyword extraction methods and approaches. J. Inf. Organ. Sci. **39**(1), 1–20 (2015)
2. Mihalcea, R., Tarau, P.: TextRank: bringing order into texts. In: Proceedings of Empirical Methods in Natural Language Processing - EMNLP 2004, pp. 404–411. ACL, Barcelona (2004)
3. Marujo, L., Viveiros, M., Neto, J.P.: Keyphrase cloud generation of broadcast news. In: Proceeding of 12th Annual Conference of the International Speech Communication Association, Interspeech (2011)
4. Medelyan, O.: Human-competitive automatic topic indexing. Ph.D. thesis. Department of Computer Science, University of Waikato, New Zealand (2009)
5. Medelyan, O., Witten, I.H.: Domain independent automatic keyphrase indexing with small training sets. J. Am. Soc. Inf. Sci. Technol. **59**(7), 1026–1040 (2008)
6. Paroubek, P., Zweigenbaum, P., Forest, D., Grouin, C.: Indexation libre et controlee d'articles scientifiques. Presentation et resultats du defi fouille de textes DEFT2012. In: Proceedings of the DEfi Fouille de Textes 2012 Workshop, pp. 1–13 (2012)
7. Kozłowski, M.: PKE: a novel Polish keywords extraction method. Pomiary Autom. Kontrola **60**(5), 305–308 (2014)
8. Beliga, S., Meštrović, A., Martinčić-Ipšić, S.: Selectivity-based keyword extraction method. Int. J. Sem. Web Inf. Syst. (IJSWIS) **12**(3), 1–26 (2016)

9. Beliga, S., Meštrović, A., Martinčić-Ipšić, S.: Toward selectivity-based keyword extraction for croatian news. In: CEUR Proceedings of the Workshop on Surfacing the Deep and the Social Web (SDSW 2014), Riva del Garda, Trentino, Italy, vol. 1310, pp. 1–8 (2014)
10. Beliga, S., Martinčić-Ipšić, S.: Network-enabled keyword extraction for under-resourced languages. In: Calì, A., Gorgan, D., Ugarte, M. (eds.) KEYSTONE 2016. LNCS, vol. 10151, pp. 124–135. Springer, Cham (2017). https://doi.org/10.1007/978-3-319-53640-8_11
11. Bird, S., Klein, E., Loper, E.: Natural Language Processing with Python. O'Reilly Media, Inc., Sebastopol (2009)
12. Balakrishnan, V., Ethel, L.-Y.: Stemming and lemmatization: a comparison of retrieval performances. Lect. Notes Softw. Eng. 2(3), 262–267 (2014)
13. Ludwig, P., Thiel, M., Nürnberger, A.: Unsupervised extraction of conceptual keyphrases from abstracts. In: Calì, A., Gorgan, D., Ugarte, M. (eds.) KEYSTONE 2016. LNCS, vol. 10151, pp. 37–48. Springer, Cham (2017). https://doi.org/10.1007/978-3-319-53640-8_4
14. Stanković, R., Krstev, C., Obradović, I., Lazić, B., Trtovac, A.: Rule-based automatic multi-word term extraction and lemmatization. In: Proceedings of the 10th International Conference on Language Resources and Evaluation, LREC 2016, Portorož, Slovenia (2016). ISBN 978-2-9517408-9-1
15. Stanković, R., Krstev, C., Lazić, B., Vorkapić, D.: A bilingual digital library for academic and entrepreneurial knowledge management. In: Proceeding of 10th International Forum on Knowledge Asset Dynamics - IFKAD 2015: Culture, Innovation and Entrepreneurship: Connecting the Knowledge Dots, Bari, Italy, pp. 1764–1777 (2015)
16. Stanković, R., Krstev, C., Vitas, D., Vulović, N., Kitanović, O.: Keyword-based search on bilingual digital libraries. In: Calì, A., Gorgan, D., Ugarte, M. (eds.) KEYSTONE 2016. LNCS, vol. 10151, pp. 112–123. Springer, Cham (2017). https://doi.org/10.1007/978-3-319-53640-8_10
17. Vitas, D., Popović, L., Krstev, C., Obradović, I., Pavlović-Lazetić, G., Stanojević, M.: The Serbian Language in the Digital Age. META-NET White Paper Series. Springer, Heidelberg (2012). https://doi.org/10.1007/978-3-642-30755-3. Rehm, G., Uszkoreit, H. (Series eds.)
18. Krstev, C., Vitas, D., Stanković, R.: A lexical approach to acronyms and their definitions. In: Mariani, Z.V.J. (ed.) Proceedings of the 7th Language & Technology Conference, pp. 219–223. Fundacja Uniwersytetu im. A. Mickiewicza, Poznan (2016)
19. Wan, X., Xiao, J.: Single document keyphrase extraction using neighborhood knowledge. In: Proceedings of the 23rd AAAI Conference on Artificial Intelligence, pp. 855–860 (2008)
20. Liu, F., Pennell, D., Liu, F., Liu, Y.: Unsupervised approaches for automatic keyword extraction using meeting transcripts. In: Proceedings of the HLT: The Annual Conference on Empirical Methods in NLP, pp. 257–266 (2009)
21. Joorabchi, A., Mahdi, A.E.: Automatic keyphrase annotation of scientific documents using Wikipedia and genetic algorithms. J. Inf. Sci. 39(3), 410–426 (2013)
22. Grineva, M., Grinev, M., Lizorkin, D.: Extracting key terms from noisy and multi-theme documents. In: Proceedings of the 18th International Conference on World Wide Web, pp. 661–670. ACM, New York (2009)
23. Lahiri, S., Choudhury, S.R., Caragea, C.: Keyword and keyphrase extraction using centrality measures on collocation networks (2014). http://arxiv.org/pdf/1401.6571.pdf

24. Medelyan, O., Frank, E., Witten, I.H.: Human-competitive tagging using automatic keyphrase extraction. In: Proceedings of the 2004 Conference on Empirical Methods in NLP, pp. 1318–1327 (2009)
25. Lahiri, S., Mihalcea, R., Lai, P.-H.: Keyword extraction from emails. Nat. Lang. Eng. **23**(2), 295–317 (2016)
26. Kim, S.N., Medelyan, O., Kan, M.-Y., Baldwin, T.: SemEval-2010 task 5: automatic keyphrase extraction from scientific articles. In: SemEval 2010 Proceedings of the 5th International Workshop on Semantic Evaluation, Los Angeles, California, pp. 21–26 (2010)
27. Yih, W.-T., Goodman, J., Carvalho, V.R.: Finding advertising keywords on web pages. In: Proceedings of the 15th International Conference on World Wide Web, pp. 213–222 (2010)
28. Lopez, P., Romary, L.: HUMB: automatic key term extraction from scientific articles in GROBID. In: Proceedings of the 5th International Workshop on Semantic Evaluation, pp. 248–251 (2010)
29. Nguyen, T.D., Kan, M.-Y.: Keyphrase extraction in scientific publications. In: Goh, D.H.-L., Cao, T.H., Sølvberg, I.T., Rasmussen, E. (eds.) ICADL 2007. LNCS, vol. 4822, pp. 317–326. Springer, Heidelberg (2007). https://doi.org/10.1007/978-3-540-77094-7_41
30. Utvic, M.: List of frequency corpus of contemporary Serbian language (in Serbian). In: Milanovic, A., Stanojcic, Ž., Popovic, Lj. (eds.) International Slavic Center, Faculty of Philology, vol. 43/3, pp. 241–262 (2014)

Methodology of Selecting the Hadoop Ecosystem Configuration in Order to Improve the Performance of a Plagiarism Detection System

Andrzej Sobecki[✉] and Marcin Kepa

Gdansk University of Technology,
ul. G. Narutowicza 11/12, 80-233 Gdansk, Poland
{andrzej.sobecki,marcin.kepa}@pg.gda.pl
http://task.gda.pl/

Abstract. The plagiarism detection problem involves finding patterns in unstructured text documents. Similarity of documents in this approach means that the documents contain some identical phrases with defined minimal length. The typical methods used to find similar documents in digital libraries are not suitable for this task (plagiarism detection) because found documents may contain similar content and we have not any warranty that they contain any of identical phrases. The article describes an example method of searching for similar documents contains identical phrases in big documents repositories, and presents a problem of selecting storage and computing platform suitable for presented method using in plagiarism detection systems. In the article we present comparison of the mentioned above method implementations using two computing platforms: KASKADA and Hadoop with different configurations in order to test and compare their performance and scalability. The method using the default tools available on the Hadoop platform i.e. HDFS and Apache Spark offers worse performance than the method implemented on the KASKADA platform using the NFS (Network File System) and the processing model Master/Slave. The advantage of the Hadoop platform increases with the use of additional data structures (hash-map) and tools offered on this platform, i.e. HBase (NoSQL). The tools integrated with the Hadoop platform provide a possibility of creating efficient and a scalable method for finding similar documents in big repositories. The KASKADA platform offers efficient tools for analysing data in real-time processes i.e. when there is no need to compare the input data to a large collection of information (patterns) and to use the advanced data structures. The Contribution of this article is the comparison of the two computing and storage platforms in order to achieve better performance of the method used in the plagiarism detection system to find similar documents containing identical phrases.

© Springer International Publishing AG, part of Springer Nature 2018
J. Szymański and Y. Velegrakis (Eds.): IKC 2017, LNCS 10546, pp. 56–69, 2018.
https://doi.org/10.1007/978-3-319-74497-1_6

1   Introduction

Along with the prevalent computerization, the number of processes in which digital documents replaced their traditional paper counterparts has largely increased. The effectiveness of using the digital documents by employees in an organization depends most on the available tools, such as the digital repositories of documents, methods used to search for the documents that comply with the defined requirements, and programs that provide the possibility of analysing the information stored in the documents. One of the obvious trends in the development of tools, used for handling the digital documents, is the increase of interest in the efficient methods of searching for similar documents. Methods of searching for similar documents may be used in different areas, according to the type of document content, e.g.

- health records with a description of treatment methods in a medical repository [1];
- court rulings in judgment document repository [2,3];
- the results of scientific research, articles and books in scientific institutes repositories [4,5];
- theses in the universities repositories [6];
- different unstructured, text documents in the plagiarism detection systems [7,8].

Areas of application for the methods of searching for similar documents are defined by the function used to calculate the degree of similarity between the two documents. We could divide these areas into two classes in which one:

- user expect documents with similar content based on e.g., keywords or a bibliography;
- user expect documents contain patterns defined by him in the request like e.g., set of text phrases;

To the first class, we could assign solutions to use in digital libraries in order to find books based on the meta-data or keywords specified by the user. In this class user generally, does not specify his requirements concern to the phrases uses in sought books. The second of a mentioned-above class includes solutions that offer for user possibility to define requirements concerning the patterns that he expects to find in sought documents. An example of such solution belong to the second class is the plagiarism detection system, where the method searches for text fragments (phrases) from published documents, which were used in a new, unpublished document, omitting the information that relates them to the sources of the borrowed fragments. One of the obstacles in common use of the methods of searching for similar documents in the plagiarism detection systems is the number of documents stored in the digital repositories.

   One of the proposed approach used to increase the performance of these methods is to perform calculations in parallel-way in the cloud [9] using the special platforms for storing documents and management of the parallel execution of tasks in the cloud computing environment. The aim of the article is to present a comparison of the storage and computing platform suitable for the problem of finding patterns in unstructured, text documents that each one is smaller than 1 MB. In the article, we have compared two platforms: KASKADA [10] (actual used) and Hadoop [11]. The analysis of these platforms was conducted using the existed plagiarism detection system SowiDocs[1]. *SowiDocs* is an anti-plagiarism system that uses the *KASKADA* platform in order to have the possibility to perform parallel computations on the data streams in real time, using the services working in the *Master/Slave* model. *KASKADA* serves the tools for creating user defined functions *UDF* in C++ language and publishes the created *UDFs* as services. This system has been developed at the Technical University of Gdansk and is used since 2010 in the University to detect plagiarism in student works. The article presents the comparison of the different method implementations for retrieving similar documents containing defined patterns, using the *KASKADA* and *Hadoop* platforms.

The Contribution of this article is the comparison results which presents advantages and disadvantages of two computing and storage platforms and their capabilities to achieve better performance of algorithms used in the plagiarism detection system to finding similar documents containing identical phrases.

2 State of Art

Algorithms for solving one of the following problems: Longest Common Substring (LCSg) [12] or Longest Common Subsequence (LCSe) [13–16] are most commonly used to detect plagiarism in the text documents. A drawback of these algorithms is their high computational complexity, which prevents the development of an efficient method for scanning the document repository in order to operate in a time acceptable to the user. One of the methods used to increase the performance of the plagiarism detection process is the pre-selection of similar documents that contain patterns defined in the analysed document. The purpose of the pre-selection is to reduce the set of input documents for algorithms that solve the problems of *LCSg* and *LCSe*. Methods used for pre-selection do not compare the original document content instead they use some kind of representation that is called a document profile. An example of methods used for pre-selection of documents based on the document profiles, are:

- inverted index [17–20],
- n-grams [21–23],
- semantic similarity [24–26],
- natural language processing [27,28],
- hashing document content [29–34].

Regardless of the methods used to pre-select the similar documents, their performance often depends on their implementation, the number of documents

---

[1] https://sowi.pg.gda.pl/.

stored in the repository and the computing platform used. The number of documents in the repositories is growing steadily, so the presented methods must be implemented in a computing platform that provides high performance and scalabilities like *KASKADA* or *Hadoop*.

The advantage of the *KASKADA* platform is mediating in the access to resources provided by cloud computing and automatic management of the running tasks. The second of the mentioned platforms is *Hadoop*, which is now one of the most popular solutions to create scalable and high-performance computing platforms. The reason for its popularity is the portability of solutions created using *Hadoop* platform tools, ease of installation and maintenance, as well as a set of additional components of the *Hadoop* ecosystem like *HBase* – a distributed, scalable, big data store (Big Table implementation [35]), *YARN* (Yet Another Resource Negotiator) and *Apache Spark* [36] – a fast and general engine for large-scale data processing.

3   Details of Our System

The *SowiDocs* system comprises of several processing stages, designed to analyse similarities between documents with increasing accuracy. The tasks are running in the cloud computing environment, according to the process described in the selected web service scenario. The scenario describes the process of the documents similarity computation in the *SowiDocs* system, using the services divided into the following stages:

- Converting – converting a received document to the text format without formatting and images,
- Mapping – computing the document profile based on the content generated by the preceding service (*Converting*) and use the following algorithms: Rabin fingerprinting [37], BSW [38] (Basic Sliding Window) and TTTD [39] (Two Thresholds Two Divisors),
- Searching – finding the similar documents by counting identical numerical values, occurring in the compared documents profiles,
- Filtering – filtering the found documents by calculating the similarity between two documents based on similarity of their contents.

An accuracy of the plagiarism detection process mostly depends on the algorithms used in the filter stage where documents are analyzed in order to find all longest common substrings. While the performance of this process mostly depends on the algorithms used in the searching stage where we try to find only this documents that contain some patterns and omit the documents that not comply with this requirement.

To achieve that in the *SowiDocs* we use document profiles that represent original text documents by fingerprint values. Each fingerprint is calculated based on the content of the sliding window. The first fingerprint value for a document is calculated based on Eq. (1) [34] and for every other position of the sliding window a single fingerprint value is calculated based on Eq. (2).

$$F_1 = (t_1 \cdot p^{n_t-1} + t_2 \cdot p^{n_t-2} + \cdots + t_{n_t}) mod 2^x \qquad (1)$$

$$F_{i+1} = (F_i \cdot p + t_{n_t-i} - t_i \cdot p^{n_t}) mod 2^x \qquad (2)$$

where:

- F_i – single i-th fingerprint value,
- p – a prime number,
- t_j – j-th char from the document,
- n_t – a length of the sliding window,
- x – exponent, e.g. 30 or 31.

4   Problem Statement

In order to achieve satisfying performance, and accuracy of the plagiarism detection process, we should find in the third stage of this process only these documents that contain patterns defined by the user. Moreover, the method used in the third stage can not omit any of the document contains that patterns. Because of that, the method using for searching for documents in the third stage was chosen to test the profitability of migrating the system from existing platform KASKADA to the Apache Hadoop Platform. The problem of a selection the platform to perform the computation arises from the number of files and its size. In one repository we have about 500.000 documents with each is smaller than 1 MB. In the one analysis process, we could use few different repositories depending on the content of the analysed document and user requirements.

Originally, the third stage of the analysis process was developed as a Master/Slave algorithm on the *KASKADA* platform. The analysed documents were saved in the repository as files in a *NFS* [40]. The task of analysing a single document was divided by the master between the slave nodes. Each slave had to compare the document with a subsection of the repository. This was done by iterating over the document profiles from the subsection and comparing them to the test document. First, every profile form the subsection was loaded into the memory as a key-value hash-map (with the fingerprints as the keys), after that, every fingerprint in the test document profile was searched for in the hash-map. A simplified scheme of processing the documents using the *KASKADA* platform can be seen in Fig. 1.

As the repository grew bigger, the time needed to process a single document grew linearly relative to its size. What's more important, limitations of the *NFS*, combined with the complexity of iterating over every file in the repository to create its hash-map, made the entire process long, even for small files.

5   Proposed Solutions

Three possible approaches were designed and tested. All three approaches were in fact MapReduce algorithms written in the *Apache Spark* environment:

- a naive approach, using a *HDFS* file repository – further called the *HDFS* approach,
- a complex approach, using a hash-map and a *HDFS* file repository – further called the *HDFS* map approach,
- a *Hbase* based approach – further called the *Hbase* approach.

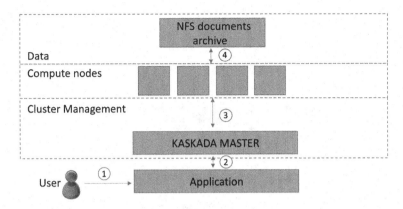

Fig. 1. *KASKADA* schema

5.1 HDFS Approaches

Both the first and the second approach work on a *HDFS* file-based repository of documents. It is important to note, that unlike in the *KASKADA* approach, the file system here is distributed among the compute nodes using *HDFS* (with data blocks replicated between nodes). A simplified scheme of documents processing in such *Hadoop* ecosystem can be seen in Fig. 2.

The first approach works by comparing every line of the profiles repository (saved as files in *HDFS*) to every line in the tested document – this means that for a document containing n fingerprints and a repository containing m fingerprints the solution does $n \cdot m$ comparison operations.

The *HDFS* map approach is an improved version of the first approach. Instead of doing $n \cdot m$ comparison operations, the tested document is converted into a key-value hash-map (with the fingerprint as the key). Because of that the search operation is simplified to m searches in the hash-map - provided there is enough system memory the computational complexity is reduced from $O(n \cdot m)$ to $O(m)$. This means that the analysis time is largely independent from the size of the tested document.

5.2 HBase Approach

The third and final approach uses, a *Hbase* implementation of a reversed index. The database was created on top of the existing data nodes of the Hadoop cluster. On each data node a *Hbase* Region server was installed. A *Hbase* master server was also installed on one of the master nodes. A simplified scheme of the Hadoop platform in the *HBase* setup can be seen in Fig. 3.

The schema of the database was designed as a reversed index:

- every row is indexed by a value of a fingerprint,
- every row contains a number of columns (part of a single column family) - each named after a single document containing this fingerprint,

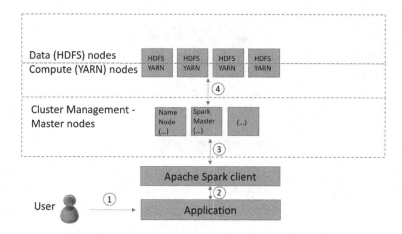

Fig. 2. Hadoop HDFS schema

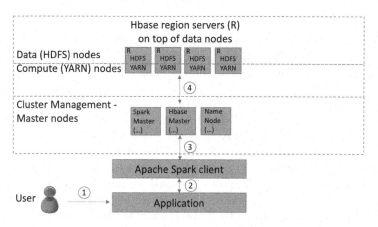

Fig. 3. *Hadoop* and *HBase* schema

- each column contains a single integer value, representing the number of occurrences of this fingerprint in the related document.

This in summary means, that the computational complexity is further reduced to be $O(n \cdot f(m))$. – where $f(m)$ is the number of operations required to retrieve a row from *HBase*. As $m \gg n$ and $f(m) < m$ this solution should be the fastest one of the three.

6   Experiments

In order to sufficiently evaluate the proposed solutions we planned a series of experiments, which was designed to test such features, as time performance and scalability in relation to the size of a repository and the size of the analysed document. Later, we run those tests in our testing environment on a supercomputer $TRYTON^2$. Mentioned tests were done on a prepared dataset, created from real-world diplomas that had been writing by students at the Gdansk University of Technology. The minimal similarity between selected documents was about 2% and it resulted from the similarity of title pages, statements and university affiliations.

6.1   Planned Tests

As mentioned before, we planned a series of tests in order to evaluate our approaches and their viability to process a constantly growing database of text documents. Details of these tests were as follows:

- the time needed to search our repository depending on its size – in total of 17 000 real and unique (excluding cases of plagiarism) documents of varying size.
- the time needed to insert a new document into the repository – as it is almost equally important to the search time (since the standard use-case consists of both similar documents search and repository inserts). As before, this time was measured for different sizes of the repository, in order to evaluate the scalability of this operation.
- the scalability of each solution – depending on the size of the tested document.
- the scalability of the $KASKADA$ and the $Hadoop$ ecosystem – depending on the number of concurrent requests and the number of available processors.

Each test was conducted on a random batch of n documents from the dataset, and all the results were averaged over this batch. Results of those tests can be seen in Subsect. 6.4.

6.2   Dataset

Our dataset consisted of around 17 000 text documents (stripped of formatting and images), varying in size from few kilobytes to one megabyte. Each document was a real and unique diploma – the repository consists of works from students of the Gdansk University of Technology. For every document there are two files in the repository – one containing its text and another, containing it's profile. Every profile contains a few hundreds to several hundred thousands of fingerprints.

6.3   Test Environment

All Hadoop tests were run in a cluster environment, comprising of eight nodes in an *openstack* environment – three master/manager nodes and five *HDFS* data nodes with *HBase* Region Servers. Each data node was equipped with 8 CPU cores and 32 GB of memory. Tests were run with *Apache Spark*, each *YARN* task was limited to 6 cores per data node, giving a total of 30 processors.

---

[2] Specification at TOP500 website: http://www.top500.org/system/178552.

All *KASKADA* tests were run in a cluster environment comprising of 8 nodes – 5 management nodes and 3 compute nodes. Each compute node was equipped with 12 CPU cores and 32 GB of memory.

6.4 Results

The first test we run was the experiment measuring the search operation time per 10 000 fingers, depending on the number of documents in the repository. The results of this test can be seen in Fig. 4. The naive iterative *HDFS* approach is a few orders of magnitude slower than the other three. The reason of that probably depends on the number of files in the repository. In this approach, we did not compact small files into larger buckets. Furthermore, the *KASKADA* map and the *HDFS* map approaches achieved similar results – the *HDFS* map approach is only two times faster. The *HBase* based approach is the fastest – achieving performance better by an order of magnitude from the original *KASKADA* approach. Also the *HBase* approach scales much better (close to logarithmically) than the *HDFS*, *HDFS* map and the *KASKADA* map approaches, which all scale close to linearly. Results for the every approach achieved the same level of accuracy.

Next, we run the import operation time test – in order to check whether the operation of importing new files into *HBase* doesn't impact the performance gain negatively. The results of this test can be seen in Fig. 5. The time of import a new document is almost independent of the repository size. Furthermore, this time is almost negligible compared to the search operation times.

The third test we run was aimed at measuring the scalability of all three solutions in relation to the processed document size. The results of this test can be seen in Fig. 6. The *HBase* and *HDFS* solutions scale close to linearly. The *KASKADA* map solution time grows very slowly depending on the size of the analysed document, the *HDFS* map solution time was almost constant.

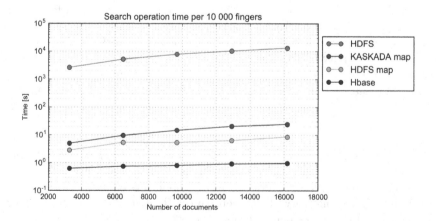

Fig. 4. Search operation time per 10 000 fingers

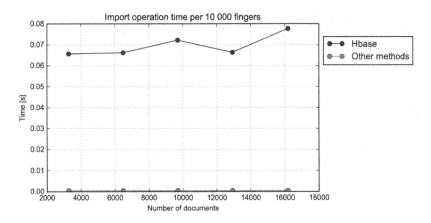

Fig. 5. Import operation time per 10 000 fingers

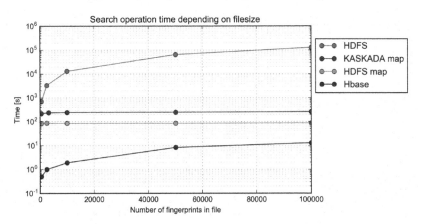

Fig. 6. Search operation time depending on file size

The fourth experiment we conducted was aimed to test the scalability of both platforms and the three fastest solutions, depending on the number of processors used in computations. The result of this test can be seen in Fig. 7. All three solutions scale fairly well in a close to linear manner.

The final experiment was run in order to test how both of the platforms handle many concurrent requests. All three platforms were limited to the same number of processors and memory. The result of this test can be seen in Fig. 8. The time of processing grows linearly with tasks load on the *KASKADA* platform. The *KASKADA* platform rejects new tasks, when there are no available resources – the number of rejected requests is represented as bars on the chart. The *Hadoop* ecosystem handles heavy load much better, no tasks were rejected and the processing times grow at a smaller pace (most likely, thanks to the advanced caching and load distribution algorithms of the platform). The sudden jump in processing time between 4 and 5 *HBase* approaches is caused by memory limitations of the system – the fifth task had to wait for free memory in order to start).

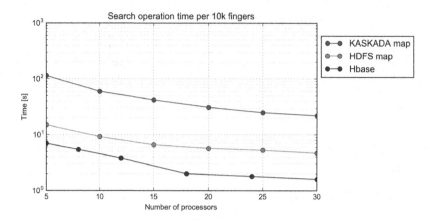

Fig. 7. Search time depending on the number of processors used

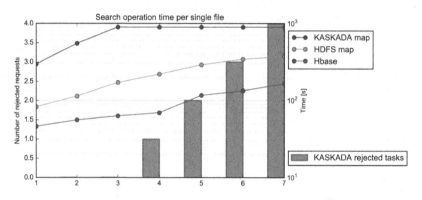

Fig. 8. Cumulative search time for n parallel tasks

7   Conclusion

Conducted experiments confirm the benefits of migrating the selected algorithm to the *Hadoop* platform from the *KASKADA* platform. The naive, iterative method, using the distributed file system *HDFS* and the integrated computing cluster *YARN* did not prove to be as effective as the original algorithm on the *KASKADA* platform. However the improved version, using a in-memory map, was measured to be several times faster than the original *KASKADA* algorithm and just as scalable. The difference is most visible when using the *HBase* database to store and analyse the documents profiles. Searching for similar documents using *HBase* is around 25× faster than the search method running on the *KASKADA* platform. This is caused by the lack of a dedicated, distributed file system for the *KASKADA* platform (which is using a standard disk matrix), as well as by the better scaling of the *HBase* algorithm. Results of experiments depends on the size of files stored in the repositories. For the plagiarism detection system where the size of files is smaller than 1 MB the most suitable computing platform configuration is HBase using reversed index as described above.

In summary, our tests proved, that the *HBase* solution is much faster and scales much better, in relation to the profiles repository size. Apart from that, the results quality was exactly the same as for the original *KASKADA* algorithm. The *KASKADA* platform allows for fast and efficient analysis of multimedia data streams, exploiting the compute power of a supercomputer or a compute cluster. The *Hadoop* platform is much better suited to support an anti-plagiarism system, since it provides efficient tools for big-data processing.

References

1. Fragidis, L.L., Chatzoglou, P.D., Aggelidis, V.P.: Integrated nationwide electronic health records system: semi-distributed architecture approach. Technol. Health Care **24**(6), 827–842 (2016)
2. Aletras, N., Tsarapatsanis, D., Preotiuc-Pietro, D., Lampos, V.: Predicting judicial decisions of the European court of human rights: a natural language processing perspective. PeerJ Comput. Sci. **2**, e93 (2016)
3. Hall, M.A., Wright, R.F.: Systematic content analysis of judicial opinions. Calif. Law Rev. **96**(1), 63–122 (2008)
4. Jurik, B.A., Blekinge, A.A., Ferneke-Nielsen, R.B., Moldrup-Dalum, P.: Bridging the gap between real world repositories and scalable preservation environments. Int. J. Digit. Libr. **16**(3–4), 267–282 (2015)
5. Beel, J., Gipp, B., Langer, S., Breitinger, C.: Research-paper recommender systems: a literature survey. Int. J. Digit. Libr. **17**(4), 305–338 (2016)
6. Tuarob, S., Bhatia, S., Mitra, P., Giles, C.L.: AlgorithmSeer: a system for extracting and searching for algorithms in scholarly big data. IEEE Trans. Big Data **2**(1), 3–17 (2016)
7. Kong, L., Zhao, Z., Lu, Z., Qi, H., Zhao, F.: A method of plagiarism source retrieval and text alignment based on relevance ranking model. Int. J. Database Theory Appl. **9**(12), 35–44 (2016)
8. Velasquez, J.D., Covacevich, Y., Molina, F., Marrese-Taylor, E., Rodriguez, C., Bravo-Marquez, F.: Docode 3.0 (document copy detector): a system for plagiarism detection by applying an information fusion process from multiple documental data sources. Inf. Fusion **27**, 64–75 (2016)
9. Buyya, R., Yeo, C.S., Venugopal, S.: Market-oriented cloud computing: vision, hype, and reality for delivering it services as computing utilities. In: 10th IEEE International Conference on High Performance Computing and Communications, 2008, HPCC 2008, pp. 5–13. IEEE (2008)
10. Krawczyk, H., Proficz, J.: KASKADA - multimedia processing platform architecture. In: Proceedings of the 2010 International Conference on Signal Processing and Multimedia Applications (SIGMAP), pp. 26–31, July 2010
11. White, T.: Hadoop: The Definitive Guide. O'Reilly Media Inc., Sebastopol (2012)
12. Kasai, T., Lee, G., Arimura, H., Arikawa, S., Park, K.: Linear-time longest-common-prefix computation in suffix arrays and its applications. In: Amir, A. (ed.) CPM 2001. LNCS, vol. 2089, pp. 181–192. Springer, Heidelberg (2001). https://doi.org/10.1007/3-540-48194-X_17
13. Hunt, J.W., MacIlroy, M.: An algorithm for differential file comparison. Citeseer (1976)

14. Levenshtein, V.I.: Binary codes capable of correcting deletions, insertions, and reversals. Soviet Phys. Dokl. **10**(8), 707–710 (1966)
15. Winkler, W.E.: The state of record linkage and current research problems. In: Statistical Research Division, US Census Bureau. Citeseer (1999)
16. Baeza-Yates, R., Navarro, G.: A faster algorithm for approximate string matching. In: Hirschberg, D., Myers, G. (eds.) CPM 1996. LNCS, vol. 1075, pp. 1–23. Springer, Heidelberg (1996). https://doi.org/10.1007/3-540-61258-0_1
17. Cutting, D., Pedersen, J.: Optimization for dynamic inverted index maintenance. In: Proceedings of the 13th Annual International ACM SIGIR Conference on Research and Development in Information Retrieval, pp. 405–411. ACM (1989)
18. Anh, V.N., Moffat, A.: Inverted index compression using word-aligned binary codes. Inf. Retr. **8**(1), 151–166 (2005)
19. Yan, H., Ding, S., Suel, T.: Inverted index compression and query processing with optimized document ordering. In: Proceedings of the 18th International Conference on World Wide Web, pp. 401–410. ACM (2009)
20. Gabrilovich, E., Markovitch, S.: Computing semantic relatedness using wikipedia-based explicit semantic analysis. In: IJCAI, vol. 7, pp. 1606–1611 (2007)
21. Mcnamee, P., Mayfield, J.: Character n-gram tokenization for European language text retrieval. Inf. Retr. **7**(1–2), 73–97 (2004)
22. Mayfield, J., McNamee, P.: Single n-gram stemming. In: Proceedings of the 26th Annual International ACM SIGIR Conference on Research and Development in Information Retrieval, pp. 415–416. ACM (2003)
23. Ogawa, Y., Matsuda, T.: An efficient document retrieval method using n-gram indexing. Syst. Comput. Jpn. **33**(2), 54–63 (2002)
24. Deerwester, S., Dumais, S.T., Furnas, G.W., Landauer, T.K., Harshman, R.: Indexing by latent semantic analysis. J. Am. Soc. Inf. Sci. **41**(6), 391 (1990)
25. Hofmann, T.: Probabilistic latent semantic indexing. In: Proceedings of the 22nd Annual International ACM SIGIR Conference on Research and Development in Information Retrieval, pp. 50–57. ACM (1999)
26. Kanerva, P., Kristofersson, J., Holst, A.: Random indexing of text samples for latent semantic analysis. In: Proceedings of the 22nd Annual Conference of the Cognitive Science Society, vol. 1036. Citeseer (2000)
27. Lewis, D.D., Jones, K.S.: Natural language processing for information retrieval. Commun. ACM **39**(1), 92–101 (1996)
28. Strzalkowski, T.: Natural language information retrieval. Inf. Process. Manag. **31**(3), 397–417 (1995)
29. Schleimer, S., Wilkerson, D.S., Aiken, A.: Winnowing: local algorithms for document fingerprinting. In: Proceedings of the 2003 ACM SIGMOD International Conference on Management of Data, pp. 76–85. ACM (2003)
30. Heintze, N., et al.: Scalable document fingerprinting. In: 1996 USENIX Workshop on Electronic Commerce, vol. 3, no. 1 (1996)
31. Forman, G., Eshghi, K., Chiocchetti, S.: Finding similar files in large document repositories. In: Proceedings of the Eleventh ACM SIGKDD International Conference on Knowledge Discovery in Data Mining, pp. 394–400. ACM (2005)
32. Willett, P.: Document retrieval experiments using indexing vocabularies of varying size. II. Hashing, truncation, digram and trigram encoding of index terms. J. Doc. **35**(4), 296–305 (1979)

33. Dhillon, I.S., Fan, J., Guan, Y.: Efficient clustering of very large document collections. In: Grossman, R.L., Kamath, C., Kegelmeyer, P., Kumar, V., Namburu, R.R. (eds.) Data Mining for Scientific and Engineering Applications. MC, vol. 2, pp. 357–381. Springer, Boston (2001). https://doi.org/10.1007/978-1-4615-1733-7_20

34. Manber, U., et al.: Finding similar files in a large file system. In: USENIX Winter, vol. 94, pp. 1–10 (1994)

35. Chang, F., Dean, J., Ghemawat, S., Hsieh, W.C., Wallach, D.A., Burrows, M., Chandra, T., Fikes, A., Gruber, R.E.: Bigtable: a distributed storage system for structured data. ACM Trans. Comput. Syst. **26**(2), 4:1–4:26 (2008). http://doi.acm.org/10.1145/1365815.1365816

36. Zaharia, M., Chowdhury, M., Franklin, M.J., Shenker, S., Stoica, I.: Spark: cluster computing with working sets. In: Proceedings of the 2nd USENIX Conference on Hot Topics in Cloud Computing, HotCloud 2010, p. 10. USENIX Association, Berkeley (2010). http://dl.acm.org/citation.cfm?id=1863103.1863113

37. Rabin, M.O., et al.: Fingerprinting by random polynomials. Center for Research in Computing Technology, Aiken Computation Laboratory, University (1981)

38. Muthitacharoen, A., Chen, B., Mazieres, D.: A low-bandwidth network file system. In: ACM SIGOPS Operating Systems Review, vol. 35, no. 5, pp. 174–187. ACM (2001)

39. Eshghi, K., Tang, H.K.: A framework for analyzing and improving content-based chunking algorithms. Hewlett-Packard Labs Technical Report TR, vol. 30, p. 2005 (2005)

40. Shvachko, K., Kuang, H., Radia, S., Chansler, R.: The hadoop distributed file system. In: 2010 IEEE 26th Symposium on Mass Storage Systems and Technologies (MSST), pp. 1–10, May 2010. https://doi.org/10.1109/MSST.2010.5496972. ISSN 2160-195X

Assessing Word Difficulty for Quiz-Like Game

Jakub Jagoda and Tomasz Boiński[✉]

Department of Computer Architecture, Faculty of Electronics,
Telecommunication and Informatics, Gdańsk University of Technology,
Gdańsk, Poland
tobo@eti.pg.gda.pl

Abstract. Mappings verification is a laborious task. Our research aims at providing a framework for manual verification of mappings using crowdsourcing approach. For this purpose we plan on implementing a quiz like game. For this purpose the mappings have to be evaluated in terms of difficulty to better present texts in respect of game levels. In this paper we present an algorithm for assessing word difficulty. Three approaches are presented and experimental results are shown. Plans for future works are also provided.

1 Introduction

During our research, mainly during the Colabmap[1] project we created a set of mappings between English Wikipedia articles and WordNet synsets [1–4]. Each mapping consists of a WordNet synset, definition of the synset and the title of Wikipedia article with special characters encoded using RFC 3986. Such mappings, when proved to be correct, will allow formalization of Wikipedia structure. The obtained set of mappings contained algorithmically created 54475 connections. We aim at creating 100% correct mappings corpora so the set required manual verification.

In 2006 Luis von Ahn proposed usage of computer games as something more than pure entertainment and thus creating the idea of so called GWAP (Game With A Purpose) [5]. GWAPs are typical games that provide standard entertainment value that users expect but are designed in a way that allows generation of added value by solving a problem requiring intellectual activity. It is worth noticing that GWAPs does not allow financial gratification for the work. The will to continue playing should be treated as the only way of gratifying users [6]. Tempted by the results obtained during the Samsung's survey we decided on implementing a GWAP for validation of those connections [7] following the Human Based Computation model [8].

The originally obtained mappings were extended with three additional "next best" mappings with the idea of presenting the user a question (definition of a synset) with 4 possible answers (Wikipedia article titles). At the beginning the 3 other answers were randomly selected from the set of Wikipedia's pages but

---

[1] http://kask.eti.pg.gda.pl/colabmap.

© Springer International Publishing AG, part of Springer Nature 2018
J. Szymański and Y. Velegrakis (Eds.): IKC 2017, LNCS 10546, pp. 70–79, 2018.
https://doi.org/10.1007/978-3-319-74497-1_7

such approach quickly proved to be incorrect as the "next best" mappings were not related at all to the question. Instead we used Wikipedia search functionality to select alternative answers (according to Wikipedia). For the purpose of verification we implemented a 2D platform game called TGame[2] ("Tagger Game") as a 2D platform game following the output-agreement model [9].

In the next step of mappings verification we decided to implement a quiz like game similar to "Who wants to be a Millionaire" (with a small difference that instead of real questions we will mostly ask about words or phrases, composed of two or more words). One of the major problems here is how to order the questions asked? It is obvious that when the player starts the game, he or she shouldn't immediately get a difficult question – otherwise the player would leave the game quickly and would be discouraged. The difficulty should start at a relatively low level and increase while the player answers next questions. For this we need to somehow order the words from the least to the most difficult. In this paper we present a method of validating word difficulty for such ordering.

The structure of the paper is as follows. Section 2 defines what is a word difficulty and presents some of the approaches. Section 3 presents the proposed approach. In Sect. 4 evaluation of the proposed algorithm is given and finally Sect. 5 presents final conclusions and proposes some works that can be done in the future to further enhance the proposed solution.

2 Defining Word Difficulty and Related Work

To assess word difficulty we need an algorithmic way of classifying words having only that word, i.e. a set of tokens (letters in this case). Such sets are not really meaningful to a computer program in a way they are meaningful to an average person.

There are many approaches to this problem. Most of them however focus on assessing the whole text [10,11] and often utilize complex techniques like Coh-Metrix [12]. In our case single word, rather than the whole text, characterization is needed. One can also find plenty of games and puzzles that are related to words and they use various scoring systems and classification strategies. For example, Scrabble uses different score per letter depending on their frequency in specified language, promoting letters that are "rare" with higher score. In this case a difficult word might be a word that consist of rare letters. In this case the meaning or complexity of the word does not matter, only the score of letters it is composed of. On the other hand, a game in which the player's task is to type words on a standard QWERTY keyboard as fast as possible might not find these rules relevant – instead, a difficult word would be a one that is difficult to write, meaning for example its letters lay in some distance between each other or involving various fingers to type it. Therefore in order to correctly classify words, we need to define what words we want to consider difficult.

---

[2] https://play.google.com/store/apps/details?id=pl.gda.eti.kask.tgame,
   http://kask.eti.pg.gda.pl/tgame/.

There are many ways for people to tell if they consider a word difficult or not. It can be assumed that an average person knows an average set of words, so most of people will classify word's difficulties more or less similarly. Of course, it will be extremely unlikely that a group of people, asked to order the words by their difficulty, would end up with exactly same lineup. It's rather about asking them to assign some labels to the words, for example "how difficult, on a scale 1–5, is that word to you?". We can consider that a difficult word for an average person is a word that the person does not see often and, when they see that word, its construction gives them only a little, if any, idea about its origin or possible meaning. It is clear that a set of common, everyday words exists and have a large common part among average people. It is also clear, that an average person that is not in any way related to some specific domain might consider words coming from that domain as difficult, because those are not everyday words for them. In our case we thus define word difficulty as a score from 1 to 5 stating how probable it is that the person knows the meaning of the word.

Research show that frequency of a word might be correlated to its difficulty [13]. The observation that the words that occurs in texts less often can be considered more difficult is one of the best and most widely used methods of estimating word's difficulty. Such observations lead to creation of statistical word assessment defining difficulty as a measure how often the word occurs in the given domain or in everyday life meaning how easy it is to be seen. If the word is often seen in text than it is treated as easy for most of the population and vice versa [13,14]. Such approach led also to many modern text assessment service implementations like Twinword API [15].

3   Our Approach

In our solution we asses difficulty of words connected with Wikipedia articles. As such we decided to use Wikipedia as the corpora for text occurrence analysis. In all cases we evaluated a subset of the mappings against over 5 000 000 pages from English Wikipedia in each case building upon the previous solution.

3.1   Naive Approach

The first algorithm (Algorithm 1) was based directly on the observations given in the Sect. 2.

The result of the algorithm is a set of words **W** sorted from the easiest to the most difficult one. This approach have some limitations:

- a short, simple word that is very rare even among various types of texts can be mistakenly classified as a difficult word, for example a word "moo", which is clearly known even to very young children.
- a lot of words get the same score.
- the corpora used must have an average distribution of the words, otherwise it can yield incorrect results, this is difficult to verify with Wikipedia.

Algorithm 1. Naive approach

1: read text corpus **T**
2: read set of words to classify **W**
3: **for all** word **w** in set **W do**
4:     count number of times **w** occurs in text **T**
5:     assign the result **r** with **w**
6: **end for**
7: Sort words in **W** by number of occurrences **r** ascending

3.2 Adding Word Length

In this approach we decided to include into the algorithm the length of the analyzed word to reduce the impact of the first two limitations given in the previous section. In this approach we can consider difficult words as the ones that are both rare and long. Short words, as well as the frequent ones, will be more likely to be classified as easy.

During the implementation we also found out that it's very hard to correctly adjust the weight coefficients (length and number of occurrences) depending on the size of text corpora and input words, therefore we decided to use the relative values. The algorithm goes as shown in Algorithm 2.

Algorithm 2. The second approach

1: read text corpus **T**
2: read set of words to classify **W**
3: select the longest word in **W** and store its length as **lMax**
4: find the word from set W that occurs most times among text T and store the number of occurrences as **oMax**
5: **for all** word **w** in set **W do**
6:     c = number of times **w** occurs in text **T**
7:     lw = length of **w**
8:     $s = \left(\frac{lw}{lMAX}\right) * \left(\frac{c}{oMAX}\right)$
9:     assign the score **s** with **w**
10: **end for**
11: Sort words in **W** by the score **s** descending

Once again the resulting set of words **W** is sorted from the easiest to the most difficult word. The score is calculated as a multiplication of length of the word and the number of occurrences in the text. In this approach the most difficult word (the lowest score) is a combination of being long and occur least times. If two words have similar frequency score, the longer one will now become more difficult. In all cases the score is calculated as relative within the available text.

3.3 The Final Approach

In this approach we tried to deal with the third issue. Imagine that our text set consist of ten texts, similar in length: five of them are academic papers on distributed computations and five of them are cake recipes. If it happens that only one cake requires bananas, word "banana" might appear less times than the word "matrix" which would mean that the former will be classified as more difficult while one might expect that for an average person it would be vice versa. To eliminate this problem, we might take into consideration whether the word originates from an easy or a difficult text and apply proper weight to the resulting score. For determining whether a text is difficult or not (in English) we can use one of the existing methods. In our solution we chose Flesch-Kincaid readability ease test [16]. This test, invented by Rudolf Flesch and J. Peter Kincaid for U.S. Navy in 1975, takes a text and applies formula 1 following to it.

$$fkScore = 206.835 - 1.015 * (\frac{totalwords}{totalsentences}) - 84.6 * (\frac{totalsyllables}{totalwords}) \quad (1)$$

The result (fkScore) is a score with most values between 0 and 100 (although scores below and above are possible to achieve). This score tells how difficult is the text to read – the lower the score, the more difficult the text. As a curiosity, one of the easiest sentences with score 116 is "The cat sat on the mat", whereas the chemical name of titin (a protein) which is 189,819 characters long and consists of 72443 syllables, scores a −6128472. The rated texts can be divided into groups show in Table 1.

Incorporation of Flesch-Kincaid score requires further changes to the algorithm. The final algorithm is shown in Algorithm 3.

As in previous approaches the resulting set of words **W** is sorted from the easiest to the most difficult word. Similar as in previous approach the final score is a multiplication of length and occurrence scores. In this case the length score of a word takes value from range <1, 2> so not to zero the whole score. In the case where classification of a multi-word phrase is needed the phrase should be split into separate words for which the score should be computed. The phrase score should be than computed as an average score of all words that it consists of.

Table 1. Groups of text difficulty

Score	Notes
90.0 and above	Very easy to read, easily understood by an 11-year old
80.0–90.0	Easy to read, conversational English for average people
70.0–80.0	Fairly easy to read
60.0–70.0	Plain English, easily understood by 13- to 15-year-old students
50.0–60.0	Fairly difficult to read
30.0–50.0	Difficult to read
30.0 and below	Very difficult to read

Algorithm 3. The third approach with Flesch-Kincaid score

1: read a set of texts **T**
2: read set of words to classify **W**
3: **for** i = 0 **to** i = size(**T**) **do**
4:     $fkScore[i] = 206.835 - 1.015 * (\frac{totalwords(T[i])}{totalsentences(T[i])}) - 84.6 * (\frac{totalsyllables(T[i])}{totalwords(T[i])})$
5: **end for**
6: **for** i = 0 **to** i = size(**T**) **do**
7:     $fkScore[i] = \frac{fkScore[i]}{max(fkScore)}$
8: **end for**
9: select the longest word in **W** and store its length as **lMax**
10: **for** i = 0 **to** i = size(**W**) **do**
11:     **for** j = 0 **to** j = size(**T**) **do**
12:         let **occurrences[i][j]** be the number of occurrences of word **W[i]** in text **T[j]**
13:         let **partialFrequencyScore[i][j]** be **occurrences[i][j]*fkScore[j]**
14:     **end for**
15:     $frequencyScore[i] = \frac{\sum_{n=0}^{size(T)-1} partialFrequencyScore[i][n]}{size(T)}$
16:     $lengthScore[i] = (2 - \frac{length(W[i])}{lMax})$
17:     $s[i] = frequencyScore[i] * lengthScore[i]$
18: **end for**
19: Sort words in **W** by the score **s** descending

4 Evaluation

For evaluation purposes we created a set of 20 words generated using Random Word Generator tool[3]. Those words were presented to a group of 90 people. Each time the words were randomly shuffled not to introduce any suggestions to the order of difficulty. Each person was asked to order the words from the easiest one to the most difficult. The results were than accumulated and merged using the following steps:

1. For each person participated, get a list of their result
2. For every list, attach scores with every word, so that the first word (the easiest, according to the participant) gets 1 point and the last (the most difficult) gets 20 points
3. For every word then calculate average score from all the lists.
4. Sort words by calculated average score ascending.

In the results we got an ordered list of words (from the easiest to the most difficult) presented in Table 2.

Just like we assumed, the common, well-known and short words occupy the beginning of the table. Some results might be considered unexpected (like "whistle"), but in those cases there might be other factors influencing their difficulty except for the ones that were considered in the formula (e.g. difference between how a word is written and pronounced – something that is common for English language).

---

[3] https://randomwordgenerator.com/.

After the survey the same set of words were classified using all three versions of the proposed solution. As text corpora, English Wikipedia was used (consisting of 4 838 000 pages).

We divided the results into four groups with equal number of words. We assume that words in one groups are close in terms of difficulty. The words in italics are the words that were assigned by the algorithm to other difficulty level than according to the survey. The results, compared with the survey, are presented in Table 3.

As we can see the naive version correctly assigned 9 words, first modification 10 words and the final version 11 words. The average difference of score (calculated in the number of levels the word was shifted) is 1.45 in the first case, 1.4

Table 2. Evaluation set of words ordered by humans

Word	Order	Word	Order	Word	Order	Word	Order
start	1	dirt	6	parcel	11	panoramic	16
cup	2	unit	7	jazzy	12	whistle	17
hard	3	rabbits	8	disagree	13	substantial	18
false	4	haircut	9	horrible	14	wobble	19
cute	5	drip	10	observation	15	tedious	20

Table 3. Comparison of words evaluation

Survey	Algorithm #1	Algorithm #2	Algorithm #3
start	cup	cup	cup
cup	start	start	*unit*
hard	*unit*	*unit*	hard
false	hard	hard	*drip*
cute	false	false	start
dirt	*substantial*	dirt	dirt
unit	*observation*	*substantial*	*wobble*
rabbits	dirt	*observation*	*false*
haircut	*whistle*	*whistle*	rabbits
drip	*parcel*	cute	*cute*
parcel	*rabbits*	parcel	jazzy
jazzy	*panoramic*	*rabbits*	*whistle*
disagree	horrible	horrible	parcel
horrible	*cute*	*panoramic*	*haircut*
observation	disagree	disagree	horrible
panoramic	*jazzy*	*drip*	*observation*
whistle	tedious	*jazzy*	tedious
substantial	*drip*	tedious	*disagree*
wobble	*haircut*	*haircut*	panoramic
tedious	wobble	wobble	substantial

in the second case and 0.9 for the final algorithm. The final solution, in most cases, switch the words between the neighboring groups.

The results obtained using the third approach suits our purposes very well. We needed to obtain an ordered list of words difficulty for the need of a quiz game. This list can be later corrected by the players themselves during the actual playing of the game. Moving words on level up or down in terms of difficulty is perfectly fine in this situation. For the purpose of the game we plan on classifying 56 000 words and assign them to 10 classes. Small differences with resulting positions are thus less likely to cause level mismatches.

The experiments performed during the evaluation revealed some unsolved problems. It was very hard to create an absolute scoring system within the algorithm. This is because the average frequency of a word in all texts depends on the number of text we use, while the average length of a word is independent of that and stabilizes at some level. This attempted to be fixed by introducing the weight coefficients for both the frequency and length parts, but it was very difficult to adjust them properly, especially when the text corpora contained millions of texts.

Flesch-Kincaid score works well for regular English texts, but sometimes within the corpora there are texts resulting in very low, negative scores, breaking the results. Such situation occurred in one of the tests. Some Wikipedia pages consists mostly of Chinese people names, which scored -2971. Such a text was not useful in our computations and introduced noise in the results. After some further tests we decided to exclude any text with a score lower than 0, since this indicated that either the text is not in English (at least partially) or we deal with something unusual, like a protein name.

The final approach is also very memory intensive. Counting occurrences of 56 000 unique words in over 4 800 000 texts takes a lot of time and uses a lot of memory. The earliest plan was to count occurrences of all of the unique words in all of the texts, but this led to exponential growth of the database. We thus decided to limit calculations only to the words we are actually interested in which allowed to keep the memory constraints in check.

5   Conclusion and Future Work

The scoring of word difficulty is a difficult task, mainly due the lack of one, standard definition what it means for a word to be difficult. Observation shows however, that the approach presented here is consistent with observation of the human behavior – if we stumble upon a word very often it is more probable that it is easier for us.

The presented approach allows us to order the set o phrases needed verification in a manner that will not be discouraging to players. Also it is worth noting that the main purpose of this algorithm is to give a preliminary classification that later might be corrected by players playing the game or manually adjusted by moderators.

In the future it could be feasible to extend the algorithm further. We should take into consideration also the pronunciation of the word. The greater the difference between spelling and pronunciation, the more difficult the word can be considered. Taking into account Scrabble-like letter ranking like promoting rare letter groups (pairs or triplets) or calculate the ratio of unique letters to the word length (more unique letters, the more difficult the word) might allow better classification independent from the domain of the word.

References

1. Korytkowski, R., Szymanski, J.: Collaborative approach to WordNet and Wikipedia integration. In: The Second International Conference on Advanced Collaborative Networks, Systems and Applications, COLLA, pp. 23–28 (2012)
2. Szymański, J.: Mining relations between Wikipedia categories. In: Zavoral, F., Yaghob, J., Pichappan, P., El-Qawasmeh, E. (eds.) NDT 2010. CCIS, vol. 88, pp. 248–255. Springer, Heidelberg (2010). https://doi.org/10.1007/978-3-642-14306-9_25
3. Szymański, J.: Words context analysis for improvement of information retrieval. In: Nguyen, N.-T., Hoang, K., Jędrzejowicz, P. (eds.) ICCCI 2012. LNCS (LNAI), vol. 7653, pp. 318–325. Springer, Heidelberg (2012). https://doi.org/10.1007/978-3-642-34630-9_33
4. Szymański, J., Duch, W.: Self organizing maps for visualization of categories. In: Huang, T., Zeng, Z., Li, C., Leung, C.S. (eds.) ICONIP 2012. LNCS, vol. 7663, pp. 160–167. Springer, Heidelberg (2012). https://doi.org/10.1007/978-3-642-34475-6_20
5. Von Ahn, L.: Games with a purpose. Computer **39**(6), 92–94 (2006)
6. Von Ahn, L., Dabbish, L.: Designing games with a purpose. Commun. ACM **51**(8), 58–67 (2008)
7. Biuro Prasowe Samsung Electronics Polska Sp. z o.o.: Prawie połowa Polaków gra codziennie w gry wideo (in Polish)
8. Wightman, D.: Crowdsourcing human-based computation. In: Proceedings of the 6th Nordic Conference on Human-Computer Interaction: Extending Boundaries, pp. 551–560. ACM (2010)
9. Boiński, T.: Game with a purpose for mappings verification. In: 2016 Federated Conference on Computer Science and Information Systems (FedCSIS), pp. 405–409. IEEE (2016)
10. Binkley, M.R.: New ways of assessing text difficulty. Readability: Its past, present and future, pp. 98–120 (1988)
11. Kauchak, D., Leroy, G., Hogue, A.: Measuring text difficulty using parse-tree frequency. J. Assoc. Inf. Sci. Technol. **68**, 2088–2100 (2017)
12. Crossley, S.A., Greenfield, J., McNamara, D.S.: Assessing text readability using cognitively based indices. Tesol Q. **42**(3), 475–493 (2008)
13. Breland, H.M.: Word frequency and word difficulty: a comparison of counts in four corpora. Psychol. Sci. **7**(2), 96–99 (1996)
14. Carroll, J.B.: An alternative to Juilland's usage coefficient for lexical frequencies. ETS Res. Rep. Ser. **1970**(2), 1–15 (1970)

15. Inc., T.: Twinword API (2011). https://www.twinword.com/api/language-scoring. php. Accessed 10 May 2017
16. Kincaid, J.P., Fishburne Jr, R.P., Rogers, R.L., Chissom, B.S.: Derivation of new readability formulas (automated readability index, fog count and flesch reading ease formula) for navy enlisted personnel. Technical report, DTIC Document (1975)

From Deep Learning to Deep University: Cognitive Development of Intelligent Systems

Mariia Golovianko[1] ⓘ, Svitlana Gryshko[2], and Vagan Terziyan[3(✉)] ⓘ

[1] Department of Artificial Intelligence, Kharkiv National University of Radioelectronics, Kharkiv, Ukraine
mariia.golovianko@nure.ua
[2] Department of Economic Cybernetics, Kharkiv National University of Radioelectronics, Kharkiv, Ukraine
svitlala.gryshko@nure.ua
[3] Faculty of Information Technology, University of Jyvaskyla, Jyvaskyla, Finland
vagan.terziyan@jyu.fi

Abstract. Search is not only an instrument to find intended information. Ability to search is a basic cognitive skill helping people to explore the world. It is largely based on personal intuition and creativity. However, due to the emerged big data challenge, people require new forms of training to develop or improve this ability. Current developments within Cognitive Computing and Deep Learning enable artificial systems to learn and gain human-like cognitive abilities. This means that the skill how to search efficiently and creatively within huge data spaces becomes one of the most important ones for the cognitive systems aiming at autonomy. This skill cannot be pre-programmed, it requires learning. We offer to use the collective search expertise to train creative association-driven navigation across heterogeneous information spaces. We argue that artificial cognitive systems, as well as humans, need special environments, like universities, to train skills of autonomy and creativity.

Keywords: Deep learning · Cognitive system · Cognitive development
Computational creativity · Exploratory search · Deep university

1 Introduction

Current research in Artificial Intelligence emphasizes the role of human-like cognition modeling for artificial systems to enable automatic handling of complex situations in realistic environments by using such traditionally human capabilities, as learning, adapting, interacting, and understanding [1]. Cognitive systems can already recognize image and speech, translate texts, identify diagnosis, filter content, make user-oriented recommendations. They are becoming more accurate in predictions, analytics and decision making due to the ability to process huge amounts of raw data and get deeper insights leveraging on deep non-linear learning models configured by people [2]. The next step is to ensure the real depth of cognition and autonomy of intelligent systems: a

© Springer International Publishing AG, part of Springer Nature 2018
J. Szymański and Y. Velegrakis (Eds.): IKC 2017, LNCS 10546, pp. 80–85, 2018.
https://doi.org/10.1007/978-3-319-74497-1_8

system should be aware of its current features and abilities, and capable of self-development, self-configuration and self-maintenance which means to have and understand its own desires, intelligently form novel ideas, theories, inventions, do research, set up own goals, reach them and understand why and how [3]. This is addressed by increase of the systems' creativity and efficiency [4–6].

In this research we focus on the techniques and architectures enabling cognitive development of intelligent systems. An intelligent system (either human or artificial one) cannot handle the complexity and the infinity of the open world at once as an input. It applies a combination of focused sensing, searching, asking, querying and browsing strategies, makes on-the-fly selections and navigations, studies and assesses search results, compares and integrates the obtained information, and finally develops new knowledge and abilities. Such exploratory search is used for exploration of the information space and satisfaction of the system's informational needs [7]. It is an iterative process comprising sequential refinement of search activities and update of search objectives by ongoing shift of search focus (specified, e.g., by keywords in Web search) of the system. Ability to switch the focus consciously is a required feature of the intelligent autonomous system. In this research we demonstrate which data models and techniques can be applied to train this ability in cognitive systems.

Information retrieval in Web is traditionally performed by use of keyword-based models. In [8] we showed a model of exploratory search in big data based on an association-driven navigation in the space of collective experience created by sets of keywords used for search queries. In this paper we argue that the same model in a more abstract form can be used for more generic creative association-driven navigation in heterogeneous information spaces.

We introduce a concept of the *university for everything or* "deep university", which can be launched as a creative, evolving and collaborative training environment for artificial and hybrid (Collective Intelligence) cognitive systems, which guides the course of cognitive processes and provides a cognitive system (a "student") with the information resources for the increase of the self-awareness and autonomy by deep-learning-driven self-development of capabilities to be curious, to ask questions (formulate queries) intelligently and creatively, find answers and make decisions.

2 Education for Everything: Universities for Cognitive Systems

2.1 Growing Fully Developed Cognitive Systems

The old-fashioned view at an Artificial Intelligence system has become obviously too primitive. According to the problem-solving paradigm, an intelligent system is capable of getting a problem (from a human) and solving it by breaking into a set of intelligent tasks characterized as either a machine-learning problem, a planning problem, a theorem-proving problem, etc., autonomously or in collaboration with humans.

However, the point is to build an intelligent system implementing human-like intellectual capacity to full extent: beginning from the ability to really want to do something or being curious to explore something, generate ideas, discover and formulate problems, define tasks intelligently, handle them creatively and consciously, and impact the environment synchronously with the self-management. Current separate machine learning techniques, even those called deep ones, cannot ensure all these, especially for heterogeneous-multi-task handling systems. Advanced machine learning must ensure that a computational cognitive system meets all functional criteria, defined by Newell for cognitive architectures [9], such as, exhibiting rational, effective adaptive behavior, using vast amounts of knowledge about the environment, ability to integrate diverse knowledge, learning from the environment, acquiring capabilities through development, exhibiting self-awareness and self-consciousness, and others.

In the human world these issues are addressed by education which is an important enabler of human development implying expansion of capabilities (also creative ones) and freedoms. Schools and universities serve as centers for intellectual capacity building, verified information share and exchange. Likewise, a modern artificial cognitive system must be well-trained. We argue that (deep) learning for a machine is a dynamic, evolutionary process, very similar to traditional higher education, however, with new challenges and features. It facilitates comprehensive acquisition of different skills at all the major cognitive levels, leveraging on collaboration in creative, dynamically changing ecosystems, similar to those built around universities.

In order to address arising motivations and, therefore, survive and be effective, a system must have some basic instincts of *curiosity, imagination and intuition*. These three contribute to a system's creativity and *proactivity,* enabling anticipatory, change-oriented and self-initiated behavior. Such preconditions for self-awareness and consciousness of a system will drive further its self-organization, self-configuration and self-maintenance.

Learning of cognitive systems as "students" in future universities is deeper than can be provided according to any traditional approach to education due to a multilayered comprehensive structure of the study. Basic features of deep universities are:

- generation of dynamic artificial curricula on demand: to satisfy a system's ongoing needs and curiosity;
- a (deep) structure of the generated curricula consisting of a set of training courses for different cognitive functions of a system;
- a deep structure of the "training courses" (smart syllabi) providing the hierarchical increase of the cognitive complexity of learning outcomes, according to the revised Bloom's taxonomy [10] and Webb's depth-of-knowledge levels [11]. Within a "training course" a system learns remembering facts, understanding them, applying them, analyzing, evaluating and, finally, creatively developing new entities;
- application of different machine learning methods for different tasks: supervised learning, unsupervised learning, semi-supervised learning, reinforcement learning.

2.2   Implementation of Developing Cognitive Architectures

System development is a process of self-configuration and self-maintenance, initiated by a system itself. A system finds a problem of an absolutely new type and needs configurational upgrades to be able to solve it. It specifies its learning requests and expectations (in terms of learning outcomes) and learns from the collaborative training environment, increasing its useful knowledge and enhancing its self-configurational abilities, i.e., skills how to choose cognitive models and adjust configurational hyper-parameters of each model for different tasks. By this interpretation a cognitive system plays both roles: a "learner" and a "university".

This idea brings us to the basic (executive) structure of a cognitive system consisting of three main components: (i) a creative idea generator, (ii) a work planner, which defines a problem as a cascade of specific tasks according to emerged ideas, and (iii) problem solvers. On the top we have a learning subsystem (deep university) training each component of the executive subsystem to perform intelligently and creatively according to the artificial curricula developed for the system (see Fig. 1).

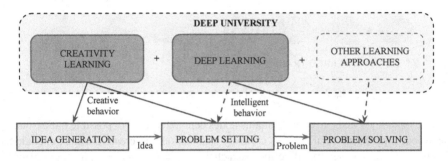

Fig. 1. Basic architecture of a typical creative cognitive system

2.3 Learning from Collective Creativity

In the era of digitalization, the cognitive mobility of the society is a new mission and a new challenge for the universities. Such mobility is achieved due to the creativity of cognition: curiosity and independent search, free and smart orientation and self-navigation in big data, the ability to ask new questions and find non-trivial tasks. Creativity and curiosity are recognized as the main 21st-Century Skills [12].

A classical university is a place of accelerated human development. One of the most important functions of a "deep university" is to train creative (exploratory) search skills based on the awareness of relevant collective experiences. Similarly to learning intelligent problem-solving skills in a human-like manner (i.e., extracting feature hierarchies with deep learning techniques), a cognitive system needs also to learn how to satisfy its curiosity and develop imagination and intuition. One possible approach is to leverage on *collective creativity* experience.

We use a TB network data model for collective experience representation. It is an evolution of a specific tree-based data structure called a TB (There-and-Back) structure [13], which we have previously used for modeling collective experience of a keyword search in [8]. We focus on the sequential, interactive and associative nature of creativity which can be viewed as exploratory search in the collaborative creative space of states. Such search is driven by a smart iterative focusing where the focus (e.g., set of keywords for search or set of queries to sensors, etc.) at each stage is defined by the system itself. Creative space is organized as a network of concepts or cognitive states (e.g., objects, events and ideas) interconnected by links or pathways reflecting the strength of association between pairs of concepts (see Fig. 2).

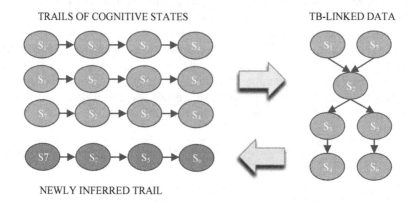

Fig. 2. An example of a creative space construction

The input layer of the network contains nodes denoted by a set of possible initial states, the output layer keeps final states – curiosity satisfaction and creative ideas generation. Creativity process is therefore described as a chain of cognitive states S_j, from motivation to satisfaction. We call them trails because we use swarm learning algorithms for machine training on top of this data model: $Trail_i := S_{i1}, S_{i2}, .., S_{in}$, where S_{i1} – motivational state, S_{in} – terminal state of satisfaction. Links in the trails are creator's associations representing a transfer from the output of one cognitive state to the input of another. The trails are combined into an associative network. The space is constructed by the algorithm of TB feeding described in details in [8]. It is an iterative process of incorporation of new trails into an existing structure. New implicit relationships, thus new creative trails, can be automatically inferred over the basic structure.

In this case creativity learning is based on exploratory search in the previously formed creativity space.

Formally, a machine interacts with the creative space in discrete time steps. At each time step, a machine observes the environmental state S_{ij} and applies an action according to the association A_{ijk}. Depending on S_{ij} and A_{ijk}, the system transfers itself into a new state and receives a real-valued reward $r \in R$. The system's goal is to maximize its expected cumulative reward, called return R. The result is a map of cognitive states that generates an action for any given state. We suggest using swarm intelligence methods, e.g., the ant colony optimization algorithms, for finding good paths in the creative space by laying down pheromone trails and calculating reward obtained by a system in each state based on it.

3   Conclusions and Future Work

Nearly magic capabilities of cognitive computing and deep learning are really impressive. Despite this obvious success, there is still a great amount of limitations and restrictions in both cognitive systems and deep learning algorithms. We believe that the most challenging, interesting and demanding issue in cognitive computing is building cognitive architectures for artificial systems with capabilities of self-exploration and self-development. Big data around and within such systems requires smart (driven by best collected practices) iterative focusing to manage it autonomously. We find it reasonable to draw a parallel between a system and a human development and argue about the need of special universities for artificial systems' comprehensive cognitive development. Within such universities a system will consciously develop its cognitive skills to explore (search, sense and understand what to search, why and how) the external physical and abstract world together with itself smartly and creatively.

Acknowledgements. This article is based upon work from COST (European Cooperation in Science and Technology) Action KEYSTONE IC1302.

References

1. Kelly, J., Hamm, S.: Smart Machines: IBM's Watson and the Era of Cognitive Computing. Columbia University Press, New York (2013)
2. LeCun, Y., Bengio, Y., Hinton, G.: Deep learning. Nature **521**(7553), 436–444 (2015)
3. Varshney, L.R., Pinel, F., Varshney, K.R., Schörgendorfer, A., Chee, Y.M.: Cognition as a part of computational creativity. In: 2013 12th IEEE International Conference on Cognitive Informatics and Cognitive Computing (ICCI* CC), pp. 36–43. IEEE, July 2013
4. Jordanous, A.: Four PPPPerspectives on computational creativity in theory and in practice. Connection Sci. **28**(2), 194–216 (2016)
5. Colton, S., Wiggins, G.A.: Computational creativity: the final frontier? In: Proceedings of the 20th European Conference on Artificial Intelligence, pp. 21–26. IOS Press, August 2012
6. Pease, A., Colton, S.: On impact and evaluation in computational creativity: a discussion of the Turing test and an alternative proposal. In: Proceedings of the AISB Symposium on AI and Philosophy, April 2011
7. Marchionini, G.: Exploratory search: from finding to understanding. Commun. ACM **49**(4), 41–46 (2006)
8. Terziyan, V., Golovianko, M., Cochez, M.: TB-structure: collective intelligence for exploratory keyword search. In: Calì, A., Gorgan, D., Ugarte, M. (eds.) KEYSTONE 2016. LNCS, vol. 10151, pp. 171–178. Springer, Cham (2017). https://doi.org/10.1007/978-3-319-53640-8_15
9. Newell, A.: Unified Theories of Cognition. Harvard University Press, Cambridge (1994)
10. Anderson, L.W., Krathwohl, D.R., Airasian, P., Cruikshank, K., Mayer, R., Pintrich, P., Wittrock, M.: A Taxonomy for Learning, Teaching and Assessing: A Revision of Bloom's Taxonomy. Longman Publishing, New York (2001). Artz, A.F., Armour-Thomas, E.: Development of a cognitive-metacognitive framework for protocol analysis of mathematical problem solving in small groups. Cogn. Instr. **9**(2), 137–175 (1992)
11. Webb, N.L.: Depth-of-knowledge levels for four content areas. Language Arts (2002)
12. New Vision for Education: Fostering Social and Emotional Learning through Technology. World Economic Forum (2016). http://www3.weforum.org/docs/WEF_New_Vision_for_Education.pdf
13. Lovitskii, V.A., Terziyan, V.: Words' coding in TB-structure. Problemy Bioniki **26**, 60–68 (1981). (In Russian)

From a Web Services Catalog to a Linked Ecosystem of Services

Fatma Slaimi, Sana Sellami, and Omar Boucelma(✉) (iD)

Aix Marseille Université, CNRS, ENSAM, Université de Toulon,
LSIS UMR 7296, 13397 Marseille, France
{fatma.slaimi,sana.sellami,omar.boucelma}@univ-amu.fr

Abstract. In this paper, we present a Linked ecosystem of Web services where both Web services, mashups and users are represented as a multigraph structure. For illustration and experimental purposes, a graph has been constructed, in gathering web services metadata from ProgrammableWeb. The graph is stored in a Neo4j graph database and serves as a repository for a realistic collection of web services for achieving services/mashups discovery and recommendation.

Keywords: Web services · Discovery · Recommendation · Linked data
Graph databases · Neo4j

1 Introduction

The advent of service oriented approaches has led to plethora of available Web services (or APIs). However, and besides the availability of these services through directories/catalogues such as ProgrammableWeb[1] (PWeb) Web services' portals still remain non-well-structured in order to ease the discovery and recommendation processes. In addition, all these services/mashups are a bit scattered on the Web and there are no materialized links among them that could facilitate their discovery. Therefore, we need an explicit WSs representation in materializing different links accordingly with different semantics.

Indeed, with the growth of social networks and the emergence of the social Web, one may collect different kind of metadata in addition to users' previous usages or users' profiles. Indeed, users (web services) can no more be considered as independent/isolated entities, but as a set of pairs characterized by other types of relationships such as follow, confidence, etc. These relationships generate graphs of interconnected (close or "similar") users, among which are those having common interests. For instance, in PWeb, users are connected by track relationships as illustrated in Fig. 1.

---

[1] https://www.programmableweb.com/.

© Springer International Publishing AG, part of Springer Nature 2018
J. Szymański and Y. Velegrakis (Eds.): IKC 2017, LNCS 10546, pp. 86–98, 2018.
https://doi.org/10.1007/978-3-319-74497-1_9

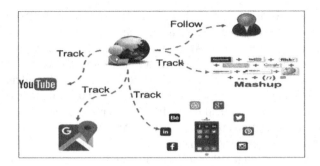

Fig. 1. Track relationships on ProgrammableWeb

Hence, the goal of this paper is to describe a vision of a *PWeb*-like ecosystem modeled as a multigraph where intra-services/mashups, intra-users and inter services/ users and mashups links are exhibited. The idea is to make leverage of the available metadata on various objects (services, mashups and users) in order to discover and to recommend services of interest to a user, accordingly with his/her profile. This vision has been materialized with a prototype built on top of Neo4j, and an experimental evaluation performed with a real dataset[2].

The remainder of this paper is organized as follows. Related work is discussed in Sect. 2. In Sect. 3, we present the *PWeb* heterogeneous multigraph. Section 4 describes the graph exploration to recommend services/mashups. Section 5 details the implementation features and the results of our approach. Section 6 concludes the paper and presents some future work directions.

2 Related Work

Several research works have been proposed to model the network of Web services as a graph in order to discover or recommend APIs or mashups [3, 6, 9]. As described in [6], authors propose a three-level graph model for visualizing the Web service ecosystem: (1) An API graph that connects services when they are used in the same mashup; (2) A domain graph that provides information about services that are more likely to be connected to produce innovative applications; and (3) A tag graph which connects two tags if there exist two APIs which are labeled with those tags and appear in the same mashup. In addition, authors in [3] propose a graph based recommendation approach to assign tags to unlabeled APIs by exploiting both graph structure information and semantic similarity.

Moreover, the convergence towards a Web of linked data[3] leads to a novel services' representation, known as "services linked by their URIs" or linked services allowing the definition of interconnected services based on their functionalities. In [2], authors propose a framework for defining a linked view over multiple repositories and for searching their content. The objective is to publish repository contents

---

[2] http://www.lsis.org/sellamis/Projects.html#WeS-ReG.
[3] http://linkeddata.org/.

and identify semantic links across them in order to exploit complementary API descriptions. The motivation of this framework are threefold: (i) the overlapping of the storage of APIs, (ii) the same API is registered multiple times within different repositories, (iii) similarities between APIs and mashups across different repositories cannot be exploited to enrich search results. Authors also identified a link (denoted simAs link) between mashups of resources which is calculated based on the comparison of their terminological items. In [5] an approach for providing new services based on service composition is proposed. Authors define the term of composite web services for a web service that does not provide requested service but delegates parts of the execution to other web services and receives the results from them to perform the whole service. However, all these models do not consider the users' interactions.

Indeed, social networks did change the nature of "useful" metadata in the discovery and recommendation processes [4]. Besides users' previous usages or users' profile, one may also take into account other types of relationships such as follow, confidence, etc. These relationships are used to generate graphs of interconnected users, which help in determining closest users or those having common interests.

The works of Deng et al. [7, 8] are based on the analysis of social networks' contents and users' relationships. Authors propose a Web service recommendation system based on trust relationships modeled by a graph and established either (i) explicitly when a user specifies his/her list of trustful connections, from the beginning, or (ii) implicitly when the same QoS evaluation is given by two different users. Note that this approach exploits preference similarities among users involved in the network, but still suffers from the lack of metadata especially for new users, e.g. preferences, previous uses, etc. In [12], authors proposed a discovery/composition model (called LinkedWS) based on social networks. This model is able to detect the interactions among Web services. The relations used by LinkedWS are: Recommendation/Partners, Recommendation/Robustness and Collaboration. The composition process implements both Recommendation/Partners and Collaboration relationships. LinkedWS can be updated by adding new nodes/relations or by modifying them.

Within this context, we propose to model the programmable Web ecosystem as a heterogeneous multi-graph. The graph considers the interest relationships between system's users and published Web services/mashups. The goal is to streamline the search for a service and also to allow the detection of users' neighborhoods. In addition, the use of such graph representation makes the system able to propose a service to a requester and to personalize a recommendation for a new user.

3   Heterogeneous Multigraph of the Programmable Web

In this section, we describe the PWeb "social network". Starting from the Linked APIs graph database presented in [11], we take into account new nodes and relationships.

3.1 Multigraph Overview

The network is modeled as a heterogeneous multigraph by means of *users/services* and *mashups relationships*. As depicted in (Fig. 2), the multigraph has a 4-levels structure, accordingly with the different nodes: Categories level, Services level, Mashups and Users levels. A service may belong to one or several categories (membership relationship); A user can follow services/mashups used by other users even if he/she is not directly connected to these users.

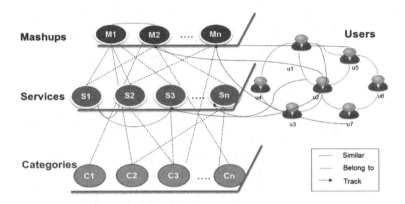

Fig. 2. Heterogeneous multigraph of the Programmable Web

The multigraph exhibits four different types of relationships among both users and services/mashups. Relationships are the edges of the multigraph. First, knowing that each service/mashup may belong to a category, e.g. twitter service belongs to social category, we came up a *Belongs_To link*. Next, services (resp. mashups) need to be related to each other. Based on the services (resp. mashups) properties, we proposed the *similar link*. We identify the *Belongs_To_mashup link* between services and mashups when a service is part of a mashup. Finally, each user can follow services/mashups and other users. We define then a *track link* between these entities.

3.2 Similarity Relationships

In this section, we describe the different relationships that may exist between users (resp. services/mashups) in order to construct the multigraph. These relationships are defined on the basis of similarities among entities. Similarities are based on follow/ track relationships and properties similarities. Track relationships are expressed by means of PWeb tracks. A user can track (follow): web services, mashups, or other users.

Services Relationships (*Similar link*). Currently, several Web services (e.g. google Maps, big Maps) that are exposed on existing platforms such as *ProgrammableWeb* are functionally equivalent. A relationship can be defined between each pair of functionally similar services. This similarity is determined by comparing services' description items, i.e., category, name, description and tags. The similarity between two services (formula 1) is calculated using the average of Information Retrieval (IR) metrics [13] as described in Table 1.

$$Sim(S_i, S_j) = \text{Average}(sim_{Cat}, sim_{Name}, sim_{Desc}, sim_{Tag}) \tag{1}$$

Table 1. IR similarity measures

Service properties	Metrics	Formula
Category	Cosine	$simCat(C1, C2) = \dfrac{|VC1 \cdot VC2|}{\|VC1\| \cdot \|VC2\|}$ $C1$ and $C2$ are categories of services $VC1$ (resp. VC2) is the vector of words of $C1$ (resp. $C2$)
Description	Cosine	$simDesc(D1, D2) = \dfrac{|VD1 \cdot VD2|}{\|VD1\| \cdot \|VD2\|}$ $VD1$(resp. VD2) is the vector of words of $D1$ (resp. $D2$)
Name	Dice	$simName(N1, N2) = \dfrac{2 * |tok(N1) \cap tok(N2)|}{|tok(N1) \cup tok(N2)|}$ $tok(N1)$ (resp. $tok(N2)$) is the set of tokens in $N1$ (resp. $N2$)
Tag	Jaccard	$simTag(T1, T2) = \dfrac{2 * |tok(T1) \cap tok(T2)|}{|tok(T1) \cup tok(T2)|}$ $tok(T1)$ (resp. $tok(T2)$) is the set of tokens in $T1$ (resp. $T2$)

Mashups Relationships (*Similar link*). We establish a link between mashups if they share one or more services. For example, twitter API belongs to **BBC Browser** and **Soccer Shots** mashups. Mashups similarities are calculated with Formula (2):

$$Sim_{Mashups}(M1, M2) = \frac{|tok(SM1) \cap tok(SM2)|}{|tok(SM1) \cup tok(SM2)|} \tag{2}$$

where *tok(SM1) (resp. tok(SM2))* is the set of services composing M1 (resp. M2).

Users Relationships (*Track link*). We consider two types of relationships between users: follow and similarity. The *follow relationship* represents a relation of interest between two users. There is a *similarity* relationship between users if two users follow the same services, mashups and eventually other users which, in this case, yields to a set of users that have likely similar interests.

The *similarity* relationship between users is determined according to the number of services and mashups that users have in common in their *watchlist*. Users deploying several common services may have similar interests and could be considered as similar. The similarity between two users u_i and u_j is measured with Formula (3) [1].

$$Sim_{user}(u_i, u_j) = \frac{\left|H_{ui} \cap H_{uj}\right|}{\left|H_{ui}\right|} \tag{3}$$

where Hu_i and Hu_j are the recent histories of users u_i and u_j respectively.

4 MultiGraph Based Recommendation Approach

We propose a hybrid recommendation approach [14] based on relationships, user's record and preferences, invocations and *watchlists* in order to recommend relevant services/mashups.

We consider a scenario where the user searches for a Web service. The recommendation process illustrated in Fig. 3 involves: (i) Web services search in order to find the most relevant services in the services graph according to the user's request; (ii) recommending relevant services according to the user's history, (iii) recommending the mashups which share the same relevant services according to the mashups relationships in the graph and the mashups tracked by the user's neighbors and (iv) ranking the resulted Web services/mashups list in terms of the services/mashups' according to theirs popularities to recommend the most relevant ones.

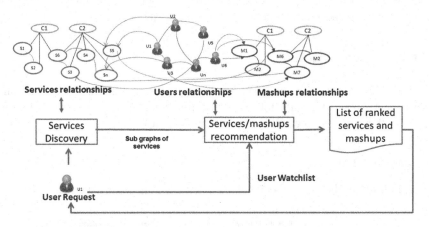

Fig. 3. Recommendation process

4.1 Web Services Discovery

Given a user query, the search process consists in retrieving the most relevant services. The process returns the top k-similar Web services that are relevant. The user query is keyword-based and may include one (or more) category (ies), a service name, tags, service's protocol (SOAP, REST, etc.). For the similarity between a user request R and each service in the graph, we combine several string similarity functions as described in Table 1 above.

4.2 Web Services/Mashups Recommendation

Services Recommendation Process. The recommendation process is based on the previously generated multigraph. To recommend Web services, we need to rank them based on their popularity scores. The popularity of a service (*Pop(s)*) denotes the number of previously recorded usages (Hu) (of the user and his/her neighbors) this service has been involved in. The neighbors of a user are those related to him/her in the graph. We choose to Top K most similar users and we compute the popularity of a service in using correspondence matrix M (users are the lines, and services are the columns):

$$M[ui, sj] = \begin{cases} 1 & \text{if } ui \text{ tracks } sj \\ 0 & \text{else} \end{cases}$$

$$Pop(s_j) = \frac{\sum_{i \in |U|} M[u_i, s_j]}{|U|} \qquad (4)$$

Mashup recommendation Process. The mashups recommendation is based on the relationships between services, mashups and users in the multigraph. The recommendation algorithm will return the popular mashups that share similar services and the mashups tracked by the user's neighbors. The popularity of mashups is computed according to the tracks relations between users and mashups.

5   Experimental Results

In this section, we describe the generation of a proposed multigraph model and the experimental obtained results following the implementation of our recommender system[4] with a real dataset crawled from *ProgrammableWeb*.

5.1   Implementation

Figure 4 illustrates the main tasks involved to generate the graph database.

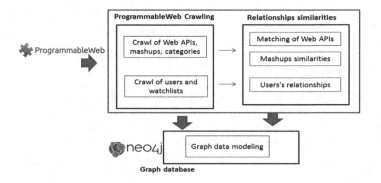

Fig. 4. Workflow of the multigraph model

For evaluation purposes, we crawled 828 users, 700 Web services, 300 mashups and 344 *watchlists* (users' previous tracks). The *relationships similarities* module (Fig. 3 above) computes similarities among services, mashups and users in order to build the

---

[4] http://www.lsis.org/sellamis/Projects.html#WeS-ReG.

graphs. We built a Neo4j graph database consisting of 1460 nodes (116 categories, 700 services, and 344 users having a *watchlist*, 300 mashups) and 1756 relationships. The users' level consists of nodes (users) and edges that are labeled as *FOLLOW* relationships between users. At the services (resp. Mashups) level, services (resp. mashups) are grouped by categories as illustrated in Fig. 5.

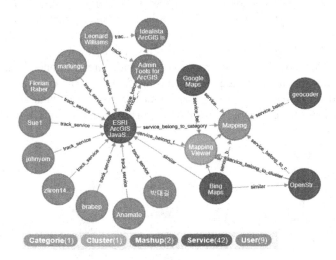

Fig. 5. Excerpt of users/services multigraph

We defined four types of relationship between nodes:

(1) *BELONGS_TO* connects a service (or mashup) to a category,
(2) *SIMILAR* is the similarity between services (resp. mashups),
(3) *BELONGS_To_Mashups* links services to their mashups, and
(4) *TRACK* is the link between users and services/mashups.

5.2 Experimental Evaluation

The goal of the experimentations is to evaluate the user's satisfaction with recommended services based on graph database exploration. The recommendation system performs graph analytics to produce a set of recommended services and mashups according to a user's request. Our assumption is that the user belongs to the user's graph. A user's query consists of a category and a set of keywords. Filtering by category is first carried out and then the similarity between user's query and services' (mashups') components is computed to find the most similar services or mashups. The recommendation system returns a set of ranked services (mashups) which may be of interest to the user. These services are retrieved from the list of discovered services and then ranked according to the service popularity.

Two types of experiments were conducted: first, we assess the performance of our system in term of CPU time. Second, we evaluate the quality of the recommendations.

Our experiments have been conducted on a dual Core i 7@2.50G PC with 8G RAM, under Windows 10.

CPU Time Evaluation

We compared the execution time of our recommendation system called WReG with that obtained by known recommendation approaches in the literature using the *librec* framework[5] namely, (i) *TrustSVD* [10] which is a trust-based matrix factorization technique recommendation system that analyzes the social trust data from real-world data sets; (ii) *Recommendation of popular services* which is inspired by *ProgrammableWeb* recommendation strategy: the most popular service is the most frequent one in mashups.

We executed 10 times our algorithm with the following random inputs: previous services used for WReG, and QoS of these same services for Popular and TrustSVD. Figure 6 illustrates the comparative results in terms of the CPU time (in seconds).

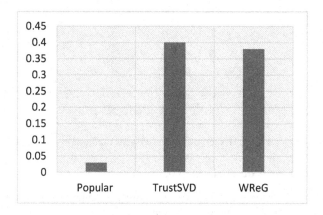

Fig. 6. Execution time (ms) of the recommendation approaches

We can see that the *recommendation of popular services* is the most. This can be explained by the fact that this approach finds out only the most frequent services involved in mashups. WReG and TrustSVD approaches are costly because of the data filtering process which explores historicity of users' neighbors'. However, WReG has potential for efficiency since it does not perform any other similarity measurements between users. These measurements are computed during the graph generation.

Quality of the Recommendation

In order to estimate the quality of recommendations generated by our system, we divide the dataset (users' tracks of services and mashups extracted from *watchlists*) into a training set and a test set. To evaluate the quality and the performance of the recommendation based graph database system, we use *precision*, *recall*, *RMSE* and *hit-rank* measures.

---

[5] http://www.librec.net/.

Let PR denotes the set of relevant recommended services, R the set of recommended services and P the set of relevant services.

Precision: Refers to a ratio of correctly predicted (satisfying user) services to the number of all recommended services.

$$Precision = \frac{|PR|}{|R|}$$

Recall: Refers to the ratio of correctly predicted services to the number of all the services satisfying the user in the testing set.

$$Recall = \frac{|PR|}{|P|}$$

RMSE: The Root Mean Squared Error (RMSE) is used in evaluating accuracy of predicted rating (r_s).

$$\text{Let } r_s = \begin{cases} 1 \text{ if } s \in P \\ 0 \text{ else} \end{cases}$$

$$RMSE = \sqrt{\frac{\sum_{u,s}(1 - r_s)}{N}}$$

where N is the number of recommended services, $u \in U$ and U represents the set of users who evaluated a service s.

Hit-rank: Takes into account the ranks of returned services.

$$Hit\text{-}rank = \frac{1}{m * |R|} \sum_{u \in U} \sum_{i=1}^{h} \frac{1}{pi}$$

where h is the number of relevant services occurring at the positions $p_1, p_2, ..., p_h$ within the recommendation list; m is the total number of users.

To compute the recall, precision and Hit-rank, we used 5 and 10 first recommended services (Fig. 7) and mashups (Top 5, Top 10) (Fig. 8). We note that the accuracy of the recommendations increases proportionally with the number of returned services/mashups. The likelihood of providing a relevant service is greater when the number of recommended services increases. Indeed, it may be difficult for recommendation algorithms to identify all intersting services for users, while it is relatively easier to recommend a subset of relevant services.

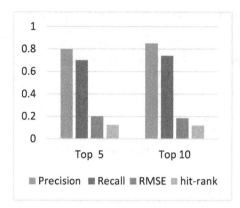
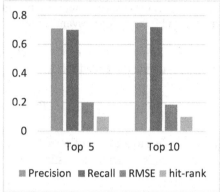

Fig. 7. Ratios-S (w.r.t the number of recommended services)

Fig. 8. Ratios-M (w.r.t the number of recommended mashups)

Table 2 shows the performance comparison in terms of precision@5, precision@10 recall@5, recall@10, hit-rank@5, hit-rank@10 and RMSE@5, RMSE@10.

Table 2. Comparison of the recommendation approaches

Approaches	Precision @5	Precision @10	Recall @5	Recall @10	RMSE @5	RMSE @10
TrustSVD	0.73	0.75	0.61	0.63	0.211	0.2
WReG	**0.80**	**0.85**	**0.70**	**0.74**	**0.2**	**0.185**
Popular	0.41	0.39	0.34	0.61	0.31	0.3

We note that WReG performs better than the other approaches. This can be justified by the fact that, unlike existing approaches, WReG recommendation algorithm is not based only on intra-services and intra-users relationships but also on users-services and users-mashups relationships. TrustSVD that is the closest to our system gives good precision values since it takes into account trust relations between users and services. But as all rating based approaches, it is not able to recommend services in the lack of rating values or invocation histories. Unlike TrustSVD, our approach provides good recommendations of services and mashups even when users do not have services in their histories. Furthermore, one may notice that *Popular,* which is the *ProgrammableWeb* approach, returns the lowest results compared to TrustSVD and WReG. This is due to the fact that *Popular* does not take into account users' interests and recommends the same services to all users. The results are not personalized.

To summarize, our graph recommender system is based on intra-relationships (between users, services, and mashups) and relationships between users and services/ mashups. Compared to existing service recommendation systems, ours performs better in most cases. The neighborhood size and the users' histories affect positively the accuracy of our approach.

6 Conclusion

Since the advent of services oriented approaches and besides the availability of services through existing directories/catalogues such as *ProgrammableWeb*, Web services' catalogues still remain not well suited for a discovery and composition processes.

In this paper, we described an approach where a graph-based model is used to structure the ecosystem composed of services (APIs), mashups and users. To illustrate the promises of this graph structure, we developed a recommendation system for web services and mashups. The system has been implemented in using Neo4j, and experiments have been conducted with real dataset crawled from *ProgrammableWeb*. Experimental results were promising although not being formally benchmarked.

In the future, we plan to extend this work to service management for IoT in order to perform IoT services discovery.

References

1. Berry, M.W., Drmac, Z., Jessup, E.R.: Matrices, vector spaces, and information retrieval. SIAM Rev. **41**, 335–362 (1999)
2. Bianchini, D., De Antonellis, V., Melchiori, M.: Link-based viewing of multiple web API repositories. In: Decker, H., Lhotská, L., Link, S., Spies, M., Wagner, R.R. (eds.) DEXA 2014. LNCS, vol. 8644, pp. 362–376. Springer, Cham (2014). https://doi.org/10.1007/978-3-319-10073-9_30
3. Liang, T., Chen, L., Wu, J., Bouguettaya, A.: Exploiting heterogeneous information for tag recommendation in API management. In: IEEE International Conference on Web Services, ICWS 2016, pp. 436–443 (2016)
4. Chen, W., Paik, I., Hung, P.C.: Constructing a global social service network for better quality of web service discovery. IEEE Trans. Serv. Comput. **8**, 284–298 (2015)
5. Chen, W., Paik, I.: Improving efficiency of service discovery using Linked databased service publication. Inf. Syst. Front. **15**(4), 613–625 (2013)
6. Lyu, S., Liu, J., Tang, M., Kang, G., Cao, B., Duan, Y.: Three-level views of the web service network: an empirical study based on ProgrammableWeb. In: IEEE International Congress on Big Data (BigData Congress 2014), pp. 374–381 (2014)
7. Deng, S., Huang, L., Yin, Y., Tang, W.: Trust-based service recommendation in social network. Appl. Math. **9**, 1567–1574 (2015)
8. Deng, S., Huang, L., Xu, G.: Social network-based service recommendation with trust enhancement. Expert Syst. Appl. **4**, 8075–8084 (2014)
9. Liang, T., Chen, L., Wu, J., Dong, H., Bouguettaya, A.: Meta-path based service recommendation in heterogeneous information networks. In: Sheng, Q.Z., Stroulia, E., Tata, S., Bhiri, S. (eds.) ICSOC 2016. LNCS, vol. 9936, pp. 371–386. Springer, Cham (2016). https://doi.org/10.1007/978-3-319-46295-0_23
10. Guo, G., Zhang, J., Yorke-Smith, N.: TrustSVD: collaborative filtering with both the explicit and implicit influence of user trust and of item ratings. In: Proceedings of the Twenty-Ninth AAAI Conference on Artificial Intelligence, pp. 123–129 (2015)
11. Aljalbout, S., Boucelma, O., Sellami, S.: Modeling and retrieving linked RESTful APIs: a graph database approach. In: Debruyne, C., Panetto, H., Meersman, R., Dillon, T., Weichhart, G., An, Y., Ardagna, C.A. (eds.) OTM 2015. LNCS, vol. 9415, pp. 443–450. Springer, Cham (2015). https://doi.org/10.1007/978-3-319-26148-5_29

12. Maamar, Z., Wives, L.K., Badr, Y., Elnaffar, S., Boukadi, K., Faci, N.: Linkedws: a novel web services discovery model based on the metaphor of Social networks. Simul. Model. Pract. Theory **19**, 121–132 (2011)
13. Jackson, D.A., Somers, K.M., Harvey, H.H.: Similarity coefficients: measures of co-occurrence and association or simply measures of occurrence? Am. Nat. **133**(3), 436–453 (1989)
14. Bobadilla, J., Ortega, F., Hernando, A., Gutiérrez, A.: Recommender systems survey. Knowl. Based Syst. **46**, 109–132 (2013)

Towards Keyword-Based Search
over Environmental Data Sources

David Álvarez-Castro, José R. R. Viqueira$^{(\boxtimes)}$ (iD), and Alberto Bugarín

Centro Singular de Investigación en Tecnoloxías da Información (CiTIUS),
Universidade de Santiago de Compostela, Santiago de Compostela, Spain
`david.alvarez.castro@rai.usc.es,`
`{jrr.viqueira,alberto.bugarin.diz}@usc.es`

Abstract. This paper describes the problem of keyword-based search over environmental data sources. Based on a number of assumptions that simplify this general problem, a prototype of a search engine for environmental data was designed, implemented and evaluated. This first solution serves as a proof of concept that illustrates its applicability in different domains, for both expert and non-expert users. The requirements analysis undertaken and the subsequent design and implementation helped in the identification of a number of new research challenges.

Keywords: Keyword-based search · Environmental data
Geo-spatial data · Fuzzy query language · Information retrieval
Scientific data

1 Introduction

The monitoring and modelling of our environment (Earth Surface) is a task to which much effort is daily devoted, especially by public administrations. Most of the produced data is used by scientist of different areas to study and try to predict many disparate types of phenomena. A well-known and probably most representative example of the above is weather forecasting. As a consequence, very large amounts of geo-spatial data are produced nowadays by different means, including sensing devices and environmental modelling processes. Most of these data is only used by experts (mainly scientists). For example, environmental, socio-demographic and geographic datasets, which include properties such as rain-fall, winds, sea and air temperature, humidity, demography and economic development may be used in the field of public health to model the behaviour of diseases such as Cholera [1] and Influenza [10]. However, such data might also be of great importance in other applications areas. An obvious example of the above is the clear impact that meteorological data has in tourism and other applications related to open air activities.

This article is based upon work from COST Action KEYSTONE IC1302, supported by COST (European Cooperation in Science and Technology).

J. Szymański and Y. Velegrakis (Eds.): IKC 2017, LNCS 10546, pp. 99–110, 2018.
https://doi.org/10.1007/978-3-319-74497-1_10

Keyword-based search technologies have already proved their effectiveness for the development of search engines in the area of Information Retrieval [7]. An example that we will use as a relevant metaphor or reference for the present work is the searching of books, which enables not only finding a book of interest for the user, but additionally to determine which parts of the book are of greater relevance for the specified set of keywords[1]. Recently, keyword-based search technologies have also been adapted to work over structured data sources, like relational databases, XML and linked open data sources [14]. The advantage over structured query languages is that the user does not need to know neither a specific syntax nor the data source schema. If we focus on geo-spatial data, keyword-based search technologies have been developed in the area of Geographic Information Retrieval [9] to search non structured datasets based on both textual and spatial criteria. Keyword-based search is also enabled to explore catalogues that contain metadata of structured geo-spatial[2] and environmental[3] datasets. Notice however that these catalogues enable the user to find a given dataset if it has been annotated with appropriate keywords, but they do not provide information about the parts of the dataset which are of greater relevance for the query, as Google Books does. Despite of all the above achievements, and to the best of these authors knowledge, none of the currently available technologies enable a scientist expert to search for datasets and specific areas and time periods within those datasets relevant for him/her. For instance, searching for areas of the planet involving "high water temperatures and rainfall close to densely populated areas" is of interest for an epidemiologist interested in cholera, since these are the conditions which help the Vibrio Cholerae bacteria to proliferate [1].

Based on the above, in this paper the problem of Keyword-Based Search over Environmental Data Sources is described. Besides, based on some assumptions that simplify the above problem, a first prototype of a search engine for environmental data was designed, constructed and evaluated. The prototype has the typical architecture composed of a Data Crawler, an Index Structure and a Search Engine. Besides, as a demonstrator of the search technology, a simple web map based graphical user interface was also developed, which enables the specification of search expressions and the navigation through spatial and temporal dimensions of the retrieved data. The construction of this prototype helped in the identification of research challenges that define interesting directions for future work.

The remainder of this paper is organized as follows. Section 2 provides a deeper description of the problem of searching environmental data sources with keywords. Related work is discussed in Sect. 3. Section 4 provides a brief description of the developed prototype. Performance evaluation is addressed in Sect. 5 and Sect. 6 concludes the paper and outlines potential future work directions.

---

[1] https://books.google.com/
  https://www.hathitrust.org/.

[2] http://www.opengeospatial.org/standards/cat.

[3] http://www.unidata.ucar.edu/software/thredds/current/tds/catalog/
  InvCatalogSpec.html.

2 Problem Statement

2.1 Environmental Data Sources

Broadly speaking, environmental data is generated by some either observation (Observation Data) or modelling (Modelling Data) process. In any case, as it is defined by the Observations and Measurements (O&M) standard specification of the Open Geospatial Consortium (OGC)[4], values of some property (*Observed Property*) of some entity of interest (*Feature of Interest - FOI*) are generated by some process (*Observation Process*) for different time instants (Phenomenon Time). Depending on the nature of the *Process* and *FOI* involved, the generated data may fit either an entity-based conventional data model or a scientific array-based data model. Thus, for example, Fig. 1(a) illustrates an entity-based dataset, which records Current-Temperature-Depth (CTD) profiles generated at various sampling stations of the coast of Galicia (NW Spain) by the regional oceanographic agency INTECMAR[5]. At each sampling campaign (weekly approximately), a ship travels through all the sampling stations (*FOIs*), and uses a CTD device (*Process*) to generate values for different properties (water temperature is illustrated in the figure) at different depths. On the other hand, Fig. 1(b) illustrates an array-based dataset, which records a 3D (2 spatial and 1 temporal dimensions) array of Sea Surface Temperature (SST) data generated by the National Oceanographic and Atmospheric Agency (NOAA) of the US government. Daily observation data obtained from sensors on board of different types of platforms (satellites, ships, buoys) is interpolated using the Optimum Interpolation method to generate a daily grid of 0.25° of spatial resolution.

It has to be remarked that, although environmental data is mainly numeric data, keywords are also present in both data and metadata. In particular, the names of entity types ("Sampling station", "Municipaliy", "Road", etc.), properties ("Sea Surface Temperature", "Elevation", "Rainfall", "Population density", etc.) and processes ("CTD", "MODIS", "Optimum Interpolation", etc.) may be used by a keyword-based search engine to locate relevant data. Besides, text properties of entities (most commonly names and descriptions) also contain keywords that may be used in queries.

2.2 Description of the Search Problem

Roughly speaking, the problem consists in the evaluation of a set of search conditions expressed with keywords to determine which are the relevant data sources that fulfill the condition and which are the regions of space and the periods of time which are relevant inside each data source. Contrary to conventional catalogues, the result is not just a list of data sources, but also a ranking of relevant regions and time periods, which should be used to download relevant data from each data source. In general, the following types of search restrictions, expressed with keywords, should be supported by a search engine.

---

[4] http://www.opengeospatial.org/standards/om.

[5] http://www.intecmar.gal/.

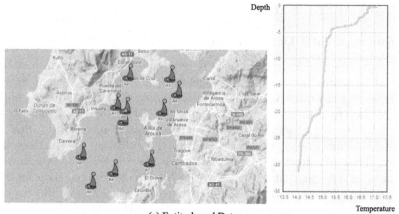

(a) Entity-based Data.
Water Temperature. Source: INTECMAR. http://www.intecmar.org/

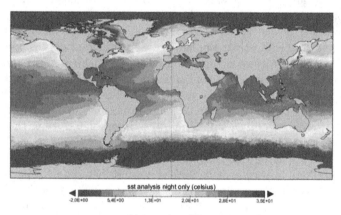

(b) Array-based Data.
Sea Surface Temperature. Source: NOAA OISST. http://www.ncdc.noaa.gov/oisst

Fig. 1. Illustration of environmental data sources.

Spatial restrictions. They determine the areas of geographic space of interest
for the user. They combine keywords of names of entity types and/or entities
with keywords that represent spatial relationships, either topological, distance
or directional. Examples of these restrictions are the following: "in Madrid",
"in a Hotel", "close to Hilton", "far from sampling station", "near the coast"
and "north of Santiago".

Temporal restrictions. They determine the periods of time of interest for the
user. They combine keywords of names of entity types and/or entities with
keywords that represent temporal relationships. Examples of these restrictions are the following: "during a storm", "just before Katrina' and "during
monsoon".

Data restrictions. They determine the values of data properties which are of interest for the user. They combine keywords of names of data properties with linguistic values, defined as terms which express value constraints for the properties. Examples of these restrictions are the following: "high sea surface temperature", "low rainfall" and "normal wind speed".

Additionally, a search engine might also support restrictions on other dimensions of the data, such as data provenance (data generated by a specific modelling software or by a concrete type of sensor) and data quality.

3   Related Work

Keyword-based search technologies are at the basis of modern search engines for digital libraries, document management and the web. Related to them, much work has been undertaken during the last decades in the area of Information Retrieval (IR) [7]. In this area, faceted search may combine text with available document metadata to improve the effectiveness. Regarding structured data sources, Full Text Search (FTS) functionality is included in query languages like SQL[6] and XQuery[7]. Limitations of these technologies include [5,14]: (i) only simple text search with limited scoring is supported, (ii) the keyword-based search functionality, supported by abstract data types is not really integrated into the DBMS query optimizer and (iii) the user must have structured query language skills and must know the database schema. To solve the first limitation more advanced ranking approaches have been proposed, including probabilistic [4] and authority-based [2] rankings. For the second limitation [5] proposes an architecture where keyword-based search functionality is supported in a layer on top of a relational storage engine. To cope with the last limitation, the user should submit a set of keywords and the system should response with a ranked list of interconnected tuples. To achieve this two main approaches have been identified in [14], namely Schema Based and Graph Based approaches. In the former a ranked list of relational expressions is generated from the keywords, which are next evaluated to obtain the expected result. In the latter, the database is materialized into a graph and graph algorithms are used to obtain the result.

Spatial Data Management (SDM) is a topic to which much research efforts have been devoted during the last 30 years. Many solutions have been developed for spatial data modelling, efficient spatial data storage and access and spatial query processing and optimization. In spite of this, research challenges still exist specific sessions are still present in the main Data Management conferences like VLDB and SIGMOD. Main application areas of SDM are Geographic Information Systems (GIS) and Environmental Data Management. Related to the present work are the advances in the so called Geo-spatial Semantic Web [8,11] and in Geographic Information Retrieval (GIR) [9]. More specifically related is

---

[6] https://www.iso.org/standard/31368.html.
[7] https://www.w3.org/TR/xpath-full-text-10/.

the semantic integration of data sources [12,13] and spatio-textual indexing ([6] provides a nice tutorial).

Finally, regarding the discovery of geo-spatial and environmental data sources, standards have been proposed that define metadata schemes[8] and catalogue service interfaces[9]. Despite of all the above efforts, it does not exist an effective technology for keyword-based search over geo-spatial environmental data sources, which enables both the discovery of relevant data sources and the effective and efficient search of their contents to determine relevant spatial zones and time periods for subsequent data download.

4   Prototype Description

In this section we describe the most relevant components of our prototype KEYWORDTERM [3], for keyword-based search over environmental data sources. Two types of data sources are considered in the current implementation of KEYWORDTERM: (i) Entity-based data sources whose data is accessible through the Open Geospatial Consortium (OGC) standard Web Feature Service (WFS)[10] interface and (ii) Raster Array data sources whose data is accessible through the NetCDF Subset[11] Web Service interface defined by Unidata. Future implementation of the system should support other well-known data access web service interfaces. Beyond data access, both data sources are required to implement also the OGC Web Map Service (WMS) standard interface, to ease data visualization tasks. In the current implementation entity-based data sources were simulated using Geoserver[12], whereas Unidata's Thematic Real-time Environmental Distributed Data Service (THREDDS)[13] was used to simulate raster data sources. It is assumed that the coordinates of all the data sources use the same projected coordinate reference system.

A *Crawler* periodically scans the data sources and updates a Spatiotemporal-textual index structure, which is next used during the search process. To ease this process, the existence of a catalog with an already harmonized vocabulary is assumed. Therefore, both data source discovery and semantic data integration and fusion are tasks, which should be undertaken in a real scenario, lie out of the scope of the current prototype.

The *Index Structure* has two parts. A first part provides access methods to evaluate data restrictions, i.e., restriction over the values of the scanned properties. Relevant structures are illustrated in Fig. 2(a). The property name vocabulary is shown at the left side of the figure. Each property name has a set of fuzzy

---

[8] https://www.iso.org/standard/53798.html.

[9] http://www.opengeospatial.org/standards/cat.
http://www.unidata.ucar.edu/software/thredds/current/tds/catalog/InvCatalogSpec.html.

[10] http://www.opengeospatial.org/standards/wfs.

[11] http://www.unidata.ucar.edu/software/thredds/current/tds/reference/NetcdfSubsetServiceReference.html.

[12] http://geoserver.org/.

[13] http://www.unidata.ucar.edu/software/thredds/current/tds/.

linguistic values, whose semantics are endowed by means of fuzzy sets [15]. At the current prototype it is assumed that those fuzzy linguistic values are defined by some expert, however, in a real scenario such expert knowledge should be combined with knowledge extracted from the data sources to generate those values. For each linguistic value, spatial and temporal indexes provide access to either membership raster tiles (for raster array properties) or membership spatio-temporal vector zones (for entity-based properties). The decomposition of the spatial dimension into tiles follows a regular Quadtree-based subdivision of space, whereas temporal semantics were considered for the temporal dimension. The second part of the structure provides methods to evaluate spatial and temporal restrictions. The implemented structure is illustrated in Fig. 2(b). The root of the structure is the Entity Type vocabulary. The entities of each type are

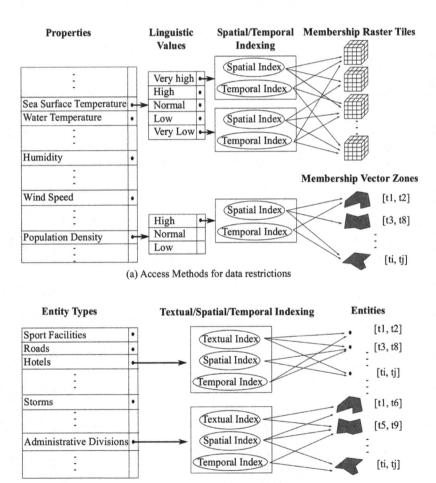

(a) Access Methods for data restrictions

(b) Access Methods for spatial and temporal restrictions

Fig. 2. Illustration of textual spatial and temporal access methods.

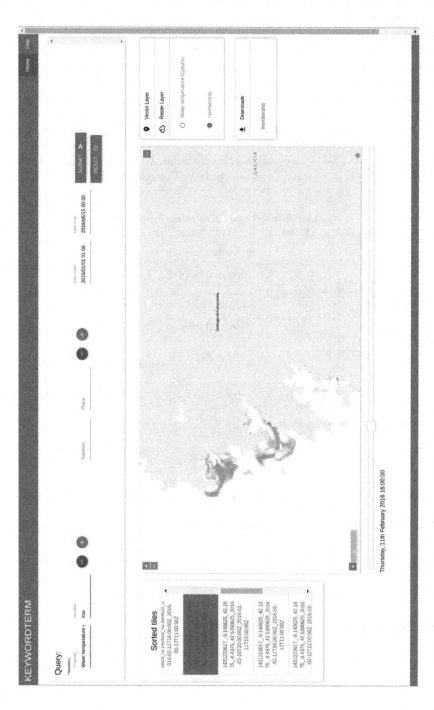

Fig. 3. Screenshot of the web GUI, showing the output (in red) of the query "Low Water Temperature". The darker the red colour the higher the fulfilment of the search condition for each point of the map. (Color figure online)

indexed by textual, spatial and temporal indexes. Both the spatial and temporal extent of each entity is recorded. Currently, the PostgreSQL+PostGIS spatial DBMS is used to implement both the index and the storage of entities. The raster array tiles are recorded with the scientific array DBMS SciDB.

The *Search Engine* is made up of three subcomponents. A concept discovery component is used by clients to discover the names of *Properties* and *Entity Types* that are available in the index. A search component enables the evaluation of combinations of data, spatial and temporal restrictions, based on the available *Properties, Entity Types* and *Entities*. The result set of spatio-temporal tiles, zones and entities may be visualized by clients through a WMS service. The query language has been limited to a conjunction of a three optional restrictions: (i) data restrictions expressed by conjunctions of expressions of the form *"LinguisticValue PropertyName"*, such as *"High Temperature and Low Salinity"*. (ii) Spatial restrictions expressed by conjunctions of expression of the form *"SpatialRelationshipName SpatialName"*, where *SpatialName* is either the name of a *Spatial Entity Type* (for example "Near Hotel") or the name of a *Spatial Entity* (for example "Within Hilton"). These restriction are still not implemented in the current version. (iii) Temporal restrictions expressed by either a time instant or a time interval (notice that keywords are not enabled in the current implementation to express temporal restrictions, but they will be in future versions).

A web based Graphical User Interface (GUI) was developed to demonstrate the functionality of the search engine and to analyse issues related to the interaction with the user, including the specification of the search restrictions and the navigation through the result. A screenshot of this interface is provided in Fig. 3 in landscape orientation. At the top of the interface, three control sets enable the specification of data, spatial and temporal restrictions. The result ranking of spatio-temporal tiles (it is reminded that spatial restrictions are still not implemented) is listed below at the left side of the interface. Currently each tile is depicted with spatial and temporal coordinates, however a better graphical representation of the spatial and temporal context of each tile is currently being implemented. At the centre of the screen a map shows the membership values of the selected tile (low water temperatures are shown in the figure). The temporal dimension of the current tile may also be navigated with the time slider at the bottom of the interface. At the right of the interface the user may chose to view in the map either the result membership or the input data. A download link enables the user to get the data of the current tile from the data source.

5 Performance Evaluation

A preliminary evaluation of the performance of the prototype was done. Although the evaluation is not exhaustive it already enables to derive some important conclusions. The index structure uses tiles that record 20 time instants and 180×360 spatial cells (10.4 MB aprox). Two datasets of different sizes (441 and 1928 Tiles) were created by crawling environmental raster data from the region of Galicia (NW Spain). The prototype was installed in a virtual machine

Table 1. Index access and membership calculation times in seconds.

Search expression (DB size)	Accessed tiles	Result tiles	Index	Membership
Low elevation (1928 tiles)	33	33	0.036	11.087
Low elevation (441 tiles)	33	33	0.003	8.526
Low air temperature and Normal wind speed (441 tiles)	6/11	6	0.021	480.086

with 6 cores (3.60 GHz) and 6 GB of RAM, running in a machine with a total of 8 cores and 8 GB of RAM.

Table 1 shows for three different search expressions over the two databases: (i) the number of membership tiles that are accessed through the index, (ii) the number of membership tiles of the result, (iii) the time (seconds) needed to navigate the index and (iv) the time (seconds) required to access and process the membership values. A first important issue is that the index access time is very small compared to the membership calculation for theses database sizes. However, it is important to note that increasing the database size around 4.5 times caused an increase of the index time of around 12 times, whereas the membership calculation was increased less than 1.5 times. It is expected therefore the a good indexing technique is a key issue to use very large datasets. Another important issue to note is the high cost of the computation of membership intersections to evaluate the last search expression. A parallel implementation of theses calculations is the only feasible approach. To complete this section, Fig. 4 shows the searching time with respect to the number of tiles selected by the index for queries involving just one property. It is obvious that search selectivity has great impact in the response time, however it is important to remind that high selectivity will, in general, come from the intersection of various restrictions, and the cost of computing those intersections is very high.

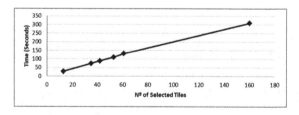

Fig. 4. Response time with respect to query selectivity.

6   Conclusions and Future Work

A first proof of concept prototype of a search engine for environmental data sources was designed and implemented. The functionality and performance of the tool is still very limited, however it has served as a starting point to get a more clear idea of the problem of keyword-based search over structured environmental dataset and to identify various research challenges that may guide future research efforts in this topic. Such issues of potential future work include the following.

- The semantic integration and fusion of different data sources for the same property or entity type. Such data integration must take into account data quality and provenance, but it might also consider other factors such as the overall reliability or authority of each data source.
- In the current prototype it is assumed that fuzzy linguistic values are provided by some expert. However, in a real scenario, the membership at each location and time should be calculated taking into account expert knowledge, knowledge extracted from the data source and also knowledge extracted from each user feedback and profile.
- The current search language is a compromise between the simplicity of list of keywords and the complexity of a full fledged structured query language. More investigation should be undertaken in this topic to find the best compromise between simplicity and expressiveness, considering the uncertainty in the definition of terms and operators involved in the queries.
- The ranking of the result tiles is currently done by aggregating membership values. In an scenario with more than one data provider for each Property and Entity Type, more sophisticated algorithms could be devised both to produce membership values for each location and time and to rank tiles and data sources based on those values.
- It was shown in Sect. 5 that the performance of the current implementation is far from being acceptable. To solve this, better spatio-temporal-textual indexing structures should be devised and distributed implementations of both crawling and searching should be undertaken, together with a rigorous evaluation of the efficiency of the implementations.

References

1. Baker-Austin, C., Trinanes, J.A., Taylor, N.G., Hartnell, R., Siitonen, A., Martinez-Urtaza, J.: Emerging vibrio risk at high latitudes in response to ocean warming. Nature Clim. Change **3**(1), 73–77 (2013)
2. Balmin, A., Hristidis, V., Papakonstantinou, Y.: ObjectRank: authority-based keyword search in databases. In: Proceedings of the Thirtieth International Conference on Very Large Data Bases, vol. 30, pp. 564–575. VLDB Endowment (2004)
3. Álvarez-Castro, D., Viqueira, J.R., Bugarín, A.: Aproximación a la búsqueda basada en términos sobre conjuntos de datos medioambientales. In: Molina, J.J.G. (ed.) XXI Jornadas de Ingeniería del Software y Bases de Datos, V Congreso Español de Informática, pp. 381–384. Ediciones Universidad de Salamanca (2016)
4. Chaudhuri, S., Das, G., Hristidis, V., Weikum, G.: Probabilistic information retrieval approach for ranking of database query results. ACM Trans. Database Syst. **31**(3), 1134–1168 (2006)
5. Chaudhuri, S., Ramakrishnan, R., Weikum, G.: Integrating DB and IR technologies: what is the sound of one hand clapping? In: Second Biennial Conference on Innovative Data Systems Research (CIDIR 2005), Asilomar, CA, USA, pp. 1–12, 4–7 January 2005

6. Chen, L., Cong, G., Jensen, C.S., Wu, D.: Spatial keyword query processing: an experimental evaluation. In: Proceedings of the 39th international conference on Very Large Data Bases, PVLDB 2013, pp. 217–228. VLDB Endowment (2013)
7. Croft, W., Metzler, D., Strohman, T.: Search Engines: Information Retrieval in Practice. Pearson, Upper Saddle River (2010)
8. Janowicz, K., Scheider, S., Pehle, T., Hart, G.: Geospatial semantics and linked spatiotemporal data - past, present, and future. Semant. Web **3**(4), 321–332 (2012)
9. Jones, C.B., Purves, R.S.: Geographical information retrieval. Int. J. Geogr. Inf. Sci. **22**(3), 219–228 (2008)
10. Lowen, A.C., Mubareka, S., Steel, J., Palese, P.: Influenza virus transmission is dependent on relative humidity and temperature. PLOS Pathog. **3**(10), 1–7 (2007). https://doi.org/10.1371/journal.ppat.0030151
11. Patroumpas, K., Giannopoulos, G., Athanasiou, S.: Towards geospatial semantic data management: strengths, weaknesses, and challenges ahead. In: Proceedings of the 22nd ACM SIGSPATIAL International Conference on Advances in Geographic Information Systems, pp. 301–310. ACM, New York (2014)
12. Regueiro, M.A., Viqueira, J.R., Stasch, C., Taboada, J.A.: Semantic mediation of observation datasets through sensor observation services. Future Gener. Comput. Syst. **67**, 47–56 (2017)
13. Vilches-Blázquez, L.M., Villazón-Terrazas, B., Corcho, O., Gómez-Pérez, A.: Integrating geographical information in the linked digital earth. Int. J. Digit. Earth **7**(7), 554–575 (2014)
14. Yu, J.X., Qin, L., Chang, L.: Keyword search in relational databases: a survey. IEEE Data Eng. Bull. **33**(1), 67–78 (2010)
15. Zadeh, L.: Fuzzy sets. Inf. Control **8**(3), 338–353 (1965)

Collaboration Networks Analysis: Combining Structural and Keyword-Based Approaches

Ana Meštrović[(✉)] [iD]

Department of Informatics, University of Rijeka,
Radmile Matejčić 2, 51000 Rijeka, Croatia
amestrovic@inf.uniri.hr

Abstract. This paper proposes a method for the analysis of the characteristics of collaboration networks. The method uses social network analysis metrics which are especially applicable to directed and weighted collaboration networks. By using the proposed method it is possible to investigate the global structure of the collaboration networks, such as *density, centralisation, assortativity* and the dynamics of network growth. Furthermore, the method proposes appropriate network centrality measures (*degree* and its variations for directed and weighted networks) for ranking the nodes. In addition the proposed method combines a keyword-based approach and Louvain algorithm for the community detection task. Next, the paper describes a case study in which the proposed method is applied to the collaboration networks emerged from STSMs on the KEYSTONE COST Action.

Keywords: Social networks analysis · Collaboration networks
Keyword-based community detection

1 Introduction

Collaboration networks are a special case of social networks in which nodes represent actors/individuals who collaborate in certain projects, jobs or scientific publications. The collaboration environment can be for example, any organisation or institutions, academic communities, or international project. Collaboration networks can represent collaborations on different levels: between individuals, between institutions or between countries as project participants. These networks can be (but not necessarily) weighted and/or directed. Weights (if they exist) may denote the number of interactions, projects or publications. Directions (if they exist) may denote direction of communication, institutional exchange, knowledge sharing, etc. In this paper the focus is on the directed and weighted collaboration networks. Social networks analysis (SNA) in general offers a wide range of metrics for data analysis on the global, middle and local network level. However not all the measures are appropriate in all networks and cases. A variety of these measures has been applied to various researches of collaboration networks.

ⓒ Springer International Publishing AG, part of Springer Nature 2018
J. Szymański and Y. Velegrakis (Eds.): IKC 2017, LNCS 10546, pp. 111–122, 2018.
https://doi.org/10.1007/978-3-319-74497-1_11

The analysis of the collaboration networks provides an insight into the quality of the relations among actors in the network. It may identify crucial actors in the network and closely related communities. This is all of great importance for studying knowledge sharing among actors and for proposing future steps and actions.

Collaboration networks have received much attention in the research for at least the past forty years. The first attempts of collaboration networks analysis were focused on the networks based on scientific publications. The simple reason is that this data is freely available to the public. Newman [17] was one of the first who intensely studied the structure of scientific collaboration networks in terms of SNA. Following this approach many authors have combined various network measures aiming to analyse the structure of the collaboration networks constructed from scientific publications [1,2,7,9,14,17]. There were less attempts to analyse scientific project collaboration networks such as FP7 or ERASMUS, as for example in [3,19,20]. Furthermore, collaboration networks are of much interest in the organisations. For example in [8,21] the authors explored how the structure of the collaboration network can influence the innovation.

Still, there is no standardised/universal methodology nor framework proposed for the project collaboration networks analysis. Each study proposes its own set of measures and approaches. The goal of this study is to propose a method that provides an integral approach that unifies the all important measures on the global, middle and local level. It proposes a network analysis in four steps, one step for each aspect. Firstly, it analyses network on the global level. Secondly, network centrality measures are used for ranking the nodes and revealing the crucial nodes in the network. Thirdly, the network is analysed on the middle level in terms of community detection. And lastly, the network dynamics is analysed based on various network stages during the network growth.

The rest of the paper is organised as follows. The following section describes the networks, network measures and methodology of the proposed approach. The third section presents a case study based on the STSMs networks analysis. The last section provides concluding remarks and plans for future work.

2   Research Methodology

2.1   Network Types

A network or graph $G = (V, E)$ is a pair of a set of nodes V and a set of edges E, where N is the number of nodes and K is the number of edges. A network is directed if the edges have a direction associated with them. A network is weighted if there is a weight function w that assigns value (real number) to each edge. In weighted networks, S denotes the sum of all weights in the network; that actually refers to all realised relations.

2.2   Network Measures

We now review some of the standard network measures [18]. Most of them can be applied to the directed and weighted networks, but some of them are suitable only for undirected and/or unweighted networks and in that case of analysed collaboration networks the directions and/or weights are omitted.

The *degree* of a node i, k_i is the number of edges incident to the node. In a directed network, *in/out-degree* of a node is the number of incoming and outgoing links. *Weighted degree* is called *strength*. The *strength* of the node i is the sum of the weights of all the links incident with the node i:

$$s_i = \sum_j w_{ij}. \tag{1}$$

In the directed network, the i*n/out strength* s of the node i is defined as the number of its incoming and outgoing links, that is:

$$s_i^{in/out} = \sum_j w_{ji/ij}. \tag{2}$$

Average degree, $\langle k \rangle$ is the sum of the degree over all nodes divided by the number of nodes. Analogously, the *average strength*, $\langle s \rangle$ is the sum of the strength over all nodes divided by the number of nodes.

Network *centralisation*, defined in [6], reflects the extent to which interactions are concentrated in a small number of individuals rather than distributed equally among all members.

$$cent = \frac{\sum_i (k_{i^*} - k_i)}{max \sum_v (k_{v^*} - k_v)}, \tag{3}$$

where i^* is the node with largest degree in a network and $max \sum_v (k_{v^*} - k_v)$ refers to network of the same size with the maximal possible centralisation which is a star network. The value of the *cent* lies between 0 and 1 and obviously, values close to 1 denote highly centralised networks. In the collaboration networks, high value of *centralisation* shows that network relations are organized around one group of actors. In general, *centralisation* may refer to the power and control structure of the network.

Network *density* represents a fraction of existing connections and the number of all possible connections. In directed networks it is calculated as:

$$d = \frac{K}{N(N-1)}. \tag{4}$$

The network *connected component* is a subgraph in which any two nodes are connected to each other by paths. The *number of connected components* is denoted by ω. When a network has a property that it has no disconnected parts, we say it is connected; otherwise it is disconnected. Each piece is usually called a component (or connected component). The largest connected component is called the giant connected component (*GCC*). In directed networks the components can be strongly or weakly connected. Weakly connected components refer to the same components as if the network were undirected. Furthermore, it is possible to measure how well the network is connected in a sense that we measure the percentage of network that belongs to a giant component. Here this measure is defined as *connectedness* and defined as follows:

$$conn = \frac{N_{GCC}}{N},$$ (5)

where N_{GCC} is the number of nodes in the giant component.

The network is said to show assortative mixing by degree if nodes tend to be connected to other nodes with a similar degree. If the opposite is true then we say that network shows disassortative mixing by degree. The degree of *assortativity* is defined as follows:

$$r = \frac{\sum_{jk} jk(e_{jk} - q_j q_k)}{\sigma_q^2}.$$ (6)

In general, values of *assortativity* lie between 1 and 1. When r close to 1, the network is said to be assortative when r is close to 0 the network is non-assortative, while when r is close to 1 the network is disassortative.

The *clustering coefficient* of a node measures the density of edges among the immediate neighbours of a node. For weighted networks the *clustering coefficient* of a node i is denoted by c_i and defined as the geometric average of the subgraph edges weights:

$$c_i = \frac{1}{k_i(k_i - 1)} \sum_{j,k} (\hat{w}_{ij}\hat{w}_{ik}\hat{w}_{jk})^{1/3},$$ (7)

where k_i is the degree of the node i, and the edges weights $\hat{w}_{ij}$ are normalized by the maximum weight in the network $\hat{w}_{ij} = w_{ij}/\max(w)$. If $k_i < 2$, then the value of c_i is 0.

The *average clustering* of a network, C, is defined as the average value of the *clustering coefficients* of all nodes in an undirected network:

$$C = \frac{1}{N} \sum_i c_i.$$ (8)

A *path* in a network is a sequence of edges, which connect a sequence of nodes that are all distinct from one another. The *shortest path* between two nodes i and j is a path with the shortest length and it is called the distance between i and j and is denoted as d_{ij}. The *average path length*, L, of a directed network is given by the equation:

$$L = \sum_{i,j} \frac{d_{ij}}{N(N-1)}.$$ (9)

Note that the *average path length* can be calculated only for a connected network. More precisely, if $\omega > 1$, L is computed for the GCC.

The *eccentricity* of the node i is the maximum distance from i to all other nodes in the network. The *diameter* D is the maximum eccentricity.

Network *modularity* m measures the quality of the network partition in the communities. The *modularity* of a network partition is a scalar value between -0.5 and 1 that measures the density of links inside communities as compared to links between communities. Communities are groups of densely interconnected nodes within a network. In other words, nodes in a community have a greater amount of connections amongst each other than with other nodes in the network. There are many algorithms proposed for this task. We chose the most commonly used and implemented Louvain algorithm [11], a greedy optimization method that optimizes the modularity of a network's partitions.

2.3   Method for Analysing Collaboration Networks

This section proposes a method for the structural investigation of the directed and weighted collaboration networks. Besides network structure, the additional step of the whole method is to analyse the semantic aspect of the network communication. The whole approach can be performed in four main steps as follows.

The first step is to analyse the global network measures that are adequate for directed and weighted networks and which have sense in the given context. The measures are described in the previous section and the final list of measures in focus is as follows: *average (weighted) degree, centralisation, density, number of (weakly) connected components, percentage of connectedness, assortativity, average clustering coefficient, distance measures*, and *modularity*.

In the second step, the goal is to find centrally positioned nodes in the network. Network *degree* and its directed and weighted variations are the most appropriate centrality measures in this case. There are many other centrality measures. However, *degree* and *strength* shows how important the node is according to the established relations. *Degree* shows the number of different relations and strength shows the number of overall relations. Additionally, the *in-* and *out- degree* and *strength* take into account whether the direction is in-going or out-going.

In the third step the focus is on the middle level. The community detection is based on the Louvain algorithm. The result is a set of communities. Furthermore, it is possible to identify additional communities according to the semantic background of the relationships if it exists. The most straightforward way to do that is to associate a list of keywords/topics to each node. The general idea is to group nodes according to the topics they share. Two nodes are in the same community if two actors have more than t common keywords. Therefore, the results of the Louvain algorithm are extended with communities identified based on keywords.

The fourth step includes the structural analysis of the network dynamics. This step refers to structural analysis of all the previously mentioned measures and their changes over time. This is how it is possible to monitor new trends in the network growth and predict future actions.

3   Case Study: STSM Networks

This section presents a case study in which proposed method is applied to the STSM collaboration networks. The initial phase is network construction and after that the integral results of the analysis are presented.

Network construction and analysis are performed in Python packages NetworkX [22] and LaNCoA [12]. Visualisations were prepared using the tool Gephi [4].

3.1   KEYSTONE-STSM Dataset and Networks Construction

COST is the European framework supporting trans-national cooperation among researchers, engineers and scholars. Short-Term Scientific Missions (STSMs) are one of the COST networking tools that allow participants to visit an institution or laboratory in another country in order to foster collaboration, share new techniques and infrastructure [5].

For the purpose of this experiment, a collaboration network is constructed, based on the data collected from the STSMs on the KEYSTONE (semantic KEYword-based Search on sTructured data sOurcEs) COST Action [10]. There were 50 STSM grants in total: 11 in the first grant period (year 2014), 14 in the second grant period (year 2015), 8 in the third grant period (year 2016) and 17 in the fourth grant period (years 2016 and 2017).

A general $STSM_{gp4}$ network is constructed from all data collected during the four grant periods. In this network, countries are nodes and a directed link between two nodes A and B exists if there was an STSM application from country A to country B. The weight denotes how many STSM applications were realised between these two countries. Furthermore, three additional networks $STSM_{gp1}, STSM_{gp2}, STSM_{gp3}$ for the first three grant periods were constructed on the same principle. The final set of four networks serves as an examination of the network growth and dynamics.

3.2   Results

Network Structure on the Global Level. The results of the first step - the global network measures of $STSM_{gp4}$ are given in the first row of Table 1. According to the results, the value of *average strength* is close to the value of *average degree*. The same consideration holds for S and K. Consequently, the impact of weights in the network is not so significant. This can be explained by the fact that STSM agreements between two countries are rarely repeated and the links are rather uniformly distributed. The network *density* is low, however this is the usual property of such networks. The value of *centralisation* measure is around 0.3. This property is indicator that collaborations of the KEYSTONE participants is not centralised. Furthermore, the network has only two components that do not belong to the giant component, more precisely 86% of nodes belong to the GCC which indicates that network is well connected. This network is not assortative, nor disassortative which means that nodes have no property to tend to connect with mostly similar nodes (with high degree), neither opposite. The *clustering coefficient* is relatively high and *distance measures* are relatively low which may indicate that this is a small-world network [23]. The *modularity* is equal 0.429 which is on the lower limit to say that the nodes tend to group into separate communities. Actually, the whole network is overall well connected

Table 1. Global network measures for networks based on the STSM agreements, *number of nodes (N), number of links (K), network strength (S), average degree (⟨k⟩), average strength (⟨s⟩), centralisation (cent), density (dens), number of components (ω), connectedness (conn), assortativity (r), average clustering (C), average path length L, diameter D, modularity m*

Network	N	K	S	⟨k⟩	⟨s⟩	cent	dens	ω	conn	r	C	L	D	m
$STSM_{gp4}$	28	43	50	1.536	1.786	0.32	0.057	3	86%	−0.27	0.102	3.054	3	0.429
$STSM_{gp3}$	23	30	33	1.304	1.435	0.368	0.059	4	70%	−0.16	0.078	2.405	5	0.385
$STSM_{gp2}$	19	23	25	1.211	1.316	0.408	0.067	3	79%	−0.350	0.042	2.57	5	0.348
$STSM_{gp1}$	11	10	11	0.909	1		0.144	0.091	1	100%	−0.102	0	2.172	4	0.475

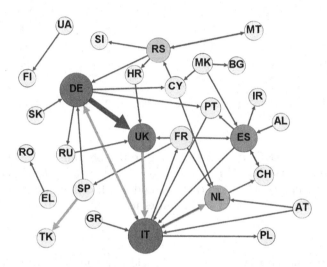

Fig. 1. $STSM_{gp4}$ directed and weighted collaboration network. Node labels are given as country acronyms based on the international 2-letters coding, ISO Alpha-2. The size of node is proportional to the node strength. The thickness of the link is proportional to the link weight

and there is no hierarchy. Obviously, there is no intentions of participants to separate in the closed communities. The overall collaboration network, $STSM_{gp4}$ is illustrated in Fig. 1.

Network Structure on the Local Level. This section presents the results of applying centrality measures to the node ranking task. The node degree and strength for undirected and directed links are examined, and therefore six variations of nodes ranking are presented. In Table 2 the first 12 of 28 nodes in total are ranked. All other nodes have centrality values 0, 1 or 2 and are not included in the table due to the limited space. In Fig. 1 node sizes are proportional to their strength. According to the results node IT has the highest centrality value except in the case of the *out degree* and *out strength* in which the node DE has the highest values. Highly ranked nodes are almost the same for all six chosen measures.

Table 2. Ranked nodes in the $STSM_{gp4}$ network

	Degree						Strength					
	Node	k_i	Node	k_i^{in}	Node	k_i^{out}	Node	s_i	Node	s_i^{in}	Node	s_i^{out}
1	IT	11	IT	7	DE	5	IT	14	IT	8	DE	8
2	DE	9	DE	4	FR	4	DE	13	UK	7	IT	6
3	ES	8	NL	4	RS	4	UK	9	DE	5	FR	4
4	NL	6	ES	4	IT	4	ES	8	NL	5	RS	4
5	RS	6	UK	4	ES	4	NL	7	ES	4	ES	4
6	FR	5	PT	2	MK	3	RS	6	PT	2	SP	3
7	UK	5	RS	2	NL	2	FR	5	RS	2	MK	3
8	CY	4	CH	2	CY	2	CY	4	TK	2	NL	2
9	PT	3	CY	2	AT	2	SP	4	CH	2	CY	2
10	CH	3	FR	1	SP	2	PT	3	CY	2	AT	2
11	SP	3	BG	1	HR	1	CH	3	FR	1	UK	2
12	MK	3	HR	1	RU	1	MK	3	BG	1	HR	1

Communities Identification. According to the Louvain algorithm there are six communities in the STSM network. Approximately 40% of the network is in the largest community which contains 11 nodes. All communities are shown in Table 3. The visualisation of all communities in the STSM network is illustrated in Fig. 2.

Table 3. Six communities for $STSM_{gp4}$ network identified using the Louvain algorithm

	Nodes	%
1	AL, AT, CH, ES, FR, GR, IT, IR, NL, PL, PT	40%
2	BG, CY, HR, MK, MT, SI, RS	25%
3	DE, RU, SK, UK	14%
4	SP, TK	7%
5	EL, RO	7%
6	FI, UA	7%

An additional insight into the existing communities is possible to be gained analysing the semantic aspect of relations/connections. The Louvain set of communities is extended by taking into account keywords from the STSM titles. The titles are adequately preprocessed: stopwords are removed and lemmatised. Certain words with too general meanings such "approach", "method", etc. are also removed from the titles. Next, the algorithm proposes that two or more

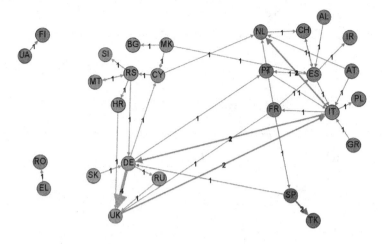

Fig. 2. Communities in network

countries are in the same community if they have more than 2 keywords in common. The final result is a set of possible overlapping communities that can be mapped onto the existing set of communities.

$SC_1 = \{MK, ES, NL, IT\}$, with a set of keywords:
$KS_1 = \{data, keyword-based, search, source\}$
$SC_2 = \{RS, DE, ES, IR\}$, with a set of keywords:
$KS_2 = \{resource, semantic, sharing\}$
$SC_3 = \{IT, PL, RS, SI\}$, with a set of keywords:
$KS_3 = \{experimenting, search, structured, techniques\}$
$SC_4 = \{MK, BG, UK, IT\}$, with a set of keywords:
$KS_4 = \{data, keyword, search\}$

Network Dynamics. Global network measures for networks constructed for the previous three grant periods are given in the last three rows in Table 1. As expected, as the network grows, the values of some measures tend to increase (k, s, C, L, m). Besides, the network growth exhibits an interesting property for this network - the participants form one connected component from the beginning. In the first grant period there is no disconnected components, while later there are only 2 or 3 components that do not belong to the GCC. This can be explained by the assumption that there has been an excellent connection and communication among participants in KEYSTONE community so they formed one coherent group from the beginning. The network growth is illustrated in Fig. 3.

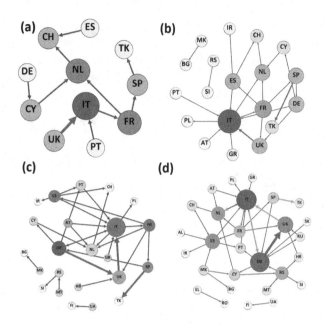

Fig. 3. Network growth in 4 grant periods: $STSM_{gp1}$ (a), $STSM_{gp2}$ (b), $STSM_{gp3}$ (c) and $STSM_{gp4}$ (d)

4   Conclusion and Discussion

This paper presents an integral method for collaboration networks analysis. The approach proposes four steps of the analysis. In the first step it proposes a set of global network measures. The chosen measures have meaningful interpretations in the context of collaboration networks. For example, they can measure how well the network is connected, whether the network is centralised or not, do nodes tend to group into communities or not, etc. In the second step, six centrality measures are chosen on the local network level for the node-ranking task. In the third step, the analysis is moved onto the middle level where communities are focused upon. The chosen algorithm is the Louvain algorithm for community detection. In addition, the proposed approach extends these algorithms with the keyword-based approach. This way, extra communities can be identified by analysing keywords that describe collaboration. In the last step, the network growth is analysed by using the same set of global measures proposed in the first step.

The approach is well suited for the directed and weighted networks with some exceptions when directions and/or weights are omitted aiming to achieve a global overview of the network from different aspects. More precisely, on the node level, the proposed approach takes into account various centrality measures some of which are applicable to the undirected networks (*degree, strength*), some are applicable only to unweighted networks (*degree, in-degree* and *out-degree*), and only two measures are applicable strictly to directed and weighted networks (*in-strength* and *out-strength*). However, all these node-level measures may be interesting for the node-ranking task. This is because from certain aspects the relations are interesting when we omit directions. Sometimes is not necessary to know the directions of scientific exchanges, only the number of exchanges. In addition, sometimes we can be interested only in exchanges with different actors - in that sense, we are not interested in the *strength*, only in the *degree*.

The network structure analysis provide information about the nature of participants and relations in the network. This knowledge can be used to improve the quality of the communication, relations, etc. As well, insight into the structure of the network can be used to foreseen future trends.

The proposed approach is tested on the STSM collaboration network of the KEYSTON COST Action. The results show that this network is well connected, not centralised. There are six communities that are well related among themselves. The network grows as one giant component from the beginning.

Note that in the presented case study only interactions between countries are considered. This could be a potential limitation because more precise results can be examined on the institutional level and on the individual level. However, in this particular case it has sense to focus only to the country level to get information how various countries collaborate in this COST Action. To get more precise insight it would be good to include a multilayer approach and involve institutional and individual perspective. Moreover, instead of number of STSMs, the duration of STSMs can be assigned as a link weight. All these ideas will be examined in the future research. There are two limitations of this study that will also be resolved in the future. First, there is only one example as a case study. The second drawback is absence of any kind of evaluation. This both limitations will be resolved in the future work by introducing, analysing and comparing more collaboration networks.

The proposed approach has two novelties. The first novelty is integrability in a sense that the proposed method combines network analysis over all the possible levels, while existing studies are mostly focused on one or two levels. The second novelty is that the approach extends the standard community detection algorithm with the keyword-based approach. The presented idea is very simple and this is still only a preliminary suggestion that need to be improved upon in future work. There are few possible directions of improvements. One possible improvement of the keyword-based analysis is to utilise ontologies [15,16]. Another direction is to analyse the collaboration network as multilayer network. Semantic in texts can be represented as suggested in [13] and it can be combined with collaboration layers.

References

1. Abbasi, A., Hossain, L., Uddin, S., Rasmussen, K.J.: Evolutionary dynamics of scientific collaboration networks: multi-levels and cross-time analysis. Scientometrics **89**(2), 687–710 (2011)
2. Abbasi, A., Altmann, J., Hossain, L.: Identifying the effects of co-authorship networks on the performance of scholars: a correlation and regression analysis of performance measures and social network analysis measures. J. Informetrics **5**(4), 594–607 (2011)

3. Balland, P.A.: Proximity and the evolution of collaboration networks: evidence from research and development projects within the global navigation satellite system (GNSS) industry. Reg. Stud. **46**(6), 741–756 (2012)
4. Bastian, M., Heymann, S., Jacomy, M.: Gephi: an open source software for exploring and manipulating networks. ICWSM **8**, 361–362 (2009)
5. Cost glossary. http://www.cost.eu/service/glossary/STSM
6. Freeman, L.C.: Centrality in social networks conceptual clarification. Soc. Netw. **1**(3), 215–239 (1978)
7. Guan, J., Yan, Y., Zhang, J.J.: The impact of collaboration and knowledge networks on citations. J. Informetrics **11**(2), 407–422 (2017)
8. Guan, J., Zhang, J., Yan, Y.: The impact of multilevel networks on innovation. Res. Policy **44**(3), 545–559 (2015)
9. Hou, H., Kretschmer, H., Liu, Z.: The structure of scientific collaboration networks in Scientometrics. Scientometrics **75**(2), 189–202 (2007)
10. KEYSTONE STSMs. http://www.keystone-cost.eu/keystone/outreach/short-term-scientific-missions-stsms/stsms-approved/
11. De Meo, P., Ferrara, E., Fiumara, G., Provetti, A.: Generalized Louvain method for community detection in large networks. In: 11th International Conference on Intelligent Systems Design and Applications, pp. 88–93. IEEE (2011)
12. Margan, D., Meštrović, A.: LaNCoA: a Python toolkit for language networks construction and analysis. In: MIPRO 2015, pp. 1628–1633 (2015)
13. Martinčić-Ipšić, S., Margan, D., Meštrović, A.: Multilayer network of language: a unified framework for structural analysis of linguistic subsystems. Phys. A Stat. Mech. Appl. **457**, 117–128 (2016)
14. Meštrović, A., Grubiša, Z.: Preliminary analysis of co-authorship networks at The University of Rijeka. Zbornik Veleucilista u Rijeci **3**(1), 159–178 (2015)
15. Meštrović, A.: Semantic matching using concept lattice. In: Proceedings of Concept Discovery in Unstructured Data, Katholieke Universiteit Leuven, pp. 49–58 (2012)
16. Meštrović, A., Calì, A.: An ontology-based approach to information retrieval. In: Calì, A., Gorgan, D., Ugarte, M. (eds.) KEYSTONE 2016. LNCS, vol. 10151, pp. 150–156. Springer, Cham (2017). https://doi.org/10.1007/978-3-319-53640-8_13
17. Newman, M.E.: The structure of scientific collaboration networks. Proc. Nat. Acad. Sci. **98**(2), 404–409 (2001)
18. Newman, M.: Networks: An Introduction. Oxford University Press, Oxford (2010)
19. Roediger-Schluga, T., Barber, M.J.: R&D collaboration networks in the European Framework Programmes: Data processing, network construction and selected results. Int. J. Foresight Innov. Policy **4**(3–4), 321–347 (2008)
20. Savic, M., Ivanovic, M., Putnik, Z., Tütüncü, K., Budimac, Z., Smrikarova, S., Smrikarov, A.: Analysis of ERASMUS staff and student mobility network within a big European project. In: IEEE Mipro (2017)
21. Schilling, M.A., Phelps, C.C.: Interfirm collaboration networks: the impact of large-scale network structure on firm innovation. Manag. Sci. **53**(7), 1113–1126 (2007)
22. Schult, D.A., Swart, P.: Exploring network structure, dynamics, and function using NetworkX. In: Proceedings of the 7th Python in Science Conferences (SciPy 2008), pp. 11–16 (2008)
23. Watts, D.J., Strogatz, S.H.: Collective dynamics of 'small-world' networks. Nature **393**(6684), 440–442 (1998)

Exploration of Web Search Results Based on the Formal Concept Analysis

Peter Butka[1](✉), Thomas Low[2], Michael Kotzyba[2], Stefan Haun[2], and Andreas Nürnberger[2]

[1] Department of Cybernetics and Artificial Intelligence, Faculty of Electrical Engineering and Informatics, Technical University of Kosice, Kosice, Slovakia
peter.butka@tuke.sk

[2] Data and Knowledge Engineering Group, Faculty of Computer Science, Otto von Guericke University Magdeburg, Magdeburg, Germany
{thomas.low,michael.kotzyba,stefan.haun,andreas.nuernberger}@ovgu.de

Abstract. In this paper, we present an approach to support exploratory search by structuring search results based on concept lattices, which are created on the fly using advanced methods from the area of Formal Concept Analysis (FCA). The main aim of the approach is to organize query based search engine results (e.g. web documents) as a hierarchy of clusters that are composed of documents with similar attributes. The concept lattice provides a structured view on the query-related domains and hence can improve the understanding of document properties and shared features. Additionally, we applied a fuzzy extension of FCA in order to support the usage of different types of attributes within the analyzed query results set. The approach has been integrated into an interactive web search interface. It provides a smooth integration of keyword-based web search and interactive visualization of concept lattice and its concepts in order to support complex search tasks.

1 Introduction

One of the challenges in information retrieval (IR) is to provide a structured view on retrieved results, which allows to better navigate within document subsets and to more easily explore the analyzed domain. While linear visualizations of result sets, i.e. simple lists of results, are still commonly used, they do not convey information about the structure of result sets, e.g. clusters of similar results. In comparison, a well-organized representation can help users to better understand the current domain of their interest and discover relationships between the retrieved documents. For this goal, we decided to study possible applications of methods of exploratory data mining known as Formal Concept Analysis (FCA) [1]. Users will be supported by an interactive visualization of a hierarchical structure of document clusters - subsets of documents with shared attributes defined within the domain. This approach can be used to support a user during an exploratory search scenario [2,3], where the user needs to get an overview of some topic or domain. Such tool can be useful in a companion technology to support interactive information access and organization.

© Springer International Publishing AG, part of Springer Nature 2018
J. Szymański and Y. Velegrakis (Eds.): IKC 2017, LNCS 10546, pp. 123–135, 2018.
https://doi.org/10.1007/978-3-319-74497-1_12

FCA provides methods that transform input data tables into concept hierarchies known as concept lattices. It has been successfully applied in several areas like conceptual data analysis, data and text mining, or information retrieval. In comparison to ontology it provides a dynamic view of actual input data table for user-specified query. In its basic version (the crisp case), FCA processes input data tables in the form of object-attribute models, also known as formal contexts. They are represented by binary relations, i.e., an object has or does not have an attribute value. Of course, there are many examples where it is natural to use formal contexts with multi-valued attributes. Hence, extensions of FCA were proposed in order to process object-attribute models, where the relationship between objects and their attributes is based on fuzzy relations, cf. [4–7].

For the purposes of practical data mining analysis, certain fuzzy FCA models, known as one-sided concept lattices, were introduced. In this case, object clusters are considered as ordinary subsets (as in the crisp case), while attributes are assumed to obtain fuzzy values [8]. In order to work with input data tables with different types of attributes an approach called Generalized One-Sided Concept Lattice (GOSCL) was introduced in [9]. This model produces a hierarchical structure of concepts from heterogeneous object-attribute models in the form of a concept lattice, which can be used in several applications for the analysis of input data. Although outputs of FCA-based methods in the form of concept lattices provide valuable information about object-attribute models, in many cases the resulting structure is too complex and hence a reduction is needed. Several approaches were already introduced, cf. [10–12]. Also for GOSCL, some methods were already tested for the reduction of concept lattices based on different ranking methods using support, stability, confidence, or other metrics, cf. [13–16].

The main goal of this paper is to apply methods like GOSCL to result sets of web search queries in order to get a structured view of the searched domain. When analyzing documents acquired from web engines using FCA-based methods, we need to prepare input tables in the form of the object-attribute model. In this case, objects are documents from the query result set and attributes are descriptive elements or features of these documents, e.g., the existence of a word within the document snippet, their importance measured by the *tf-idf* score, metadata of the document, etc. Then, a concept lattice can be created and visualized to the user. However, showing a concept lattice to the user is not straightforward due to the complex nature of its graph-like structure. Our goal is to support a user in interactively exploring a search domain. We hypothesize that visualizing search results as a concept lattice would support users during the process of search and exploration. In our first experiments, we integrated FCA-based methods into the graph visualization tool known as the creative exploration toolkit (CET) [17]. The main idea and some first work-in-progress details were introduced in [18]. In order to extend our system, we decided to re-use the back end of CET and its search functionality and add new interactive visualizations based on selected Javascript libraries (D3[1] and gojs[2]).

---

[1] D3: https://d3js.org/.

[2] gojs: https://gojs.net/.

In comparison to our previous work, we were able to extend the features of our visualizations and therefore gain a better understanding how users benefit from the visualized concept lattice of search results.

The remainder of this paper is organized as follows: Sect. 2 provides information on related work, introducing how FCA methods can be used in information retrieval tasks and extended to fuzzy FCA approaches. Section 3 describes necessary details regarding the theory of FCA, especially details regarding the GOSCL model and notes on the reduction of concept lattices. Section 4 is devoted to our proposed approach and designed visualizations. Section 5 describes our experiments with the system and discusses results. Finally, we draw conclusions and present ideas for future work.

2   Related Work and Motivation

FCA-based methods were already used in information retrieval systems and tasks. A survey on this topic can be found in [19]. Usually, approaches are divided into:

- *Direct usage for exploration:* A concept lattice is created and directly used for search and navigation in the space of hierarchically organized clusters of documents acquired from the query result set.
- *Usage for reduction:* The original concept lattice is first reduced (in order to simplify results for better and more understandable visualization) and then it is used for search and navigation.
- *Usage as a ranking function:* Methods from FCA are used as an analytical function in order to support the process of linear (re)ordering of the results according to the structure of the concept lattice and its features.

Examples are the CREDO system [20] and its extension CreChainDo [21], which visualize a hierarchy of document clusters or concepts. User feedback on the relevance of concepts is used to adapt the hierarchy, i.e., it is an interactive and adaptive exploration tool for documents from query result sets. Concepts are presented and organized in a tree structure, so it is a simplified and reduced version, i.e., a subpart of the concept lattice, which can be built on such data. In its extension, it is able to support a chain of the interactive steps and manage them. Similarly, in [22] an approach is described which uses an FCA lattice for navigation and attributes for query tuning. In [23] an approach for the enhancement of keyword-based search has been proposed, where local FCA models with agglomerative clustering were used in order to obtain a linear ranking of documents based on a combination of full-text and conceptual search. More work on this topic can be found in the aforementioned survey.

The main disadvantage of these approaches is that only the classic framework for FCA is used, i.e., every description of objects and their sets is based on binary attributes. Our vision is to apply a one-sided fuzzy approach, where objects are considered in a binary way. Defined clusters still are subsets, i.e., the object is or is not part of a concept or cluster. However, attributes can obtain fuzzy values. In this case particular documents are described by the set of different types of attributes, i.e., not only binary attributes are used, but we can describe the documents within the query result set also by some nominal, ordinal, numeric, or general lattice attributes, in order to have a more natural description of them according to user without the possibility for specific preprocessing and transformation (called conceptual scaling) to a binary input data table (which can be less interpretable for users). Here fuzzy approaches, like our generalized one-sided concept lattice (an approach which is able to combine different types of attributes within one heterogeneous data table), can be very useful and their application to interactive exploration should be analyzed. As it was already mentioned, we provided some first work-in-progress version of the system in [18]. Here, we would like to propose an extension of our visualization with the help of specific javascript libraries and some additional experiments with the new system.

3   Generalized One-Sided Concept Lattices

Before discussing details on GOSCL [9], we would like to introduce the standard FCA approach. If we have some set of attributes A and set of objects B, the fact that some object from B has some attribute from A is written in binary incidence relation I. Then (B, A, I) is called formal context and it is object-attribute model of input data, where $B, A \neq \emptyset$ and $I \subseteq B \times A$. Then, we are able to define a pair of mappings $\uparrow : 2^B \to 2^A$ and $\downarrow : 2^A \to 2^B$, for every $X \subseteq B$ and $Y \subseteq A$, as follows[3]:

$$X^\uparrow = \{y \in A : (x, y) \in I \text{ for all } x \in X\},$$

$$Y^\downarrow = \{x \in B : (x, y) \in I \text{ for all } y \in Y\}.$$

This pair of mappings forms Galois connection, which leads to concept lattice. Consequently there is given a set

$$\mathcal{B}(B, A, I) = \{(X, Y) : X \subseteq B, Y \subseteq A, X^\uparrow = Y, X = Y^\downarrow\}.$$

$\mathcal{B}(B, A, I)$ forms a complete lattice called concept lattice and pairs of subsets (X, Y) (fixed points of Galois connection) are called formal concepts.

This crisp model can be easily extended to one-sided fuzzy concept lattice, if one-side of the model will be defined as fuzzy set. In [8] author proposed model where the input consists of an L-context (B, A, R), with L as a complete lattice and relation $R : B \times A \to L$ as a binary L-fuzzy relation. It means that attributes now obtains values from L. Thanks to one-sided property, it is simple to define a pair of mappings $\beta : 2^B \to L^A$ and $\alpha : L^A \to 2^B$, which forms Galois connection (and produces so-called one-sided fuzzy concept lattice) and is defined as follows:

$$\beta(X)(a) = \bigwedge_{b \in X} R(b, a),$$

---

[3] Note that 2^S denotes the power set of the set S, i.e., the set of all subsets of S.

$$\alpha(g) = \{b \in B : \text{ for each } a \in A, \ g(a) \le R(b, a)\}.$$

A problem of the previous model is that one truth value structure L is applied for every attribute. Naturally, data tables are often heterogeneous with different types of attributes. Therefore, another generalization (Generalized One-Sided Concept Lattice - GOSCL) was proposed in [9], where every attribute is able to obtain values from its own truth value structure. Now we provide some basic details of GOSCL.

A 4-tuple (B, A, L, R) is *generalized one-sided formal context* if the following conditions are fulfilled:

(1) B is a non-empty set of objects and A is a non-empty set of attributes.
(2) $L : A \rightarrow CL$ is a mapping from the set of attributes A to the class of all complete lattices. Hence, for an attribute $a \in A$, $L(a)$ denotes a complete lattice, which represents a structure of truth values associated to the attribute a.
(3) R is generalized incidence relation (input data table), i.e., $R(b, a) \in L(a)$ for all $b \in B$ and $a \in A$. Thus, $R(b, a)$ represents a degree from the structure $L(a)$ in which the object b has the attribute a.

Similarly to previous approaches, Galois connection will form concept lattice thanks to defined mappings, i.e., we have mappings between the classical subsets of the set of all objects $\mathbf{P}(B)$ and the direct products of complete lattices $\prod_{a \in A} L(a)$ presented in a generalized one-sided formal context.

Given a generalized one-sided formal context (B, A, L, R), the concept forming operators (which again form Galois connection) $^{\perp} : \mathbf{P}(B) \rightarrow \prod_{a \in A} L(a)$ and $^{\top} : \prod_{a \in A} L(a) \rightarrow \mathbf{P}(B)$ are defined by

$$X^{\perp}(a) = \bigwedge_{b \in X} R(b, a),$$

$$g^{\top} = \{b \in B : \forall a \in A, \ g(a) \le R(b, a)\}.$$

Formal concepts are defined as the fixed points of the concept forming operators. Formally, $\mathcal{C}(B, A, L, R)$ is defined as the set of all pairs (X, g), where $X \subseteq B$, $g \in \prod_{a \in A} L(a)$, satisfying $X^{\perp} = g$ and $g^{\top} = X$. Then X is called the *extent* and g *intent* of a concept (X, g). Moreover, we can define the partial order on $\mathcal{C}(B, A, L, R)$ as:

$$(X_1, g_1) \le (X_2, g_2) \quad \text{iff} \quad X_1 \subseteq X_2 \text{ iff } g_1 \ge g_2.$$

Then, if (B, A, L, R) is a generalized one-sided formal context, the set of all concepts $\mathcal{C}(B, A, L, R)$ with the partial order defined above forms a complete lattice, which is also called generalized one-sided concept lattice corresponding to the generalized one-sided formal context (object-attribute model) (B, A, L, R).

We have also provided incremental algorithm for the creation of GOSCL model in several papers related to GOSCL (including [9]). We will skip it, because it is not necessary for understanding of GOSCL model. Now we add some small

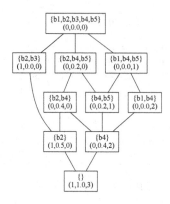

Table 1. Input for GOSCL model.

R	a_1	a_2	a_3
b_1	0	0.0	2
b_2	1	0.5	0
b_3	1	0.0	0
b_4	0	0.4	2
b_5	0	0.2	1

Fig. 1. Output GOSCL model.

illustrative example, how input data table and its corresponding GOSCL model looks like.

Let $B = \{b_1, b_2, b_3, b_4, b_5\}$ are objects and $A = \{a_1, a_2, a_3\}$ are attributes. Here, a_1 is binary attribute represented by two element chain with values 0 and 1, attribute a_2 is numeric attribute with values from real interval $<0, 1>$ and attribute a_3 is ordinal attribute represented by chain lattice with values from $0, 1, 2, 3$. Example of data table is presented in Table 1 and corresponding generalized one-sided concept lattice constructed based on this data table is presented in Fig. 1.

One of the problems of FCA-based methods is that number of generated concepts can be large, therefore it is sometimes necessary to use some reduction technique in order to achieve a more comprehensive result or visualization. For the purpose of this work most important methods are ranking methods which reduce concepts using some metric. It means that some concepts are removed according to fact that their value in some criterion is lower than selected threshold. Especially useful for reduction of too specific concepts is the application of support metric. It means that all concepts with a number of objects lower than selected percentage of the number of all objects are removed.

4   Our Tool for FCA-Based Exploration of Search Results

The main idea for our approach is to provide a tool, where concept lattices of web search results are provided to the user. Hence, the user is able to explore the clusters of results in a structured way, where groups are composed of results which share some part of attributes similarly to any concept lattice. Additionally, the user is able to navigate through these clusters, select them and browse particular links to original web pages. While there were several approaches that tried FCA-based methods in information retrieval, our approach is unique due to the usage of the whole structure of concept lattice or its reductions, possibility to provide both general and focused view of output structure, as well as the application of generalized one-sided approach for processing of different types of input attributes.

The basic idea for implementation of the approach was to integrate FCA approach into aforementioned CET Search tool, where the user can interact with the model of query result set and explore the searched domain. CET provides the possibility to an input query, call the search API (e.g., Bing API like in the first prototype, or Google API, etc.), analyze the results, generate the graph of nodes and edges, visualize them and then explore them in the user interface. After the testing of the first prototype, which was described in [18], we decided also analyze other possibilities for extension of the approach. Currently, many javascript libraries provide various interactive visualizations, which could be easily integrated, adapted and provided to users in usual web browser interface (while CET Search tool frontend is a desktop application). Therefore, for new experiments with the FCA-based exploration, we decided to use some of them. For more focused visualization we selected Double tree graph implemented in D3 javascript library, for a general graph with DAG (Directed Acyclic Graph) layout we tried GO.JS project (which is commercial, but it is possible to use it for research or education with some restrictions).

In more details, if we would like to integrate FCA-based methods (especially fuzzy extension) into graph-based visualization, we need to create object-attribute model from query results set (use weighting of terms in results to reach fuzzy extension), then create output model in the form of concept lattice with nodes (representing concepts = clusters of web engine results), connect them using edges (relation of generalization/specification between concepts) to create hierarchy of concepts, and provide interactivity to all visualization of output model. When some reduction is applied, it should be possible to select some threshold or setup.

Now we will describe some details about the current implementation. The process how the system works follow these steps:

1. User input query to system - user is able to select type of visualization graph (global or focused), number of results to process (10 is default), support value for reduction (0 for no reduction is default), check for use of vector (fuzzy) or binary (crisp) model,
2. System will use API (Bing, Google) to get search results (query results set),
3. System will preprocess model (metadata and snippets are extracted, snippets are used to create object-attribute model), create concept lattice (or its reduction) according to settings, prepare JSON file for selected visualization, push JSON to visualize part of application (provide output HTML code),
4. System will provide use fuzzy extension of FCA in order to analyze weighting of terms in results (vector model from extracted words) and/or metadata descriptions of different types,
5. provide the possibility to apply some reduction (like support-based reduction).

In order to illustrate these visualizations, we show two small examples for binary models. First, global visualization of concept lattice (see example in Fig. 2,

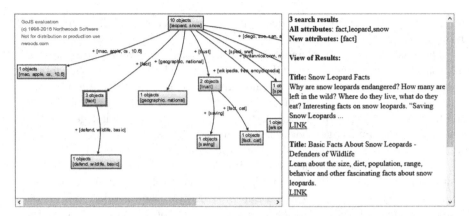

Fig. 2. Example of global visualization in DAG layout - query{snow, leopard}, 10 results, support 10%. Left part - reduced concept lattice, right part - details on selected concept.

10 web search results for specified query, reduced output) has two main parts. On the left side, concept lattice (or its reduction) is shown, where concepts are ordered in DAG layout supported by GO.JS implementation. It means that most general concepts (with all objects) are at the top, then other more specific concepts have an edge to parent concept. Also, the difference to parent concept is visualized on the edge, additional attributes (in this case terms, words in snippets of particular objects in concept) that specify more this concept are shown. The user is able to select one of the concepts and then on the right side, the details of selected concept (highlighted) are shown (at the start, details for top concept are shown). As we can see, the description shows a number of objects, shared attributes of this concept (in the fuzzy model also with their values), as well as information on new attributes according to the parent(s). Then particular results are shown for the current concept, including the link to the original source for every query result.

Another possibility for the user is to use interactive Double tree graph, which provides focused visualization (see Fig. 3) on one concept (in the middle of the left part) and its parents (upper to current node) and children nodes (lower to current node). Again, it is possible to see which words make difference between levels, also, nodes (concepts) are described by their most specific words. On the right side is detailed information on the current concept (same as in the previous type of visualization). The user is able to explore the concept lattice by click on some parent or child. Then clicked node will be focused in the middle (with all necessary changes to parents, nodes and detailed information). At the top of the double tree part, the user is also able to use droplist and quickly select any specific concept from the concept lattice defined by its specific words.

When setup for visualization is different, it will apply necessary changes. Thanks to GOSCL it is possible to use vector (fuzzy) model of snippets (from text of snippet, or original document, as well as add metadata attributes) and

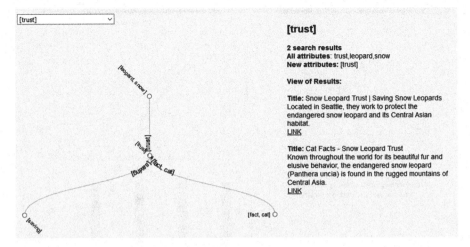

Fig. 3. Example of focused visualization in Double tree graph - query {snow, leopard}, 10 results. Left part - focused view on selected concept and its neighbours, right part - details on selected concept.

create concept lattice. Then visualization is updated and together with specified name of attribute also change in value should be shown. In current version we only tested fuzzy model containing term frequency of snippet words, but the application is able to work with generally any type of attributes (and their combinations) which are supported by GOSCL model.

5   Experiments

In order to test our tool we did some preliminary experiments with 10 different queries. We would like to see how many concepts are produced, and how effective is the reduction. From this, we were able to estimate more suitable input parameters for visualization tool, i.e., which size of query results set and reduction give us still reasonable output of concept lattice. Then, it was interesting to see if the tool is able to be enough fast in the computation of models. For every experiment, where it was needed, we did more (usually 10) runs of the process and results are based on average numbers.

In the first experiment, we studied the relation between a number of concepts and number of searched results. We did two separate measurements based on the type of input context (binary, or fuzzy - with a minimum of term frequency 1) and no reduction of output. The result is available in Fig. 4, top-left graph, where we can see that difference in our experiments is relatively small. The main reason is the usage of snippets, were term frequencies are not very high and also input table is very sparse (as it is usual in any term-based model of documents). With a longer description of documents and additional metadata attributes, a number of fuzzy concepts will rise faster.

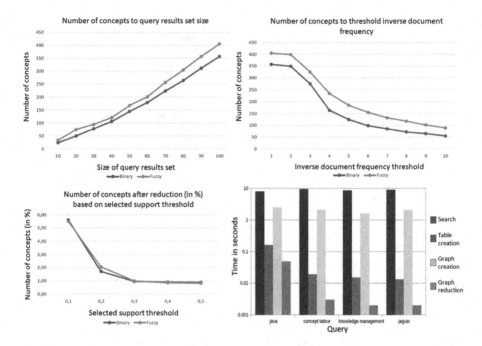

Fig. 4. The results of experiments with our tool (for more details see Sect. 5).

Another experiment tried to show a change in a number of concepts if we setup threshold for a minimum number of term existence in different documents within the query result set, i.e., terms that are in at least n documents are used for the creation of input context. We have used 100 results for the experiments, no reduction was used after creation of concept lattice. In the top-right graph of Fig. 4 we can see that number of concepts decrease fast until value 6, then decrease is linear and slower. Such reduction is good if we want to have more words which are not so specific (like only for one document in query result set), but still are able to discriminate clusters of web results.

The next experiment was related to seeing how support reduction reduce the output (see Fig. 4, bottom-left graph). As you can see, the value of support greatly reduces the number of concepts. Already at the lowest tested value of support (0.1), the number of concepts is reduced to 5%–6% in average. At 0.3, both for binary and fuzzy contexts, practically only 1% of concepts remains after the reduction phase.

The last graph available in Fig. 4 (bottom-right part) shows the computation aspects of the application within Google API. Here we found that for different queries, the most consuming part of the process is actually the step for the search of results through API, and the creation of graph. The processing times of particular operations for 100 objects in results set (on different queries) is shown in provided graph. For smaller query results sets (under 20–50 objects, depends on the usage of support reduction) with a reasonable amount of visualized concepts, the processing time of application is usually under half of one second. Therefore, there is no real limitation for usage of the tool if we want to get some useful result.

In conclusion to our preliminary experiments, we also summarized feedback from several users. The readability and usability of resulted output structure are limited to the setup of query result set size to less than 15–20 objects when the reduction is not applied. Otherwise, the structure provided by the system is too large for the user in order to get a useful understanding of clusters and their connections. If we apply reduction techniques (like support function), the readability of output structure depends on its value. By our experiments, we found that even for a maximum of 100 results, we reached a readable and good structure for navigation for support threshold with a value of 0.2. Then understanding and discrimination (or disambiguation) of subgroups of results was relatively good. In the future, other reduction techniques and extensions can help to make even better structuring and visualization of query results set. In the future, we would like to run more experiments with various inputs and setups, as well as provide more reduction techniques and user test studies based on the usage of the system by more users.

6   Conclusions

The main goal of this paper was to provide information on a tool for exploration of search results (to selected query) from web engine using Formal Concept Analysis. While some approach in this area were proposed, we decided for interactive visualization of the concept lattice (and its reductions) based on the one-sided fuzzy FCA approach, which is able to involve different types of attributes about the results of the analysis. Our tool is able to support exploration of query results set using such approaches and help in understanding the structure of the domain. In next steps, we want to extend the functionality of the tool, as well as prepare user study and larger experiments with the system.

Acknowledgments. This work was done with the help of Short Term Scientific Mission visit supported by the COST action IC1302 KEYSTONE (semantic KEYword-based Search on sTructured data sOurcEs), and partially within the Transregional Collaborative Research Centre SFB/TRR 62 "A Companion-Technology for Cognitive Technical Systems" funded by the German Research Foundation (DFG) and Slovak VEGA research grant 1/0493/16.

References

1. Ganter, B., Wille, R.: Formal Concept Analysis: Mathematical Foundations. Springer, Heidelberg (1999). https://doi.org/10.1007/978-3-642-59830-2
2. Marchionini, G.: Exploratory search: from finding to understanding. Commun. ACM **49**, 41–46 (2006)

3. Gossen, T., Nitsche, M., Haun, S., Nürnberger, A.: Data exploration for bisociative knowledge discovery: a brief overview of tools and evaluation methods. In: Berthold, M.R. (ed.) Bisociative Knowledge Discovery. LNCS (LNAI), vol. 7250, pp. 287–300. Springer, Heidelberg (2012). https://doi.org/10.1007/978-3-642-31830-6_20

4. Medina, J., Ojeda-Aciego, M., Ruiz-Calviño, J.: Formal concept analysis via multiadjoint concept lattices. Fuzzy Set. Syst. **160**, 130–144 (2009)

5. Pocs, J.: Note on generating fuzzy concept lattices via Galois connections. Inf. Sci. **185**(1), 128–136 (2012)

6. Antoni, L., Krajči, S., Krídlo, O., Macek, B., Pisková, L.: On heterogeneous formal contexts. Fuzzy Set. Syst. **234**, 22–33 (2014)

7. Pócs, J., Pócsová, J.: Basic theorem as representation of heterogeneous concept lattices. Front. Comput. Sci. **9**(4), 636–642 (2015)

8. Krajči, S.: Cluster based efficient generation of fuzzy concepts. Neural Netw. World **13**(5), 521–530 (2003)

9. Butka, P., Pocs, J.: Generalization of one-sided concept lattices. Comput. Inform. **32**(2), 355–370 (2013)

10. Kumar, C.A., Srinivas, S.: Concept lattice reduction using fuzzy K-Means clustering. Expert Syst. Appl. **37**(3), 2696–2704 (2010)

11. Antoni, L., Krajči, S., Krídlo, O.: On stability of fuzzy formal concepts over randomized one-sided formal context. Fuzzy Set. Syst. **333**, 36–53 (2018)

12. Kardoš, F., Pócs, J., Pócsová, J.: On concept reduction based on some graph properties. Knowl. Based Syst. **93**, 67–74 (2016)

13. Butka, P., Pócs, J., Pócsová, J.: Reduction of concepts from generalized one-sided concept lattice based on subsets quality measure. In: Zgrzywa, A., Choroś, K., Siemiński, A. (eds.) New Research in Multimedia and Internet Systems. AISC, vol. 314, pp. 101–111. Springer, Cham (2015). https://doi.org/10.1007/978-3-319-10383-9_10

14. Butka, P., Pócs, J., Pócsová, J.: On intent stability index for one-sided concept lattices. In: Proceedings of 10th Jubilee IEEE International Symposium on Applied Computational Intelligence and Informatics (SACI 2015), pp. 79–84 (2015)

15. Butka, P., Pócs, J., Pócsová, J.: Two-step reduction of GOSCL based on subsets quality measure and stability index. In: Zgrzywa, A., Choroś, K., Siemiński, A. (eds.) Multimedia and Network Information Systems. AISC, vol. 506, pp. 419–429. Springer, Cham (2017). https://doi.org/10.1007/978-3-319-43982-2_36

16. Smatana, M., Butka, P., Cöveková, L.: Tree based reduction of concept lattices based on conceptual indexes. In: Borzemski, L., Grzech, A., Świątek, J., Wilimowska, Z. (eds.) Information Systems Architecture and Technology: Proceedings of 37th International Conference on Information Systems Architecture and Technology – ISAT 2016 – Part I. AISC, vol. 521, pp. 211–220. Springer, Cham (2017). https://doi.org/10.1007/978-3-319-46583-8_17

17. Haun, S., Nürnberger, A., Kötter, T., Thiel, K., Berthold, M.R.: CET: a tool for creative exploration of graphs. In: Balcázar, J.L., Bonchi, F., Gionis, A., Sebag, M. (eds.) ECML PKDD 2010. LNCS (LNAI), vol. 6323, pp. 587–590. Springer, Heidelberg (2010). https://doi.org/10.1007/978-3-642-15939-8_39

18. Butka, P., Low, T., Kotzyba, M., Haun, S., Nurnberger, A.: FCA-supported exploratory web search. In: 1st International Symposium on Companion-Technology (ISCT 2015), pp. 131–136 (2015)

19. Poelmans, J., Ignatov, D.I., Viaene, S., Dedene, G., Kuznetsov, S.O.: Text mining scientific papers: a survey on FCA-based information retrieval research. In: Perner, P. (ed.) ICDM 2012. LNCS (LNAI), vol. 7377, pp. 273–287. Springer, Heidelberg (2012). https://doi.org/10.1007/978-3-642-31488-9_22
20. Carpineto, C., Romano, G.: Exploiting the potential of concept lattices for information retrieval with CREDO. J. Univ. Comput. **10**(8), 985–1013 (2004)
21. Nauer, E., Toussaint, Y.: CreChainDo: an iterative and interactive Web information retrieval system based on lattices. Int. J. Gen. Syst. **38**(4), 363–378 (2009)
22. Spyratos, N., Meghini, C.: Preference-based query tuning through refinement/enlargement in a formal context. In: Dix, J., Hegner, S.J. (eds.) FoIKS 2006. LNCS, vol. 3861, pp. 278–293. Springer, Heidelberg (2006). https://doi.org/10.1007/11663881_16
23. Butka, P., Pócsová, J., Pócs, J.: A proposal of the information retrieval system based on the generalized one-sided concept lattices. In: Precup, R.E., Kovács, S., Preitl, S., Petriu, E. (eds.) Applied Computational Intelligence in Engineering and Information Technology. Topics in Intelligent Engineering and Informatics, vol. 1, pp. 59–70. Springer, Heidelberg (2012). https://doi.org/10.1007/978-3-642-28305-5_5

Challenges in Applying Machine Learning Methods: Studying Political Interactions on Social Networks

Chaya Liebeskind[1(✉)] and Karine Nahon[2,3]

[1] Jerusalem College of Technology, Lev Academic Center, Jerusalem, Israel
liebchaya@gmail.com
[2] Interdisciplinary Center (IDC) Herzliya, Herzliya, Israel
[3] University of Washington, Seattle, USA
karineb@uw.edu

Abstract. This document discusses the potential role of Machine Learning (ML) methods in social science research, in general, and specifically in studies of political behavior of users in social networks (SN). This paper explores challenges which occurred in a set of studies which we conducted regarding classification of comments to posts of politicians and suggests ways of addressing these challenges. These challenges apply to a larger set of online political behavior studies.

Keywords: Comment relevance classification · Machine learning · Social media
Supervised learning · Political content · Political behavior

1 Introduction

The growing use of social media have resulted in vast amounts of user-generated content, that are digital traces which network actors leave behind. With the proliferation of social media, content analysis of big data became an opportunity in social science for research to understand behavioral questions and are used extensively. However, some ethical and practical challenges arise around questions of how to collect, keep, analyze and provide the data [1–3]. Manual content analysis requires high levels of efforts and time to code and analyze even small amounts of data. This is where ML may introduce a great opportunity for social scientists, as it can analyze vast amounts of data automatically. This promise does not come without challenges.

In this paper we discuss how to overcome challenges which occur while planning and employing supervised Machine Learning (ML). Supervised ML algorithms (e.g., Decision Trees, Bayesian, Support Vector Machines, and Neural Networks) use a training data of input examples with their desired output to study a function generalize and predict the value of the function for any unseen valid input [4]. In contrast to supervised ML algorithms. Our examples and application of ML are drawn from a set of studies we conducted in the field of information politics.

© Springer International Publishing AG, part of Springer Nature 2018
J. Szymański and Y. Velegrakis (Eds.): IKC 2017, LNCS 10546, pp. 136–141, 2018.
https://doi.org/10.1007/978-3-319-74497-1_13

2   Studying Political Behavior with ML Methods

The literature of political-orientated classification tasks which used supervised machine learning (ML) methods is meager. To mention few:

Recently, Shah et al. developed an automatic coding tool of policy issues (based on supervised ML) and applied their tool to news articles and parliamentary questions [5]. Hopkins et al. argued that most social science studies, which manually or automatically code text, are primarily interested in broad characterizations about the whole set of documents, such as unbiased estimates of the proportion of documents in given categories [6]. Existing supervised ML methods have focused on optimizing the goals of computer science, which for the most part involve maximizing the percentage of documents that are accurately classified into a given set of categories. Thus, they developed methods which provide approximately unbiased estimates of category proportions even when the classification accuracy is poor. Hopkins et al. applied their nonparametric method to analyze opinions in the blogosphere regarding the politician John Kerry. They computed the proportion of opinions on blogs each day or week in each of seven categories. Their research illustrated that by developing methods for analyzing textual data that optimize social science goals directly, they are able to considerably outperform standard computer science methods developed for a different purpose. In our research, we measure the classification accuracy. However, we suggest exploring the performance of a classification model. This exploration may reveal an interesting insight into the strengths and weaknesses of the classifier.

Grimmer and Steward discussed in their article the promises and pitfalls of automatic content analysis methods for political texts [7]. They outlined the three steps of supervised ML algorithm: (1) constructing a training set; (2) applying the supervised learning method; and (3) validating the model output and classifying the remaining documents. They demonstrated the use and validation of supervised learning methods while using the example from Stewart and Zhukov study concerning Russian military discourse. Stewart and Zhukov compared the stances on foreign policy activism that civilian and military elites articulate in their public statements [8]. Stewart and Zhukov collected a corpus of 7920 statements and designed a codebook so that human coders could classify statements as having a restrained, activist, or neutral position on the Russian use of force. They randomly sampled three hundred documents, coded them, and employed four different machine learning approaches in their ensemble classifier: K-Nearest Neighbor, Adaboost.M1 algorithm, Random Forest and Support Vector Machine. Grimmer and Steward used the same sample for training a Random Forest model to first learn the relationship between words and classes and then apply this relationship to classify the remaining documents. To assess how well the Random Forest algorithm was able to replicate human coders, they performed a ten-fold cross-validation using the training data. This facilitates a direct comparison of machine and human classifications. In this paper, we adopt a similar approach. We detail the three steps of supervised ML algorithm and emphasize additional challenges in adopting such a method for social science. We demonstrate the use of supervised ML algorithms in another political classification task and domain.

3   Challenges in Classifying Relevance of Political Comments While Using Supervised ML Techniques

The general outline of supervised ML algorithms follows three steps: (1) **preparing a dataset for training** which includes defining the variables of the study and labeling a subset of examples. (2) **training a classifier on the labeled (coded) dataset.** This means feature extraction – deciding as researchers which text-based features are relevant for the classifier, such as words, n-grams, part-of-speech tags, emojis, hashtags, and punctuation marks. Then, the next phase is selecting a classifier and running it on the labeled dataset. and (3) **predicting classification of big data.**

We will exemplify the challenges of applying ML techniques in social science research in a recent study which aims to identify the relevance of political comments to posts of Israeli politicians on Facebook. To simplify our task, we defined classification task as binary (a relevant or irrelevant comment to the content of the politician).

Step 1: Challenges in preparing a dataset for training

We have downloaded via Facebook Graph API all posts of Members of Knesset (MKs) between 2014–2016 (n = 130 MKs, m = 33,537 posts). The data included also the comments to these posts (n = 5.37 M comments posted by 702,396 commentators) [9]. During the process of preparing the dataset for training, we have encountered few challenges that ought to be mentioned:

- **Creating the initial dataset** - Since we collected the data not in real-time, there is always a risk that some comments were deleted, either by the person who runs the page of the MK, or by the commentator herself or by the platform (if the commentator breached its policy guidelines). See also Driscoll and Walker who discuss this issue in depth [10].
- **Preparing a coding scheme** for manually classifying the content is an iterative process which requires further refinement of the coding guidelines, until reaching an appropriate inter-rater reliability of agreement among the referees. We had to conduct 3 rounds of manual pilot coding with 3 judges of pilot sets to train the coders and refine the guidelines of coding (100, 100 and 47 comments), until reaching an appropriate inter-rater reliability of Fleiss Kappa [11] (0.82). Three rounds were a reminder of the difficulty to reach a consensus regarding political content.
- **Preparing a sample for manual coding** (n = 1489 comments). The selection of the subset of training examples should follow the distribution of the data. In our study, the data followed a power law, where certain users receive high number of comments relative to others, and the subset was chosen along the same lines. The cost of was that our sample resulted in under-sampling MKs on the 'long tail', which had very few comments originally.

Step 2: Challenges in Training a classifier

- **Extracting a feature set** - The first step in training a classifier is deciding what features of the text are relevant, and how to encode these features. We investigated three types of features: **(1) word representation**, where each of the words in the comment is considered as a feature. We compared four semantic vector representations for the comment relevance classification task. Each of the representations was generated by a different dimension reduction method, which produces word vectors that collapse similar words into groups. We examined different types of large unlabeled data for learning the distributional representations, namely comment texts, post texts and both post and comment texts. LSA dimensional reduction method outperforms the other methods for comment relevance classification of political content on Facebook. However, the best obtained accuracy was 64.97% [12]. **(2) character n-grams representation**. In character n-grams representation, each comment is considered as a character ngrams, i.e., strings of length n. For instance, the character 3-grams of the string "politics" would be: "pol", "oli", "lit", "iti", "tic", and "ics". Even though, this representation produces a considerably larger feature set, there is much less character combinations than word combinations, Therefore, this representation partly overcomes the problem of sparse data that arises when using word representation. We experiment four configurations of the character n-grams representations: $n = 2$, $n = 3$, $n = 4$ and $n = 5$. Table 1 shows a comparison of the character n-grams configurations for the comment relevance classification task. The optimal configuration was $n = 3$. In our experiments, we used the Support Vector Machines (SVM) classification method with polynomial kernel. We estimated the accuracy rate the method by a 10-fold cross-validation test. We ran these ML methods by the WEKA platform [13, 14] using the default parameters. **(3) metadata features** - We excluded features and metadata which later we would like to use as variables. For example, since our research involved analyzing the correlation between gender and positive attitude toward content of posts, we avoided using 'gender' as a feature of the classifier.

Table 1. A comparison of the character n-grams configurations

Character N-grams	Accuracy (%)	F-Measure
n = 2	63.72	0.75
n = 3	69.23	0.78
n = 4	68.48	0.77
n = 5	69.57	0.78

- **Applying feature selection methods** - the challenge here is to reduce the number of features. Fewer features are desirable since it decreases the complexity of the model. we filtered out non-relevant features using a well-known feature selection method: Correlation-based Feature Subset (CFS) [15]. The results presented in this section include CSF feature selection which significantly improved the accuracy of all the character n-grams representations. We note that feature selection was not beneficial for any of the semantic reduced vector representations.
- **Enriching the feature set to optimize the classification performance** - Achieving a high accuracy is one of the most challenging tasks of our method. We investigated whether expanding the input of the comment relevance classification task to include also the post text would increase the classification accuracy. We found that the expansion did not improve the classification results of the four semantic (reduced) representations [12]. We tested weather this expansion would increase the

classification accuracy of the character n-grams representations: n = 2, n = 3, n = 4 and n = 5. Table 2 shows a comparison of the character n-grams configurations for the comment relevance classification task, where the input is both the post and the comment text. The optimal configuration was n = 4. The advantage of the optimal configuration over all the comment-based configurations (Table 1) is statistically significant according to the paired t-test at level 0.05.

Table 2. A comparison of character n-grams configurations, where the input is both the post and the comment text.

Character N-grams	Accuracy (%)	F-Measure
n = 2	68.14	0.74
n = 3	59.7	0.78
n = 4	**76.79**	**0.82**
n = 5	72.9	0.8

- **Selecting a supervised learning algorithm** – Since there is no single learning algorithm that works best on all supervised learning problems, the challenge is to choose the right learning algorithm taking into account the classification task and the special characteristics of the dataset. Table 3 shows the classification results of seven supervised ML methods on the optimal configuration: Random Forest, Decision Tree, Bagging, Adaboost, Bayes Network, Supported Vector Machine (SVM) and Logistic Regression.

Table 3. Comparison of results obtained by seven ML methods

ML method	Accuracy %	F-Measure
RandomForest	73.52	0.78
Decision Tree	63.1	0.72
Bayes Network	59.9	0.72
Supported Vector Machine (SVM)	76.79	0.82
Logistic Regression	**79.17**	**0.83**
Bagging	71	0.77
AdaBoost	60.11	0.73

- **Analyzing the classification results** - this step aims at analyzing the types of error of a classification model. In this section the challenge is to increase the accuracy levels. We found that in some cases the accuracy level for a sub-task (e.g. – classifying only not relevant comments) is higher than the complete task (e.g. – classifying both relevant and not-relevant comments). In our example, this is why we chose the SVM method over the logistic regression, since the SVM method for classifying only not-relevant comments was 88% (with F-Measure of 0.66), while the logistic regression for both relevant and not relevant comments was 79.17%, and the logistic regression for classifying irrelevant comments is 81%. Both are lower than the SVM method.

Step 3: Predicting Classification

In order to achieve a higher accuracy at the prediction phase, we can set a threshold on the probability score for each item in the set, and then choose the subset which comprise only the items that passed the threshold. Not all the supervised ML algorithms provide a probability distribution over a set of classes. The following algorithms produce probabilities of membership (*P(class|input)*): Logistic Regression and Neural Networks with a logistic or softmax output and SVM.

We are currently running our trained classifier to predict the comment relevance classification of over than 5 M comments. The feature selection method reduced the number of features in our feature set from 22,660 (character 4-grams with frequency > 2) to 187. This feature reduction made the prediction of large amount of texts computationally feasible.

References

1. Boyd, D., Crawford, K.: Critical questions for big data. Inf. Commun. Soc. **15**, 662–679 (2012)
2. Dalton, C.M., Taylor, L., Thatcher (alphabetical), J.: Critical data studies: a dialog on data and space. Big Data Soc. **3**, (2016). https://doi.org/10.1177/2053951716648346
3. Nahon, K.: Where there is social media there is politics. In: Bruns, A., Enli, G., Skogerbo, E., Larsson, A.O., Christensen, C. (eds.) The Routledge Companion to Social Media and Politics. Routledge, New York (2016)
4. Mitchell, T.M.: The discipline of machine learning. Machine Learning Department, School of Computer Science, Carnegie Mellon University (2006)
5. Shah, D.V., Cappella, J.N., Neuman, W.R., Burscher, B., Vliegenthart, R., De Vreese, C.H.: Using supervised machine learning to code policy issues: can classifiers generalize across contexts? Ann. Am. Acad. Pol. Soc. Sci. **659**, 122–131 (2015)
6. Hopkins, D.J., King, G.: A method of automated nonparametric content analysis for social science. Am. J. Polit. Sci. **54**, 229–247 (2010)
7. Grimmer, J., Stewart, B.M.: Text as data: the promise and pitfalls of automatic content analysis methods for political texts. Polit. Anal. **21**, 267–297 (2013)
8. Stewart, B.M., Zhukov, Y.M.: Use of force and civil–military relations in Russia: an automated content analysis. Small Wars Insur. **20**, 319–343 (2009)
9. Liebeskind, C., Nahon, K., Hacohen-Kerner, Y., Manor, Y.: Comparing sentiment analysis models to classify attitudes of political comments on Facebook. Polibits Res. J. Comput. Sci. Comput. Eng. Appl. (2017)
10. Driscoll, K., Walker, S.: Big data, big questions| working within a black box: transparency in the collection and production of big Twitter data. Int. J. Commun. **8**, 20 (2014)
11. Landis, J.R., Koch, G.G.: The measurement of observer agreement for categorical data. Biometrics **33**, 159–174 (1977)
12. Liebeskind, C., Liebeskind, S., HaCohen-Kerner, Y.: Comment relevance classification in Facebook. In: CICLING 2016, the Eighteen International Conference on Computational Linguistics and Intelligent Text Processing, Budapest, Hungary (2017)
13. Witten, I.H., Frank, E.: Data Mining: Practical Machine Learning Tools and Techniques. Morgan Kaufmann, San Francisco (2005)
14. Hall, M., Frank, E., Holmes, G., Pfahringer, B., Reutemann, P., Witten, I.H.: The WEKA data mining software: an update. SIGKDD Explor. Newsl. **11**, 10–18 (2009)
15. Hall, M.A.: Correlation-based Feature Selection for Machine Learning (1999)

Wikidata and DBpedia: A Comparative Study

D. Abián[1,2], F. Guerra[3], J. Martínez-Romanos[1(✉)], and Raquel Trillo-Lado[1]

[1] University of Zaragoza, María de Luna, 1,
Ada Byron building, 50018 Zaragoza, Spain
{702089,raqueltl}@unizar.es
[2] Wikimedia España, Vega Sicilia, 2, 47008 Valladolid, Spain
davidabian@wikimedia.es
[3] University of Modena and Reggio Emilia, Modena, Italy
francesco.guerra@unimore.it

Abstract. DBpedia and Wikidata are two online projects focused on offering structured data from Wikipedia in order to ease its exploitation on the Linked Data Web. In this paper, a comparison of these two widely-used structured data sources is presented. This comparison considers the most relevant data quality dimensions in the state of the art of the scientific research. As fundamental differences between both projects, we can highlight that Wikidata has an open centralised nature, whereas DBpedia is more popular in the Semantic Web and the Linked Open Data communities and depends on the different linguistic editions of Wikipedia.

1 Introduction

Since its creation in 2001, Wikipedia has become one of the most important sources of reliable information on the Web. The English version of Wikipedia contains more than five million English articles and there are more than 280 active versions of Wikipedia in different languages that evolve independently. Wikipedia articles are typically split into two parts: (1) a body of unstructured text with details on the article subject and (2) an optional semistructured box (i.e., the *infobox*), that summarizes the most important facts about the article.

A number of big and important projects, such as Google's Knowledge Graph, Microsoft's Satori, and DBpedia [1], have exploited infoboxes for their purposes. In particular, DBpedia, created in 2007 by Free University of Berlin and Leipzig University in collaboration with the company OpenLink Software, extracts data from Wikipedia and builds an RDF graph. This project aims to extract structured information from Wikipedia and to make it available on the Linked Data Web. More recently (in 2012), Wikimedia Deutschland proposed the Wikidata project [2]. Its main goal is providing high-quality structured data acquired and maintained collaboratively to be directly used by Wikipedia to enrich its contents. Both projects, DBpedia and Wikidata, have become important in the current Linked Data Web. Thus, according to [3], DBpedia is the second node

© Springer International Publishing AG, part of Springer Nature 2018
J. Szymański and Y. Velegrakis (Eds.): IKC 2017, LNCS 10546, pp. 142–154, 2018.
https://doi.org/10.1007/978-3-319-74497-1_14

with more incoming links on the Linked Data Web, whereas Wikidata has been continuously increasing its popularity since its creation [4].

In an ideal situation, DBpedia and Wikidata should contain equivalent content, since Wikidata aims to improve the maintenance of structured data in Wikipedia and avoid data inconsistencies among the editions of Wikipedia in different languages, while DBpedia was created upon Wikipedia to make data from Wikipedia available on the Linked Data Web. However, currently, the content of these data sources is not equivalent, and through this paper we aim to provide a comparison of the quality of the data collected by these sources.

The structure of this paper is as follows. In the next section, a brief overview of the main features of Wikidata and DBpedia is introduced. After that, the criteria or dimensions considered to compare these data sources and the comparative analysis are presented in Sect. 3. Finally, some related work is analyzed in Sect. 4, and conclusions and future work are depicted in Sect. 5.

2 Overview and Evolution

On one hand, DBpedia defines itself as "a crowd-sourced community effort to extract structured information from Wikipedia and make this information available on the Web" to allow users "to ask sophisticated queries against Wikipedia and to link the different data sets on the Web to Wikipedia data"[1]. Thus, DBpedia uses different software components to extract different parts of Wikipedia articles (mainly, infoboxes) and to translate them into RDF statements. For every Wikipedia article representing a resource, DBpedia defines a URI with the following pattern: `http://dbpedia.org/resource/<Title_of_Wikipedia_Article>`. For example, the English Wikipedia article about the city of Zaragoza titled *Zaragoza*[2] corresponds to the resource identified by the URI http:// dbpedia.org/resource/Zaragoza in DBpedia. After that, different statements in RDF describing the resource identified by that URI are extracted from the article. For example, the statement (http://dbpedia.org/resource/Zaragoza, http:// dbpedia.org/property/website, http://www.zaragoza.es/) which indicates the address of the Zaragoza city website.

On the other hand, Wikidata, as Wikipedia, is an open, collaborative project hosted and supported by the Wikimedia Foundation[3], whose main goals are: (1) to act as central storage for the structured data of its Wikimedia sister projects including Wikipedia, Wikisource, etc., and (2) to provide data to other third-party projects and initiatives. Every resource or entity in Wikidata is represented by a URI that follows the pattern `http://www.wikidata.org/entity/ <QX>` where X is an integer. For example, the city of Zaragoza is represented by the URI http://www.wikidata.org/entity/Q10305. Analogously to DBpedia, Wikidata allows the definition of property-value pairs to provide descriptions of

---

[1] http://wiki.dbpedia.org/about.

[2] http://en.wikipedia.org/wiki/Zaragoza.

[3] https://wikimediafoundation.org.

entities/resources. Moreover, Wikidata also allows to specify *qualifiers*. Qualifiers refer to an assertion of a property-value pair for an entity; i.e. qualifiers allow people to define additional subordinate property-value pairs referred to assertions of a property-value pair for an entity. For example, the property-value pair (http://www.wikidata.org/wiki/Property:P1082, 732.765) of the entity with URI http://www.wikidata.org/entity/Q10305 is qualified with the pair (http://www.wikidata.org/wiki/Property:P585, 2013), indicating that the population of Zaragoza city was 732,765 habitants in the year 2013. Nevertheless, the value of the same property in 2012 was 679,624 habitants.

In contrast to URIs created in DBpedia, URIs in Wikidata do not depend upon a specific language. Besides, all data in Wikidata is international, i.e., although its display may be language-dependent, data are processed and stored in a format independent from the language adopted. For example, the number 1,003.5 is written "1.003,5" in Spanish but it is written "1 003.5" or "1,003.5" in English. However, different versions or chapters of DBpedia are maintained for each language (English DBpedia, Spanish DBpedia, etc.), so inconsistencies among the different chapters can appear. Thus, for example, in the English DBpedia, the values of the property http://dbpedia.org/ontology/leader for the resource about Spain are Felipe VI of Spain and Mariano Rajoy; whereas the values of an equivalent property in the Spanish version (http://es.dbpedia.org/property/dirigentesNombres) are Juan Carlos I of Spain (the previous king) and Mariano Rajoy[4]. Finally, DBpedia uses the standard RDF to model and store its content, whereas Wikidata uses a non standard custom model. Nevertheless, Wikidata offers web services to export data in several standard and commonly adopted formats and models such as JSON and RDF.

Summarizing, both projects, DBpedia and Wikidata, are strictly related to Wikipedia. As a consequence of this, Wikipedia, DBpedia and Wikidata form a bulky network of data flows, some of them directly assumed by the vast community of Wikipedia and Wikidata editors, open to the general public; and some of them algorithmically planned by the more-restricted community of DBpedia contributors. In more detail, DBpedia periodically retrieves information from the different chapters of Wikipedia by using statistic and data mining techniques, whereas Wikidata provides structured data to Wikipedia in real time (see Fig. 1). Moreover, DBpedia and Wikidata are different concerning their nature, structure and functioning. The maintenance of the different chapters of DBpedia is spread along a number of organizations; for example, Spanish DBpedia is maintained mainly by the Ontology Engineering Group of the Technical University of Madrid (Spain). Nevertheless, the different DBpedia chapters are coordinated by a common committee called DBpedia Internationalisation Committee. In contrast, Wikidata is maintained by an open community, hosted and supported by the Wikimedia Foundation, and actively developed by Wikimedia Deutschland.

---

[4] This data was obtained the May 15th, 2017.

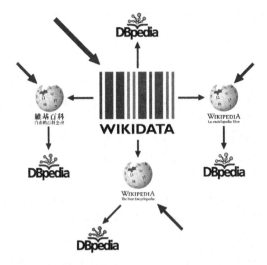

Fig. 1. Wikipedia, DBpedia and Wikidata create a bulky network of data flows, where incoming arrows represent users editing the resources.

3   Data Quality Analysis

The dimensions adopted in the literature [5–7] (see Sect. 4 for more details) to evaluate the quality of the data available in Wikipedia, DBpedia and Wikimedia are typically grouped in categories as it follows:

- *Intrinsic.* This category includes dimensions which do not depend on either the context or the task in which the data source is used. Generally, the dimensions in this category focus on whether the data properly represents the real world and on whether this representation is consistent.
- *Contextual.* This category refers to dimensions which depend on the task that users have at hand in a specific environment and time.
- *Representational.* This category refers to the design features of the data sources. It mainly focuses on how the data are stored, the ease of interpreting the data, and the interfaces and roles of the systems to interact with the data sources.
- *Accessibility.* This category refers to features related to how to obtain and access the data sources (typically via the Web) and to which extent data are sufficiently interlinked to other resources.

In this paper, we compare the data sources by using the mentioned categories and, for each of them, the dimensions proposed by at least two papers (among the ones in the literature considered as a reference) in the same category.

3.1   Intrinsic Category

Intrinsic category includes the accuracy, objectivity, consistence and reputation dimensions.

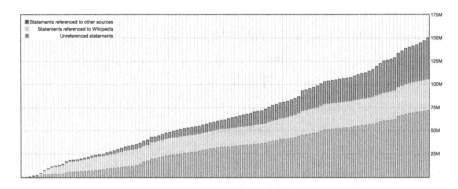

Fig. 2. Evolution of the number of references in Wikidata from 4th February 2013 to 15th May 2017. Extracted from: https://tools.wmflabs.org/wikidata/-todo/stats.php.

Accuracy. The generally adopted definition for this dimension is "the degree of correctness and precision with which information represents states of the real world" [5], i.e., to which extent data is error-free and represents the real world.

The statements in Wikidata should be verifiable and should include qualifiers that refer to trusted sources which they are based on, such as books, scientific papers, articles, etc. In particular, there exist two types of references: (1) *stated in*, to indicate the text in a media or publication where the statement is presented, and (2) *reference URL*, to refer to web sites and databases. However, if a statement represents general knowledge (for example, "the Earth is a planet") or if there exists an external identifier that immediately corroborates the statement (for example, ""Don Quixote", with ISBN-10: 0060934344, is a book") or if the statement is the information source (for example, "the name of "Miguel de Cervantes Saavedra" is "Miguel""), then references are not required. Therefore, we consider that a statement in Wikidata is precise and correct when it is conformed to the references. When references are not included, a statement is considered precise and correct when it represents the real world. According to the Fig. 2, nowadays (May 2017), almost 50% of data in Wikidata do not include references. Hence, some of these data could be considered imprecise or incorrect.

On the other hand, DBpedia incorporated N-Quads [9] from its version 3.5 (released on April 2010) onwards[5]. N-Quads allows to extend RDF triplets with an optional value in the 4th position of the statement. This value is used in DBpedia to include a provenance URI to indicate the exact origin in Wikipedia from which the associated triplet was extracted. In particular, the provenance URI is composed of the URI of the article from Wikipedia and several parameters indicating the source line from where the statement was extracted [10].

Therefore, Wikidata allows to refer to primary sources of information and its editors foster the inclusion of reliable sources and criticize the absence of these. In contrast, DBpedia can not indicate primary sources, but intermediate pages of Wikipedia which Wikidata does not consider as valid sources.

---

[5] http://wiki.dbpedia.org/changelog.

Objectivity Objectivity is typically defined as "the degree to which data is unbiased, unprejudiced and impartial" [6].

Both Wikipedia and Wikidata are edited by open communities, while DBpedia only admits editions of invited members and extracts most of its data from Wikipedia. Despite the fact that users can erroneously or intentionally include biased or partial data in Wikipedia and Wikidata, incorrect data are usually detected and fixed by other users. When no agreement among users editing an article is achieved, privileged users block the edition of conflicting data and keep only fact-based or well-referenced information. Other mechanisms to avoid vandalism are based on: (1) blocking ranges of IP addresses that have recently included false data and (2) developing bots to automatically detect and revert vandalism act[6].

Due to the fact that DBpedia automatically extracts most of its content from Wikipedia infoboxes, some noise could be introduced during this process. On the other hand, data in Wikidata is directly edited by users or by adhoc processes specifically designed to incorporate data from primary information sources (e.g., different national institutes of statistics). For this reason, we can consider the objectivity of Wikidata slightly higher than the one of DBpedia.

Reputation There is not a widely adopted definition of reputation of a data source. In this paper, we consider it as the degree of trustworthiness/reliability of the data and the extent to which third parties use or recommend such source.

Both Wikidata and DBpedia allow to include references to the sources where data is extracted. Besides, Wikidata and Wikipedia log the editions performed by the different users. Hence, analyzing the activities of the users along time and consulting the state of the data source in a certain time is possible. Regarding the extent to which third parties use both projects, we can consider DBpedia as the most important/referred node of the Linked Open Data Web according to the LOD cloud diagram [11] (a diagram that shows the relationships among datasets that have been published in Linked Data format based on metadata provided by Data Hub https://datahub.io). On the other hand, despite the fact that six entries for the query "Wikidata" are retrieved by the Data Hub's data source search engine, Wikidata is still not represented in the LOD cloud diagram.

Therefore, it can be considered that DBpedia is definitely more popular than Wikidata in the Linked Open Data community. Nevertheless, it must be emphasized that the number of users of, and requests to, Wikidata is increasing since its creation in 2012 [4], and that, recently, it has been announced that Wikidata and DBpedia will be federated [8].

Consistency The definition generally adopted for this dimension is the degree to which data in a data source "is free of (logical/formal) contradictions with respect to a particular knowledge representation and inference mechanisms" [6]. So, the conceptual and formal model of the data source must consistently represent the domain knowledge and no contradictions should be found in the model and data of the data source.

---

[6] https://wiki.data.org/wiki/Wikidata:ORES.

Both DBpedia and Wikidata use a model based on RDF which allows hierarchies of classes and properties, and instances of classes. However, the DBpedia model is semantically richer than the Wikidata model as it has been defined by means of OWL, while the core of the semantic constraints of Wikidata is defined in RDFS [12]. DBpedia does not apply semantic reasoners to effectively detect and reject data not satisfying constraints in ontologies. This is motivated by the fact that DBpedia reflects the Wikipedia data, where inconsistencies are introduced by users (e.g., in the infobox templates) [14]. On the other hand, Wikidata allows users to define ad hoc constraints for properties concerning a wide range of aspects (the most used constraints are listed in https://www.wikidata.org/wiki/Template:Constraint). Moreover, Wikidata also provides mechanisms to detect and remove data that does not satisfy those constraints. Finally, we would like to remark that, currently, DBpedia is working on the development of mechanisms to improve the data consistency [13].

3.2 Contextual Category

Contextual category includes the following dimensions: timelessness, completeness, relevancy and appropriate amount of data.

Timelessness Timelessness refers to the degree to which data are actual at the current moment. So, the update rate is one of the best metrics for this dimension.

The update rate of Wikidata depends on the activity of its users. Users can edit the content of Wikidata collaboratively by means of different interfaces, or/and they can program and execute bots to edit data. According to [4], in 2014, the edition frequency in Wikidata was up to 500 editions/minute. In contrast, updates in DBpedia are less frequent. DBpedia is updated approximately once per month[7]. Finally, it must be noticed that DBpedia also offers a live synchronization module (DBpedia Live System) [3] that allows the changes in Wikipedia to be propagated to DBpedia when an article is updated. However, this module is not running in all DBpedia chapters (e.g., it is not deployed in the Spanish chapter).

Completeness Although there is not a widely adopted definition for completeness, this dimension usually refers to the degree of data available in a specific context, i.e., the degree to which information is not missing. Different authors also define different types of completeness: schema vs column vs population completeness, completeness on schema level vs on data level, schema vs population completeness, etc. [6]. In this paper, we consider two perspectives: *completeness in depth* and *completeness in wideness*, being *wideness* the amount of entities represented in the data source and *depth* the average extent of the entities, i.e., the relation between the total of declarations and the total of entities of the data source.

---

[7] http://wiki.dbpedia.org.

In December, 2016, in Wikidata, there were 125 millions of statements distributed in 24.5 millions of items, which could be translated into one or more RDF triplets. So, Wikidata had an average depth of 5.1 declarations per element. In contrast, in the release published in April 2016 of DBpedia, 6 millions of entities were defined by means of 9500 millions of RDF triplets. So, this version contains 28.66 millions of instances with an average of 331.5 triplets per instance. The completeness of Wikidata and DBpedia cannot be compared in a non-biased way considering the previous data as the measurements for the data sources are not equivalent. Nevertheless, it can be concluded that both projects have the same order of magnitude of wideness, being Wikidata probably wider since it contains entities that does not correspond to a Wikipedia article. As well, it can be concluded that the depth of DBpedia is probably higher than the depth of Wikidata, although DBpedia resources are less structured than Wikidata entities.

Relevancy The most popular definition is "the extent to which information is applicable and helpful for the task at hand" [6]. Therefore, relevancy largely depends on the context, on the user performing the task and on the mechanisms provided by the data source to analyze and retrieve relevant resources.

Both DBpedia and Wikidata are generic data sources that provide tools for: (1) navigating and visualizing data, (2) formally querying data via SPARQL endpoints, (3) performing keyword-based searches, and (4) retrieving information about how to use the data and the different Key Performance Indicators (KPIs) that can help users to do their tasks.

Appropriate Amount of Data This dimension depends on the particular task and on the context where the data source is used. It is usually defined as the amount of data available and appropriate for a particular task.

Three SPARQL queries requesting for old, recent and very recent data, respectively, were used to provide a preliminary view of this dimension in Wikidata and in the English version of DBpedia (the most complete one) as, unfortunately, it is not possible to query all DBpedia chapters together. In particular, the following queries were submitted to both data sources on 4th January 2017:

- *Query 1*: Obtaining Spanish people born in the 20th century. DBpedia retrieved 1086 different resources, while Wikidata provided 39854 different entities.
- *Query 2*: Obtaining people who died in December, 2015. DBpedia retrieved 341 different resources, while Wikidata provided 1184 different entities.
- *Query 3*: Obtaining people who died in January, 2017. DBpedia retrieved 2 different wrong resources, while Wikidata provided 1184 different entities.

In all cases, Wikidata returns significantly more results than the English DBpedia. Other queries provided similar results. It can be concluded that Wikidata offers more appropriate data than the English DBpedia and, consequently, more appropriate data than any isolated version of DBpedia.

3.3   Representation Category

The dimensions considered in this category are: interpretability, ease of understanding, representational consistency and concise representation.

Interpretability There is not a widely adopted definition of interpretability of a data source. Nevertheless, all definitions of this dimension refer to the technical representation of the data in the data source.

Both DBpedia and Wikidata use self-descriptive formats including metadata. Moreover, resources are identified by means of global unique identifiers. However, the URIs stability is not the same in both projects. In DBpedia, the titles of the Wikipedia articles are used as identifiers. So, different versions of DBpedia can have different identifiers for the same resources (e.g., the city of London is identified by http://dbpedia.org/resource/London in the English DBpedia and by http://es.dbpedia.org/resource/Londres in the Spanish DBpedia). Moreover, the same resource can change its identifier in different versions of DBpedia (e.g., the Russian city St. Petersburg was previously named Leningrad). On the other hand, Wikidata uses auto-numeric identifiers, which are semantically independent from the resources that they represent. Thanks to this independence, URIs are stable and are not updated when even all data of the resource that they are identifying is edited. There are some rare exceptions to this rule of randomness in Wikidata IDs: Q1–Q5, Q13 and Q666 which are kept to represent specific resources.

Understandability Understandability is generally defined as the degree to "which data is easily comprehended by the information consumer, without ambiguity" [6]. So, the language of the data source labels and the representation model adopted are key for this dimension.

Although English is the default language of the interface of Wikidata, Wikidata is a multilingual project designed to centralize all data from different chapters in different languages of Wikipedia. In 2013, the Wikimedia Foundation's Linguistic Committee decided that Wikidata would accept all languages of the world with three basic considerations[8]: (1) the language has an ISO-639-3 code (a numeric code used in computer systems); (2) historical languages are permitted; and (3) constructed languages are allowed. Currently, in Wikidata, there are labels, descriptions and aliases for more than 400 languages and dialects. On the other hand, DBpedia has a different version for each language. Nevertheless, DBpedia community would like to integrate and merge multi-language instances by linking different versions of DBpedia [3].

In December 2016, the set of elements of Wikidata had a total of 136.85 millions of labels (14 millions in English) and 222.80 millions of descriptions (13.59 millions in English); while DBpedia was available in 125 languages and offered a total of 38 millions of labels and abstracts (abstracts are referred as descriptions in Wikidata).

---

[8] https://blog.wikimedia.org/2013/11/06/any-language-allowed-in-wikidata.

Representational Consistency Althought there is no consensus definition for this dimension, different authors agree on that it evaluates the degree to which information is represented in an uniform way with the purposes of increasing the interoperability and reusing intra and inter data sources. So, this dimension is extremely related to the dimension *Interlinking*.

As previously mentioned, the stability of the identifiers (URIs) is bigger in Wikidata than in DBpedia. So, we could consider that the representational consistency is bigger in Wikidata. However, if we consider inter data sources relationships, the inter-data-sources interoperability and reuse are bigger for DBpedia than for Wikidata according to the information provided by Data Hub.

Representational Conciseness Few frameworks and authors consider this dimension [6], which is usually defined as the degree to which data is compactly represented being complete. So, representational conciseness is measured by considering the length of the identifiers, and the representational language and format used by the data source.

As previously exposed, the identifiers of DBpedia depend on titles of articles in Wikipedia, while Wikidata uses shorter specific numeric identifiers. With respect to the representational language and format, DBpedia uses Virtuoso as platform to manage content based on RDF and OWL whose representational formats are quite verbose due to the fact that they are mainly based on text codification [15]. In contrast, Wikidata uses Wikibase, a specific software to manage large amounts of structured data that basically consists of two MediaWiki extensions: (1) Wikibase Repository and (2) Wikibase Client. As far as we know, Wikibase content is neither stored nor code in a standard way. Finally, we would like to remark that both, DBpedia and Wikidata, allows to export their contents to different common formats such as JSON, RDF, XML and even CSV.

3.4 Accessibility

Only the interlinking dimension is considered in this category.

Interlinking refers to the degree to which the data are linked with other data in both ways (in-going and out-going links) as it is important that each element of a data source is related to other elements (equivalent or not) defined in other data sources. Different types of interlinking are possible, being the *linked data interlinking* one of the most relevant in the Semantic Web and Web of Data.

Both Wikidata and DBpedia allow their elements to be referred from other data sources and to establish links between their elements and other resources. As previously mentioned, the number of inter-data-sources links in DBpedia is quite higher than in Wikidata. On the other hand, Wikidata has a stronger relationship with Wikimedia projects (e.g. Wikipedia or Wikispecies) than DBpedia.

4   Related Work

Knowledge bases and ontologies as DBpedia, Freebase, OpenCyc, Wikidata, and YAGO have been experimented in a large number of projects and are now adopted in commercial applications. Therefore, it is important, not only for the academic but also for the industrial community, to have a description of the main features of these knowledge sources. To the best of our knowledge, even if a complete description of these sources is available in many papers, an approach providing a critical comparison is still missing.

We started this work by focusing on Wikidata and DBpedia. In particular, we extended [8], where it is shown how Wikidata is incorporated into DBpedia and some relevant statistics about both knowledge bases are provided. This paper extends that analysis by providing a more general and complete framework for evaluating Wikidata and DBpedia. The dimensions adopted in our framework for evaluating the data quality have been selected according to the ones available

Table 1. Frameworks to evaluate the quality of data sources

Dimension Categories	Wang and Wrong (1996) [5]	Zaveri et al. (2015) [6]		Wikidata (2016) [7]
Intrinsic	Accuracy Objectivity Reputation Believability	Accuracy Consistency Conciseness Timeless		Accuracy Objectivity Reputation Consistency
Contextual	Timeliness Completeness Relevancy Value-added Amount of data	Amount of data Completeness Relevancy Verifiability Reputation Believability		Timeliness Completeness: Schema Item Population
Representational	Interpretability Understandability Consistency Conciseness	Interpretability Understandability Versatility Consistency Conciseness		Interpretability Understandability
Accessibility	Accessibility Access security	Interlinking Availability Security Performance Licensing		Interlinking
Others	Flexibility Traceability Cost-effectiveness Ease of operation Variety	Trust	Objectivity Verifiability Reputation Believability	Believability Relevancy Accessibility Access security Value-added
		Dataset Dynamicity	Timeless Currency Volatility	Amount of data Consistency Conciseness

in the state of the art. In particular, [5,6] classify the dimensions in a number of categories as Table 1 shows.

Starting from these categories, Wikidata opened a "Requests for comment" [7], where users are asked to provide their opinion on a data quality framework for Wikidata. Our proposal takes into account the work done and identified the relevant dimensions as shown in Table 1. The table highlights the dimensions which only appear in one of the proposed frameworks (in blue in Table 1), in two frameworks but in different categories (in green in Table 1) and in three frameworks but in three different categories (in red in Table 1). These dimensions were discarded[9] in our analysis since there is no consensus among different authors. After the filtering process, 11, 13 and 12 dimensions from the frameworks [5–7], respectively, have been considered in our analysis (these dimensions are represented in black color in Table 1).

5 Conclusions and Future Work

The number of structured data sources available on the Web has been increasing during the last decade. Two popular data sources commonly used are DBpedia and Wikidata. So, we have compared them by considering the criteria defined in the main frameworks to evaluate the quality of structured data sources.

As future work, we would like to develop a tool to audit the quality of data sources by considering the standard UNE 178301 Smart Cities and Open Data and the methodologies used in this paper to compare DBpedia and Wikidata. Currently, this kind of evaluations (audits) are made by considering the opinion of experts on the topic, who provide a value between zero and four for each dimension.

Acknowledgments. This work has been partially funded by: Action COST Keystone IC-1302, TIN2016-78011-C4-3-R (AEI/FEDER, UE), TIN2013-46238-C4-4-R. We thank Á. Poc, D. Martínez, X. Pan and F. del Molino for their support on this work.

References

1. Auer, S., Bizer, C., Kobilarov, G., Lehmann, J., Cyganiak, R., Ives, Z.: DBpedia: a nucleus for a web of open data. In: Aberer, K., et al. (eds.) ASWC/ISWC 2007. LNCS, vol. 4825, pp. 722–735. Springer, Heidelberg (2007). https://doi.org/10.1007/978-3-540-76298-0_52
2. Vrandečić, D.: Wikidata: a new platform for collaborative data collection. In: 21st International Conference on World Wide Web, pp. 1063–1064. ACM, France (2012)

---

[9] Dimensions "Cost-effectiveness" and "Flexibility" defined in [5] are considered very related to "Performance" and "Versatility" defined in [6], respectively, so they are represented in color green. Notice also that, despite the fact that "Interlinking" is in green, it is not discarded because it appears in the same category in [6,7].

3. Lehmann, J., Isele, R., Jakob, M., Jentzsch, A., Kontokostas, D., Mendes, P., Hellmann, S., Morsey, M., van Kleef, P., Auer, S., Bizer, C.: DBpedia - a large-scale, multilingual knowledge base extracted from wikipedia. Semantic Web J. 6(2), 167–195 (2015)
4. Vrandečić, D., Krőtzsch, M.: Wikidata: a free collaborative knowledgebase. Commun. ACM 57(10), 78–85 (2014)
5. Wang, R.Y., Strong, D.M.: Beyond accuracy: what data quality means to data consumers. J. Manag. Inf. Syst. 12(4), 5–33 (1996)
6. Zaveri, A., Rula, A., Maurino, A., Pietrobon, R., Lehmann, J., Auer, S.: Quality assessment for linked data: a survey. Semantic Web 7(1), 63–93 (2015)
7. Wikidata discussion page about Data Quality. https://www.wikidata.org/wiki/Wikidata:Requests_for_comment/Data_quality_framework_for_Wikidata. Accessed May 2017
8. Kontokostas, D., Auer, S., Lehmann, J., Hellmann, S.: Wikidata through the Eyes of DBpedia. CoRR, vol. abs/1507.04180 (2015)
9. Carothers, G., Machina, L.: RDF 1.1 N-Quads. A line-based syntax for RDF datasets. W3C Recommendation (2014)
10. Provenance meta-data in DBpedia Datasets. http://wiki.dbpedia.org/services-resources/datasets/dbpedia-datasets#h434-17. Accessed May 2017
11. The Linking Open Data diagram. http://lod-cloud.net. Accessed June 2017
12. Antoniou, G., Harmelen, F.: A Semantic Web Primer. The MIT Press, Cambridge (2008)
13. Rodríguez, I.: DBpedia Mappings Front-End Administration. Google Summer of Code Project (2017)
14. Rodriguez-Hernandez, I., Trillo-Lado, R., Yus, R.: WikInfoboxer: a tool to create wikipedia infoboxes using DBpedia. XXI Jornadas de Ingeniería del Software y Bases de Datos at Congreso Español De Infomática (2016)
15. Fernández, J.D., Martínez-Prieto, M.A., Gutierrez, C., Polleres, A.: Binary RDF Representation for Publication and Exchange (HDT). W3C Member Submission (2011)

Multi-Lingual LSA with Serbian and Croatian: An Investigative Case Study

Colin Layfield[1]([⊠]), Dragan Ivanović[2], and Joel Azzopardi[1]

[1] University of Malta, Msida, Malta
{colin.layfield,joel.azzopardi}@um.edu.mt
[2] University of Novi Sad, Novi Sad, Serbia
dragan.ivanovic@uns.ac.rs

Abstract. One of the challenges in information retrieval is attempting to search a corpus of documents that may contain multiple languages. This exploratory study expands upon earlier research employing Latent Semantic Analysis (so called Multi-Lingual Latent Semantic Indexing, or ML-LSI/LSA). We experiment using this approach, and a new one, in a multi-lingual context utilising two similar languages, namely Serbian and Croatian. Traditionally, with an LSA approach, a parallel corpus would be needed in order to train the system by combining identical documents in two languages into one document. We repeat that approach and also experiment with creating a semantic space using the parallel corpus on its own without merging the documents together to test the hypothesis that, with very similar languages, the merging of documents may not be required for good results.

1 Introduction

The classic Information Retrieval (IR) scenario generally consists of a corpus of documents in the same language that can be searched via queries in the same language. With the far-reaching implications of the Internet, specifically the World Wide Web (WWW), encountering documents in many different languages is no longer unusual. The same reasoning applies to repositories of information as with easier distribution of new information the need naturally arises to extend IR technologies to cater for this. Much research has already been carried out regarding the task of Cross Language Information Retrieval (CLIR - querying in one language and possibly retrieving results in several languages) and Multi-Language Information Retrieval (MLIR - asking questions in more than one language and retrieving results from documents that are in potentially different languages) [5].

The scenario we are examining seeks to exploit the strong similarity between languages in the Balkan region; in this case specifically Croatian and Serbian. Some researchers are actually engaged in investigating the hypothesis that these languages are actually the same. The main intention of the project Languages and Nationalism (http://jezicinacionalizmi.com/) is to start an open dialogue between linguists and other experts about the existence of four "political" languages in Bosnia and Herzegovina, Montenegro, Croatia and Serbia which have

J. Szymański and Y. Velegrakis (Eds.): IKC 2017, LNCS 10546, pp. 155–164, 2018.
https://doi.org/10.1007/978-3-319-74497-1_15

grown from the one language of the former Yugoslavia (the Serbo-Croatian language). The whole question of the status of Serbian and Croatian languages is very sensitive, because of cultural and political implications [8]. However, the outside linguists suggest it is the same language with multiple dialects taking into account the numerous shared features and easy mutual comprehension [3]. Due to the similarity of these languages the research question being investigated is whether or not LSA can be utilised in a multi-linguistic capacity to enable IR from a mixed language corpus of documents without the requirement of merging parallel documents - specifically those which are very similar.

2 Background

This section will first take a brief look at what methods are utilised already in the field of multi-lingual IR. Next a description of Latent Semantic Analysis (LSA) will be presented followed by a description of how this has been applied to the MLIR problem in the past.

2.1 Methods of Multi-Lingual Information Retrieval

As alluded to previously there has already been a considerable amount of research investigating multi-lingual IR approaches. Several reviews on methods used for tackling these issues have been published in the last few years that give an overview on the techniques used for this problem [5,7,11]. The approaches utilised generally fall into the categories of query and document translation. The idea behind these approaches is to employ various techniques (such as dictionary, machine translation or parallel corpora [5]) to translate either the query or the documents in the corpora themselves in order to allow IR to take place. [11] highlights challenges in this area to include translation disambiguation, quality/comprehensiveness of dictionaries employed and usage of technical terms.

2.2 Latent Semantic Analysis (LSA)

Latent Semantic Analysis is a technique whose roots are found in factor analysis. The idea behind LSA is to generate a classic $m \times n$ term by document matrix (which we call A) from a corpus of documents. This matrix is then reduced into three factors via *singular value decomposition* such that:

$$A = TSD^T \tag{1}$$

where T is a $m \times r$ matrix, D^T is a $r \times n$ matrix where each of these matricies has its vectors comprised of orthonormal eigenvectors, and a $r \times r$ diagonal matrix consisting of the singular values of the decomposition (r also represents the *rank* of the matrix A) [4]. The rows of matrix T represent the terms in the newly created *semantic space* and the columns of D^T represent the documents. These document vectors can now be used for similarity comparisons between one another or with additional documents (or queries) that are projected into the semantic space by multiplying the new document vector by TS^{-1}; this operation is also referred to as *folding-in* a document into the preexisting semantic space). Comparisons between documents (vectors) in this study will be done using the popular cosine operator (further details on LSA and the mechanics can be found in [1,4,9]).

The power of LSA is derived from the ability to perform *dimensionality reduction*. To do this we pick a value, say k, which is less than r and reduce the dimensionality of the singular value matrix such that it now only has k dimensions. The end result is that both term and document vectors are now represented by k dimensions. This reduced vector space is then used in comparison operations. This reduced dimensionality reduces noise and brings to the foreground any underlying "latent semantics" present in the corpus of documents [4]. The selection of k is somewhat arbitrary but a value of 300 was used in this work (as typically used in research). A good introduction to LSA can be found in [9].

2.3   Multi-Lingual Latent Semantic Analysis

Typically if a multi-lingual LSA solution is going to be employed it is generally required that a parallel training corpus is used. The parallel corpus will contain copies of the same document in the target languages - so in our case it will contain a set of identical documents in both Serbian and Croatian. The next step will be to combine these identical documents together such that each document contains the text for both languages. A term by document matrix would be generated from this combined corpus and SVD would be applied to it as described above in Sect. 2.2.

[6] carried out a study utilising ML-LSA with this approach. The parallel corpus they utilised consisted of the Hansard Collection which is a collection of Canadian parliament interactions. As Canada is a bilingual country the collection of the exchanges exists in both official languages, namely English and French. The evaluation metric they used was to perform a 'mate-retrieval' test. A mate-retrieval test involves selecting the same document in both languages (that does not exist in the semantic space) and folding one into the LSA semantic space and using the remaining document to 'search' for its mate with the document itself acting as the query. This dataset consisted of 2,482 documents. 1,500 were selected randomly for training the system (French/English documents combined and a semantic space generated). The remaining 982 were used as a test set for performing the evaluation. The test set documents were folded into the semantic space and the English document was used to search for its French mate and vice versa. The average success rate of this test was 98.4%.

A similar study was carried out by [13] using the Bible as a parallel corpus (many researchers use this as it is one of the most translated works in the world and is split up nicely to utilise as a parallel corpus). They try two approaches, one involves creating a common base of terms to generate a cross language semantic space, the second combines small portions of each document across the entire database (of the Bible). The languages used were English and Greek.

It is difficult to compare results directly as it could be the case that the document being searched for (in the other language) was already included in the semantic space and, thus, in the SVD computation which we are not doing. One conclusion reached, however, is that a good variety of documents included in the semantic space did seem to increase their precision and recall scores.

Research was carried out by [2] regarding the effects of language relatedness on multilingual information retrieval (with a focus on Indo-European and Semitic languages). In essence they experimented, using LSA in a similar fashion to the above (including usage of the Bible to create the semantic space but the Koran text was used for search), the effect of combining parallel corpus documents from multiple languages and whether or not the language "type" had any type of positive influence. They concluded that adding additional languages from a parallel corpus can be beneficial and the types of languages added can have an impact on the quality of results.

3   Experiment

The hypothesis we are testing in our experiment is that due to the similarity of Croatian and Serbian we may be able to use a semantic space that is comprised of documents from each instead of using the typical ML-LSA approach of concatenating documents from a parallel corpus. We will be experimenting with both scenarios using documents from the parallel corpus.

3.1   Dataset Used

For this experiment we needed a parallel corpus of Serbian and Croatian in order to compare both scenarios. The SETIMES dataset is used which is a collection of parallel news articles in the Balkan languages extracted from the http://www.setimes.com website [12] which consists of 9 languages overall. The dataset we employed was Croatian and Serbian parallel corpora. This corpora consisted of 170,466 aligned sentences which made up the 29,391 news articles which we will treat as documents in this study.

As with any exercise in language processing there were several steps that had to be performed in order to transform the data into a usable format. The data itself was in several large XML files which had to be processed to strip out the text[1]. Next the text was tokenized, transformed into lower case and Cyrillic characters (these only existed in the Serbian language documents) were transformed to their Latin equivalent by mapping between Cyrillic and Latin codes of Unicode character set. A small Serbian and Croatian stop word list was utilised and a Snowball stemmer[2] applied to all the text; the last step entails

---

[1] As a side effect, the XML turned out to be badly formed in places and needed to be fixed by hand.

[2] http://snowballstem.org.

the removal of diacritics from the text[3]. It should be noted that this process was applied to both Croatian and Serbian text in an identical fashion as the rules for these are virtually the same including usage of one common stemmer for Serbian and Croatian languages due to the similar morphology of those two languages [3].

The paragraphs were further processed to ensure that they contained a minimum number of words. The average number of words per document in the Hansard Collection used by [6] was 84 words in English and 86 words in French so we opted for a minimum word count of 60. This reduced the number of suitable documents from 29,391 to 19,842. It should be also be noted that this dataset contained a number of blank sentences/documents as well as documents that were entirely in English which were removed via testing documents to see if any passed a threshold of having more than 25% English stopwords[4]. The term by document matrix, before SVD is calculated, is subjected to Term Frequency - Inverse Document Frequency or Log-Entropy weighting (as described in [1,10]). In addition to this any term in the matrix that did not have a document frequency of at least 2 was discarded.

3.2 Method

Two sets of experiments were run with the dataset. The first experiment replicates the mate-retrieval test done in [6] and the second experiment tests our hypothesis. These are:

1. Perform the mate-retrieval test using the classic ML-LSA approach.
2. Perform the mate-retrieval test where each document in the semantic space consists only of a single language.

Each test was run 10 times. We varied the number of documents used in the semantic space 3 times using values of 1,000, 2,500 and 5,000 for a total of 6 sets of experiments. For each experiment, from the set of documents not used in the semantic space, 5,000 were chosen at random to perform the mate-retrieval test as in [6]. This set of experiments was run twice: once for Term Frequency-Inverse Document Frequency weighting and once for the application of the Log-Entropy weighting scheme as outlined earlier.

4   Results

The results from the experiment can be found in Table 1. These results are all of the averages from 10 runs as outlined above in the experiment description

---

[3] Diacritics are added to the top or bottom of a letter to indicate appropriate stress, special pronunciation, or unusual sounds not common in the Roman alphabet. In Serbian and Croatian, these markings indicate special pronunciation, like the difference between the pronunciation of C compared to Ć.

[4] The stop word list is available at http://www.lextek.com/manuals/onix/stopwords1. html. Note that single character stop words were not included as it was found that many Serbian/Croatian documents were flagged as English when they were present in the list.

in Sect. 3.2. The first column represents the dataset size in the experiment run. Note that in the case where the parallel documents are *not* combined into one the actual size of the semantic space will be double the dataset size as each document is put into the space individually. So a dataset size of 2,500 that does not have the parallel documents combined will actually contain 5,000 documents. The next two-columns indicate whether or not the term by document matrix was weighted using Term Frequency-Inverse Document Frequency (tf-idf) or Log-Entropy (l-e)[5]. The following column indicates whether or not it's a combined dataset (Serbian/Croatian documents combined into one). The next two columns indicate the result from the mate retrieval exercise. The 'Srb → Cro' column indicates the percentage of the time that the Serbian document used as a search document for its mate found it as the closest match, the column after is the opposite case. The next two columns indicate the percentage of the time during the mate retrieval exercise the correct document appeared in the top 5 returned results. The last two columns contain the average number of words in the semantic space as well as the average document length.

Table 1. Results for experiment runs

Dataset Size	tf-idf	l-e	Comb	Srb → Cro	Cro → Srb	top5Srb	top5Cro	Words	Doc Length
1000	✓		✓	98.1%	98.1%	98.9%	98.9%	8248.8	266.2
1000		✓	✓	99.2%	99.1%	99.7%	99.6%	8248.8	266.2
1000	✓			82.3%	82.3%	89.6%	89.2%	11237.4	135.2
1000		✓		90.1%	90.2%	94.5%	94.5%	11237.4	135.2
2500	✓		✓	97.7%	97.8%	98.2%	98.2%	13427.2	271.0
2500		✓	✓	98.7%	98.8%	99.1%	99.1%	13427.2	271.0
2500	✓			78.9%	79.0%	86.3%	86.3%	17506.4	136.3
2500		✓		86.4%	86.7%	91.4%	91.6%	17506.4	136.3
5000	✓		✓	97.5%	97.6%	97.8%	97.9%	18802.3	276.6
5000		✓	✓	98.3%	98.3%	98.7%	98.7%	18802.3	276.6
5000	✓			75.1%	75.3%	83.3%	83.2%	24066.7	137.1
5000		✓		83.4%	83.7%	88.6%	89.5%	24066.7	137.1

In addition to this data we calculated the average same similarity[6] scores of the twinned documents used in the mate retrieval exercise as well as the average of the closest match in the semantic space excluding the target document. These values can be found below in Table 2.

---

[5] We discovered, serendipitously, that the results of using tf-idf and l-e were actually superior when the folded-in search queries were only weighted using raw term-frequency. This was unexpected and will be a topic of future research. The results reported here use the commonly accepted approach of weighting the query appropriately with the weighting method used for the creation of the semantic space.

[6] The same similarity score is the cosine similarity between the two 'mate' documents.

Table 2. Average similarity values

Dataset Size	tf-idf	l-e	Combined	Avg SS	Average Best Srb Sim	Average Best Cro Sim
1000	✓		✓	0.951	0.614	0.613
1000		✓	✓	0.947	0.561	0.561
1000	✓			0.777	0.640	0.640
1000		✓		0.800	0.592	0.595
2500	✓		✓	0.956	0.686	0.686
2500		✓	✓	0.954	0.634	0.635
2500	✓			0.797	0.703	0.705
2500		✓		0.813	0.659	0.662
5000	✓		✓	0.959	0.720	0.720
5000		✓	✓	0.957	0.661	0.662
5000	✓			0.799	0.735	0.737
5000		✓		0.809	0.683	0.686

5   Discussion

First, it is interesting to note that the performance of the classic ML-LSA approach slightly out-performs the English/French mate retrieval experiment described in [6] so this acts as another confirmation of the ML-LSA approach (with l-e). A more detailed comparison on this test is difficult to realise as many details of how LSA was employed are left out. For example the number of dimensions used in the dimensional reduction is not specified nor was it mentioned if any weighting was applied to the generated term by document matrix which makes an exact replication of the scenario impossible.

Overall, it should also be noted, that Log-Entropy gives superior results compared with Term Frequency-Inverse Document Frequency every time. It should also be noted that the quality of results from the non-combined results outperformed most of the results reported in the study, [2], referred to in Sect. 2.3 although, to be fair, they were using much more challenging languages for their experiments; however this lends some support to our view that very closely related languages can be treated more like a 'regular' LSA implementation.

Next it should be observed that the performance of the non combined document test runs were somewhat worse than was expected. The accuracy, however, would still be reasonable for an information retrieval system so they can be viewed as positive overall. It is also surprising that as the dataset size increased the results started to worsen. The average similarity values found in Table 2 may offer some insight as to why this may be the case. In all the test scenarios explored there is a trend where as the data size increases so does the average best similarity for a search in the semantic space (including the same similarity average between the document mates with one close exception). These increases in average value are not inconsiderable - especially the average values representing the best similarity value in the semantic space with the Serbian or Croatian query document.

It is also worthy to note that the average number of words present in the semantic space for each increases as the number of documents used to form it increases. One of the co-authors of this paper is fluent in both Serbian and Croatian and spent some time going through a sample of several of the cases where the mate-retrieval test returned a different document than the targeted one. It was found that the news stories in question were actually related and it would have been viewed as a valid candidate for the search performed. For instance, there were some political issues in the Balkan region over a short timeframe and, as a result, there were several news articles addressing this topic in the corpus that contained similar information. It was not feasible to validate this for all the missed searches but it did seem to be a very strong theme throughout. The fact the average similarity values are increasing as the semantic spaces increases would seem to support this view; especially as the gap between the best same similarity and best similarity between the query document and the semantic space is narrowing considerably. As the variety and richness of words in the search space increases further underlying relationships of documents may be linked to potentially boost the similarity values of documents compared. Without a more exhaustive search of the scenarios where the mated document is not returned as the top choice, however, this cannot be said with certainty.

There are pros and cons to using an approach where a parallel corpus is not needed. One obvious advantage is all that may be required is a set of documents in the languages you wish to support; this alone may be sufficient to act as a useful training corpus for creating a semantic space. The downside to this is, of course, increased complexity as more documents may be required than what a parallel corpus could offer which would, therefore, increase the number of documents in our semantic space that we need to process. Performing the SVD computation is not cheap but on modern computers, in work unrelated to this, it was found that performing SVD on the Wikipedia corpus took a little under 2 weeks of computation time on a modestly powered server (the largest constraint was having enough RAM for the computation). The complexity barrier is not as inpeneratrable as it was 10 years ago so this could still be considered a viable option.

6   Conclusion and Future Work

The overall results from this exploratory early study shows some promising results. It does appear that, using the mate retrieval test, a mixed language semantic space can distinguish between the two separate languages being used. The fact that the languages are very closely related almost certainly plays a role in this result. As has been shown in other studies, even using ML-LSA, results between very different languages (in the morphological sense, say English and Arabic) are much more difficult to use in a multi-lingual search environment so this can be viewed as a special case.

This research leaves plenty of scope for future work. There are additional Balkan languages that could be added to the current Croatian and Serbian dataset to further test the applicability of this method with respect to similar languages. Besides Serbian and Croatian, there are the Bosnian and Montenegrin languages which appeared after the former Yugoslavia was broken-up. In addition, between Bosnian-Croatian-Montenegrin-Serbian (BCMS) there are the numerous shared features and easy mutual comprehension [3]. Almost 15 million people from the former Yugoslav region can have benefit of Multi-lingual IR tools and systems for BCMS languages.

The research paper discussed in Sect. 2.3 regarding the Hansard collection also utilised additional evaluation methodologies other than the mate retrieval test [6]. One such test attempted to simulate more realistic queries by finding the 5 nearest terms to each English test document and using these as a query. Presumably these would be expected to find the natural mate for the document the terms originated from but this could potentially involve a more customised search space to verify the results (they repeated a similar experiment using yellow pages categories and enhanced their semantic space by folding in a number of these too in order to see if the other language's version of these categories could be searched).

Additional experiments can be run using the same method discussed in this paper but, instead, with a semantic space generated randomly from the documents available to it rather than with matched pairs. It would also be useful to perform the same experiments again but with the creation of a semantic space that just contains roughly equal amounts of documents from each language that are not from a parallel corpus at all; this opens the possibility of trying this approach with more than 2 languages.

The corpus we are utilising is split down into the word/sentence level. A repeat of this experiment at the sentence level may also yield interesting results.

Acknowledgements. This article is based upon work from COST Action KEY-STONE IC1302, supported by COST (European Cooperation in Science and Technology).

References

1. Berry, M.W., Browne, M.: Understanding Search Engines: Mathematical Modeling and Text Retrieval, 2nd edn. SIAM, Philadelphia (2005)
2. Chew, P., Abdelali, A.: The effects of language relatedness on multilingual information retrieval: a case study with Indo-European and semitic languages. In: Proceedings of the 2nd International Workshop on "Cross Lingual Information Access" Addressing the Information Need of Multilingual Societies, pp. 1–9, January 2008. http://anthology.aclweb.org/I/I08/I08-6.pdf#page=10
3. Corbett, G.G., Browne, W.: Serbo-croat: Bosnian, Croatian, Montenegrin, Serbian. In: The World's Major Languages, pp. 330–346. Routledge, London (2009)
4. Deerwester, S., Dumais, S.T., Furnas, G.W., Landauer, T.K., Harshman, R.: Indexing by latent semantic analysis. J. Am. Soc. Inf. Sci. **41**(6), 391–407 (1990)
5. Dhavachelvan, P., Pothula, S.: A review on the cross and multilingual information retrieval. Int. J. Web Semantic Technol. **2**(4), 115–124 (2011)

6. Dumais, S.T., Letsche, T.A., Littman, M.L., Landauer, T.K.: Automatic cross-language retrieval using latent semantic indexing. AAAI Technical Report SS-97-05, pp. 18–24 (1997)
7. Dwivedi, S., Chandra, G.: A survey on cross language information retrieval. Int. J. Cybern. Inform. 5(1), 127–142 (2016)
8. Greenberg, R.D.: Language politics in the federal republic of Yugoslavia: the crisis over the future of serbian. Slavic Rev. 59(3), 625–640 (2008)
9. Landauer, T.K., Foltz, P.W., Laham, D.: An introduction to latent semantic analysis. Discourse Process. 25, 259–284 (1998)
10. Manning, C.D., Raghavan, P., Schütze, H.: Introduction to Information Retrieval. Cambridge University Press, New York (2008)
11. Sharma, M., Morwal, S.: A survey on cross language information retrieval. Int. J. Adv. Res. Comput. Commun. Eng. 4(2), 384–387 (2015)
12. Tyers, F.M., Alperen, M.S.: South-East European Times: a parallel corpus of Balkan languages. In: Proceedings of the Workshop on Exploitation of Multilingual Resources and Tools for Central and (South) Eastern European Languages, LREC 2010, pp. 49–53 (2010). http://xixona.dlsi.ua.es/~fran/publications/lrec2010.pdf
13. Young, P.G.: Cross-language information retrieval using latent semantic indexing. Master's thesis. University of Knoxville, Tennessee (1994)

Item-Based Vs User-Based Collaborative Recommendation Predictions

Joel Azzopardi[✉]

University of Malta, Msida, Malta
joel.azzopardi@um.edu.mt

Abstract. The use of personalised recommendation systems to push interesting items to users has become a necessity in the digital world that contains overwhelming amounts of information. One of the most effective ways to achieve this is by considering the opinions of other similar users – i.e. through collaborative techniques. In this paper, we compare the performance of *item-based* and *user-based* recommendation algorithms as well as propose an *ensemble* that combines both systems. We investigate the effect of applying LSA, as well as varying the neighbourhood size on the different algorithms. Finally, we experiment with the inclusion of content-type information in our recommender systems. We find that the most effective system is the *ensemble* system that uses LSA.

1 Introduction

Recommendation systems counter the information overload problem by 'pushing' relevant information to the user. One of the most effective recommendation approaches is *Collaborative Filtering* – whereby recommendations are issued based on the opinion of other similar users. Collaborative Filtering Methods are typically divided into: *user-based* methods whereby item recommendations are calculated depending on ratings by similar users; and *item-based* methods where the ratings for an item are predicted based on how similar items have been rated [10,11,13]. *Item-based* methods reportedly achieve better performance [9–11,13].

In this research, we use the MovieLens-1M dataset [7] to compare the performance of *user-based* and *item-based* approaches. We also analyse the performance of an *ensemble* of both such approaches – something that we have not encountered in literature. In addition, we use *Latent Semantic Analyses* (LSA) techniques as proposed in [5] – LSA is typically used in content-based systems, but we apply it to collaborative recommender systems. We also investigate the effect of incorporating content-based features (namely movie type information) in our collaborative recommender systems.

2 Related Work

Recommendation systems are typically divided into: *content-based* recommendations whereby recommendations are issued on the basis of similarity between

© Springer International Publishing AG, part of Springer Nature 2018
J. Szymański and Y. Velegrakis (Eds.): IKC 2017, LNCS 10546, pp. 165–170, 2018.
https://doi.org/10.1007/978-3-319-74497-1_16

the items' content and the user model; and *collaborative* recommendations where a user-item rating is predicted based on the ratings provided by similar users, or by the user on similar items [4,12,13].

Content-based approaches are able to calculate recommendations for items that do not have ratings, or that have a high-turn-over – in fact, a popular use for them is online news recommendation [2,8]. Such systems need to perform content analysis [11], and textual content is most generally represented using the *Bag-of-Words* model [4,8]. Keyword-based representations may be further extended using techniques such as *Latent Semantic Analysis* (LSA) [1,5,8].

Collaborative approaches have been found to be more effective than content-based approaches [1,9,10]. Their advantages include simplicity, and increased likelihood of including novelty and serendipity in their recommendations [3,9,11]. On the other hand, they suffer from: *sparsity* – i.e. they require substantial overlap in ratings; and the *cold-start problem* – recommendations for new users or items can not be issued if they have no ratings [3,4,9,11,12]. As described in Sect. 1, such approaches are further subdivided into *User-based* and *Item-based* methods [10,11,13] and *Item-based* methods are found to achieve better results [9–11,13]. However, the evaluation of *ensemble* methods combining both methods seems to have been rarely performed in previous research.

An important aspect underlying collaborative recommendation performance is the neighbourhood size. Prediction accuracy increases in proportion to the neighbourhood size [12]. [9] reports that accuracy improves as the neighbourhood size approaches 30, but then remains quasi uniform for further increments.

Problems faced by collaborative systems can be partially relieved by incorporating content-based features when calculating similarities [4,9,12]. While [9] and [4] report improved results when incorporating content features, the incorporation of content features in [6] caused a deterioration of results. [11] states that there is no consensus on how such techniques should be combined, and suggests a number of different hybrid types. When comparing different hybrid types, [3] found that *cascade recommendation* (i.e. a priority is given to each recommender, and the lower-priority ones are used to break ties) resulted to be the most effective hybrid technique.

3   Methodology

In this research, we compare the performance of *user-based* and *item-based* collaborative recommenders. We analyse the effect of LSA – LSA has been very rarely applied in collaborative scenarios. We also investigate the effectiveness of an *ensemble* combining both *user-based* and *item-based* approaches. Additionally, we identify the best neighbourhood sizes to use. Finally, we also experiment with the incorporation of movie-type information in collaborative recommenders.

3.1   Collaborative Recommendation Algorithms

The *user-based* recommendation algorithm is based on the *kNN* algorithm whereby each 'vote' is weighted by the similarity of the other user to the current user. The neighbourhood consists of the k most similar users that have also rated the item under consideration. The algorithm is shown below:

```
predictRating-SimUsers (UserSimMatrix, UserID, ItemID, k)
  CandidateRatings ← φ
  SimUsers ← getSimilarUsers (UserSimMatrix, UserID)
  curk ← 0

  while (curk < k)
    user ← getNextMostSimilarUser (SimUsers)
    SimUserRating ← getUserItemRating (user, ItemID)

    if (exists(SimUserRating))
      updateCandidateRatings (CandidateRatings, SimUserRating,
                                          Similarity(user, UserID))
      k ← k + 1
    end if
  end while

  return (getHighestWeightedCandidate (CandidateRatings))
end
```

The parameter $UserSimMatrix$ refers to a matrix containing the similarity between each pair of users. This matrix is constructed by representing each user as a vector of ratings, and using Pearson similarity to calculate each pairwise similarity. In the LSA variant of this algorithm, the user-by-item ratings matrix is decomposed using SVD, and only the top-most dimensions are used to construct the pair-wise user similarity matrix.

The *item-based* recommendation algorithm is equivalent to the *user-based* recommendation algorithm, where instead of user pair-wise similarity, item pair-wise similarity is used. Predicted ratings are calculated based on how the current user rated the items that are most similar to the item in question.

The ensemble algorithm uses both the user pair-wise similarity matrix, and the item pair-wise similarity matrix. It obtains separate candidate recommendations lists ($CandidateRatings$) from both the *user-based* and the *item-based* recommendation algorithms described previously. The predicted recommendation is set to highest weighted candidate after merging both lists together.

3.2 Incorporation of Content-Type Information

The *MovieLens 1M* dataset classified each movie under multiple categories. To incorporate this information, we constructed a feature-by-item matrix where the items are the movies, and the features are the movie categories. We kept the sum of each column in this feature-by-item matrix uniform to 5 (the maximum MovieLens rating). Hence, the category score of each movie is set to be 5 divided by the total number of categories pertaining to that movie. For our hybrid recommendation algorithms, we appended the category-by-item matrix to the original user-by-item matrix. This matrix is then used to calculate the pair-wise similarity matrices in the algorithms described previously.

4 Evaluation

We evaluated our algorithms using the *MovieLens 1M* dataset [7], that consists of 1000209 ratings for 3883 movies by 6040 different users. A typical approach is to use 80% of the dataset for training, and the remaining 20% for testing [12]. We split the dataset on a user by user level – i.e. we placed the oldest 80% of the ratings for each user in the training set, and the remaining (newer) ratings in the test set. This resulted into a training set consisting of 800193 ratings, and a test set composed of 200016 ratings. We evaluated the predictions using *Mean Average Error* (MAE) metric as described in [4,10,11].

We compared a total of 13 different algorithms – summarised in Table 1. In the cases of algorithms that utilised LSA, we evaluated their performance across a range of different dimensions between 100 and 1000 in intervals of 100. The column "LSA Dimensions Used" shows the number of dimensions that gave the best results across all neighbourhood sizes.

Results in Fig. 1 show that *Item-based* recommenders perform considerably better than the *user-based* equivalent. Whilst LSA has a beneficial effect on *user-based* recommendations, it has an overall negative effect on the *item-based* recommendation results. The *ensemble* system that uses LSA (Algorithm 6) gives slightly better results across practically all neighbourhood sizes than the pure *item-based* system that does not use LSA. In fact, the best result obtained is for this *ensemble* setup (Algorithm 6) with a neighbourhood size of 80.

Increasing the neighbourhood size beyond 40 has marginal improvement in recommendation accuracy. Whilst *item-based* recommenders are most effective with a neighbourhood size of 40 with a slight deterioration of results for larger

Table 1. Recommendation algorithms

Algorithm index	Similar items	Similar users	Item category	LSA dimensions used
1	✓			-
2	✓			300
3		✓		-
4		✓		1000
5	✓	✓		-
6	✓	✓		300
7			✓	-
8	✓		✓	-
9	✓		✓	300
10		✓	✓	-
11		✓	✓	1000
12	✓	✓	✓	-
13	✓	✓	✓	300

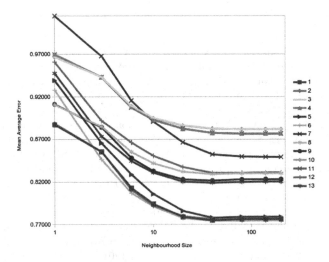

Fig. 1. Results obtained by the different algorithms

sizes, the performance of *user-based* recommenders keeps improving (albeit very slightly) as neighbourhood sizes are increased. The ensemble algorithm that uses LSA (Algorithm 6) obtains the best results with a neighbourhood size of 80, and results degrade slightly with larger neighbourhoods.

Results also show that incorporation of movie-type information cause an overall deterioration of results when used as a hybrid with the other collaborative systems. These observations confirm the observations reported in [6] where hybrid systems performed worse than purely collaborative systems.

5   Conclusions and Future Work

In this research, we compared *item-based* recommendation approaches with analogous *user-based* approaches, as well as with an *ensemble* approach combining both. We analysed the effect of LSA as well as the variation of neighbourhood size. Our best performing system is the *ensemble* system that uses LSA. However, this is followed closely by the *item-based* system that does not use LSA. Our *item-based* system performs best with a neighbourhood size of about 40, whilst the *ensemble* system performs best with a neighbourhood of size 80.

Our experiments have also shown that purely collaborative recommendation systems perform better than hybrid systems that incorporate item types. However, an interesting avenue for future research would be an investigation of the different methods of how content-type features may be incorporated in collaborative systems.

References

1. Azzopardi, J., Ivanovic, D., Kapitsaki, G.: Comparison of collaborative and content-based automatic recommendation approaches in a digital library of Serbian PhD dissertations. In: Calì, A., Gorgan, D., Ugarte, M. (eds.) KEYSTONE 2016. LNCS, vol. 10151, pp. 100–111. Springer, Cham (2017). https://doi.org/10.1007/978-3-319-53640-8_9
2. Azzopardi, J., Staff, C.: Automatic adaptation and recommendation of news reports using surface-based methods. In: Pérez, J., et al. (eds.) Highlights on Practical Applications of Agents and Multi-Agent Systems. AINSC, vol. 156, pp. 69–76. Springer, Heidelberg (2012). https://doi.org/10.1007/978-3-642-28762-6_9
3. Burke, R.: Hybrid web recommender systems. In: Brusilovsky, P., Kobsa, A., Nejdl, W. (eds.) The Adaptive Web. LNCS, vol. 4321, pp. 377–408. Springer, Heidelberg (2007). https://doi.org/10.1007/978-3-540-72079-9_12
4. Choi, Y.S.: Content type based adaptation in collaborative recommendation. In: Proceedings of the 2014 Conference on Research in Adaptive and Convergent Systems, RACS 2014, pp. 61–65. ACM, New York (2014)
5. Deerwester, S., Dumais, S.T., Furnas, G.W., Landauer, T.K., Harshman, R.: Indexing by latent semantic analysis. J. Am. Soc. Inf. Sci. 41(6), 391–407 (1990)
6. Garcin, F., Zhou, K., Faltings, B., Schickel, V.: Personalized news recommendation based on collaborative filtering. In: Proceedings of the The 2012 IEEE/WIC/ACM International Joint Conferences on Web Intelligence and Intelligent Agent Technology - Volume 01, WI-IAT 2012, pp. 437–441. IEEE Computer Society Washington (2012)
7. Harper, F.M., Konstan, J.A.: The movielens datasets: history and context. ACM Trans. Interact. Intell. Syst. 5(4), 19:1–19:19 (2015)
8. Lang, K.: Newsweeder: learning to filter netnews. In: Proceedings of the 12th International Machine Learning Conference, ML 1995, pp. 331–339. Morgan Kaufman (1995)
9. Li, Q., Kim, B.M.: An approach for combining content-based and collaborative filters. In: Proceedings of the Sixth International Workshop on Information Retrieval with Asian Languages - Volume 11, AsianIR 2003, pp. 17–24. Association for Computational Linguistics, Stroudsburg (2003)
10. Patel, V., Hasan, M.: Parallel ratio based CF for recommendation system. In: Proceedings of the 7th International Conference on Computing Communication and Networking Technologies, ICCCNT 2016, pp. 34:1–34:4. ACM, New York (2016)
11. Schafer, J.B., Frankowski, D., Herlocker, J., Sen, S.: Collaborative filtering recommender systems. In: Brusilovsky, P., Kobsa, A., Nejdl, W. (eds.) The Adaptive Web. LNCS, vol. 4321, pp. 291–324. Springer, Heidelberg (2007). https://doi.org/10.1007/978-3-540-72079-9_9
12. Stanescu, A., Nagar, S., Caragea, D.: A hybrid recommender system: User profiling from keywords and ratings. In: Proceedings of the 2013 IEEE/WIC/ACM International Joint Conferences on Web Intelligence (WI) and Intelligent Agent Technologies (IAT) - Volume 01, WI-IAT 2013, pp. 73–80. IEEE Computer Society, Washington (2013)
13. Xia, C., Jiang, X., Liu, S., Luo, Z., Yu, Z.: Dynamic item-based recommendation algorithm with time decay. In: 2010 Sixth International Conference on Natural Computation, vol. 1, pp. 242–247, August 2010

An Integrated Smart City Platform

Paolo Nesi[1], Laura Po[2], José R. R. Viqueira[3], and Raquel Trillo-Lado[4]([⊠])

[1] Information Engineering Department, University of Florence,
Via di Santa Marta, 3, 50139 Florence, Italy
paolo.nesi@unifi.it

[2] "Enzo Ferrari" Engineering Department, University of Modena and Reggio Emilia,
Via Vivarelli, 10, 41125 Modena, Italy
laura.po@unimore.it

[3] Centro Singular de Investigación en Tecnoloxías da Información (CiTIUS),
Universidade de Santiago de Compostela, Santiago de Compostela, Spain
jrr.viqueira@usc.es

[4] Depto. de Informática e Ingeniería de Sistemas (DIIS) e I3A,
Universidad de Zaragoza, Zaragoza, Spain
raqueltl@unizar.es

Abstract. *Smart Cities* aim to create a higher quality of life for their citizens, improve business services and promote tourism experience. Fostering smart city innovation at local and regional level requires a set of mature technologies to discover, integrate and harmonize multiple data sources and the exposure of effective applications for end-users (citizens, administrators, tourists ...). In this context, Semantic Web technologies and Linked Open Data principles provide a means for sharing knowledge about cities as physical, economical, social, and technical systems, enabling the development of smart city services. Despite the tremendous effort these communities have done so far, there exists a lack of comprehensive and effective platforms that handle the entire process of identification, ingestion, consumption and publication of data for Smart Cities.

In this paper, a complete open-source platform to boost the integration, semantic enrichment, publication and exploitation of public data to foster smart cities in local and national administrations is proposed. Starting from mature software solutions, we propose a platform to facilitate the harmonization of datasets (open and private, static and dynamic on real time) of the same domain generated by different authorities. The platform provides a unified dataset oriented to smart cities that can be exploited to offer services to the citizens in a uniform way, to easily release open data, and to monitor services status of the city in real time by means of a suite of web applications.

Keywords: Data integration · Open data · Linked data
Smart city platform · Smart Cities · Ontology

© Springer International Publishing AG, part of Springer Nature 2018
J. Szymański and Y. Velegrakis (Eds.): IKC 2017, LNCS 10546, pp. 171–176, 2018.
https://doi.org/10.1007/978-3-319-74497-1_17

1   Introduction

"A Smart City is an Information and Communication Technologies (ICT) enabled development which extensively uses information as a way to improve quality of life for its citizens and population at large" [1]. In this context, sensors, social media, web activities, tracking devices, etc. generate various and large amount of real-time data that Smart Cities need to deal with. This paper proposes a platform for the European national administrations, citizens and companies for implementing data integration processes that short the time and costs in enabling the data gathering for smart city applications and services. Starting from local services available to citizens such as public transport information, commercial data, etc., it will build a unified dataset by using consolidated technologies and tools. This dataset that can be used and queried by several applications for exploring the data, searching for information, extracting statistical indicators or publishing open data. The proposed platform is based on four open-source mature tools that covers the entire process of the data value chain (see Fig. 1). These tools have been used for several years in specific areas such as data integration (MOMIS [2,3]), data aggregation and reconciliation towards a Smart City Ontology (ETL tools and KM4City [4]), integration of environmental sensor data (SOS-SM [5–7]) with respect to the Semantic Sensor Network W3C ontology (SSN ontology) and population and update of ontologies (Infoboxer [8]).

This paper is devoted to describe how the proposed platform works, and how it can be used. The rest of the paper is structured as follows. In the next Section, related work is analyzed. After that, in Sect. 3, the proposed data value chain is depicted. Moreover, some of the web applications that interact with the unified RDF dataset are briefly described. Finally, in Sect. 4 conclusions and future work are depicted.

2   Related Work

The amount of data generated and collected by public administrations (city councils, regional administrations, etc.) has been exponentially increasing since the beginning of the digital era. Besides, since all nations of the Organization for Economic Co-operation and Development (OECD) signed a declaration establishing that all publicly-funded data should be made publicly available[1], Open Data Initiatives have emerged to ease the development of methodologies, technologies and standards in order to publish these data. One of the most successful Open Data Initiatives has been the Linked Open Data Initiative[2], which is focused on improving the access and integration of public data coming from different sources by using machine readable datasets.

In this context, numerous projects and different initiatives to exploit all these data in order to improve the management of cities and the quality of life of their

---

[1] http://goo.gl/XYhfEb.
[2] http://linkeddata.org/.

citizens have arisen: CitySDK[3], [9,10], etc. These projects are focused on specific domains (e.g. energy, pollution, transport, tourism) or challenges (e.g. how to make predictions on a specific topic, integrating specific datasets, publishing data, ...). However, up to our knowledge, there is not a general platform that takes into account all the data value chain to offer smart city services by considering all the affected agents (administrations, citizens, companies, etc.). So, in this paper, we propose such a platform by integrating previous consolidated solutions focused on specific problems (data integration, ontology population, etc.).

3   The Data Value Chain

The steps that guides users from the discovery of raw data and its ingestion to the analysis and exploitation of results realize the *data value chain*, as "in a Data Value Chain, information flow is described as a series of steps needed to generate value and useful insights from data" [11]. The proposed platform covers the entire process of the data value chain that is composed of four phases (see Fig. 1).

Phase I (Data Sources Search) starts with the definition of a specific goal. Then, a deep and wide search of the relevant data sources (local, regional, national and international sources) is performed. Both public and private data sources are analyzed and selected w.r.t. the domain of the smart city project [12,13]. The platform allows an iterative process, so new data sources can be incrementally considered to enrich the project.

Phase II (Data Integration) is devoted to the integration and mapping of the different selected data sources w.r.t. the Knowledge Model for City (KM4City) and the Semantic Sensor Network Ontology (SSN)[4]. Both KM4City and SSN

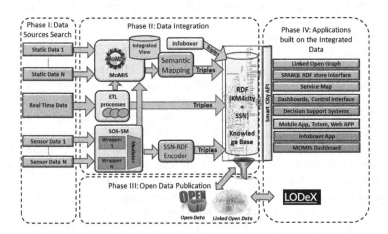

Fig. 1. The integrated smart city platform and the 4 phases of the data value chain.

---

[3] http://www.citysdk.

[4] http://w3c.github.io/sdw/ssn/.

are domain-specific ontologies; whereas KM4City focuses on providing a vocabulary to improve the effectiveness of smart city applications, SSN is an ontology developed by the W3C Semantic Sensor Networks Incubator Group (SSN-XG) to describe sensors and their observations. Integration and mapping are performed with different tools by considering the type of the selected data-sources. Thus, sensor data are processed by Sensor Observation Service Semantic Mediation (SOS-SM); real time data are filtered and transformed by means of Extraction Transformation and Load (ETL) tools (such as Pentaho[5]); and static heterogeneous data-sources are integrated by means of MOMIS[6], which can aggregate data coming from both structured or semi-structured data sources in a semiautomatic way to bring out new information from apparently unrelated existing data. The created integrated view is transformed into RDF triples. Moreover, this obtained RDF Knowledge Base can be extended or updated by using Infoboxer[7]. A tool oriented to non-technical users that helps to link the values introduced to existing entities in the data source and enforces semantic constraints on them.

Ingesting data from different kind of public and private sources necessarily requires to deal with aspects such as: variability, complexity, variety, geo-spatial aspects, integration and size of these data sources. So, data ingestion and aggregation processes must address the "Big Data" issues described in [2,4,14,15]. This problem can be partially solved by using specific reconciliation processes to make these data interoperable with other ingested and harvested data. The velocity of data is related to the frequency of data update, and it allows distinguishing static from dynamic data.

Phase III (Open Data Publication) makes the resulting value-added information public and searchable on the Web as Linked Open Data. The owner of the data can choose or filter a portion of the RDF Knowledge Base and publish it as Open Data or Linked Open Data. In particular, the goal of this phase is to enable users to publish one or a set of datasets according to the 5-stars deployment scheme for the Linked Open Data proposed by Berners-Lee [16]. Thus, linking the dataset to external sources is unavoidable in order to create a proper 5-stars dataset.

Phase IV (Applications built on the Integrated Data) takes as input the integrated information and provides specialized applications such as tools for geographical querying, for exploring and navigating LOD sources, for analyzing statistical information, etc. In more detail, these applications exploit the RDF-Knowledge Base by making queries [17–20] and offer different services to different types of users (citizens, companies, tourist, staff of public administrations, mobile operators, etc.). For example: searching services around a certain GPS point such as looking for an area where restaurants are available, services to detect and predict critical conditions or discover cause-effect relationships, recommendation services tuned on the basis of statistical data, decision support services, dash-boards that allow to analyze Key Performance Indicators such

---

[5] http://community.pentaho.com/projects/data-integration/.

[6] http://www.datariver.it/data-integration/momis/.

[7] http://sid.cps.unizar.es/Infoboxer.

as MOMIS-dashboard, etc. All the services can communicate with the system asking for data or providing data to the servers through the Smart City API [4].

4 Conclusions and Future Work

In this paper, we presented a platform to turn the potential of data for the economy and society into reality where public and private data sources can be exploited in order to improve the management of cities and the quality of life of their citizens. The proposed platform is a suite of four open-source mature solutions focused on: the integration of data sources (MOMIS), the publication of smart data related to cities by considering a unified view (KM4city), and the population and update of data sources by considering data provided by users (Infoboxer) and by sensor observation services (SOS-SM). Moreover, other mature tools, such as MOMIS dashboard, are also considered to enrich the platform.

The different components of this platform have been already tested and deployed in several contexts, successfully, but the integrated solution has not been tested yet. So, as future work, we would like to study how to improve the performance of the integrated solution and how to audit its deployments by considering standard metrics, such as the ones defined in the norm UNE 178301 "Smart Cities and Open Data".

References

1. Mamkaitis, A., Bezbradica, M., Helfert, M.: Urban enterprise: a review of smart city frameworks from an enterprise architecture perspective. In: IEEE International Smart Cities Conference (ISC2), Trento, Italy, 12–15 September, pp. 1–5. IEEE (2016)
2. Bergamaschi, S., Beneventano, D., Corni, A., Kazazi, E., Orsini, M., Po, L., Sorrentino, S.: The open source release of the MOMIS data integration system. In: Proceedings of the Nineteenth Italian Symposium on Advanced Database Systems (SEBD), Maratea, Italy, 26–29 June, pp. 175–186 (2011)
3. Bergamaschi, S., Po, L., Sorrentino, S.: Automatic annotation in data integration systems. In: Meersman, R., Tari, Z., Herrero, P. (eds.) OTM 2007. LNCS, vol. 4805, pp. 27–28. Springer, Heidelberg (2007). https://doi.org/10.1007/978-3-540-76888-3_14
4. Bellini, P., Benigni, M., Billero, R., Nesi, P., Rauch, N.: Km4city ontology building vs data harvesting and cleaning for smart-city services. J. Vis. Lang. Comput. 25(6), 827–839 (2014)
5. Regueiro, M.A., Viqueira, J.R.R., Taboada, J.A., Cotos, J.M.: Virtual integration of sensor observation data. Comput. Geosci. 81, 12–19 (2015)
6. Regueiro, M.A., Viqueira, J.R.R., Stasch, C., Taboada, J.A.: Semantic mediation of observation datasets through sensor observation services. Future Gener. Comput. Syst. 67, 47–56 (2017)
7. Regueiro, M.A., Viqueira, J.R.R., Stasch, C., Taboada, J.A.: Sensor observation service semantic mediation: generic wrappers for in-situ and remote devices. In: Comyn-Wattiau, I., Tanaka, K., Song, I.-Y., Yamamoto, S., Saeki, M. (eds.) ER 2016. LNCS, vol. 9974, pp. 269–276. Springer, Cham (2016). https://doi.org/10.1007/978-3-319-46397-1_21

8. Yus, R., Mulwad, V., Finin, T., Mena, E.: Infoboxer: using statistical and semantic knowledge to help create Wikipedia infoboxes. In: 13th International Semantic Web Conference (ISWC), vol. 1272, Riva del Garda, Italy, pp. 405–408. CEUR-WS, October 2014

9. Khan, Z., Anjum, A., Soomro, K., Tahir, M.A.: Towards cloud based big data analytics for smart future cities. J. Cloud Comput. **4**(1), 2 (2015)

10. Albino, V., Berardi, U., Dangelico, R.M.: Smart cities: definitions, dimensions, performance, and initiatives. J. Urban Technol. **22**(1), 3–21 (2015)

11. Curry, E.: The big data value chain: definitions, concepts, and theoretical approaches. In: Cavanillas, J.M., Curry, E., Wahlster, W. (eds.) New Horizons for a Data-Driven Economy - A Roadmap for Usage and Exploitation of Big Data in Europe, pp. 29–37. Springer, Cham (2016). https://doi.org/10.1007/978-3-319-21569-3_3

12. Beneventano, D., Bergamaschi, S., Gagliardelli, L., Po, L.: Open data for improving youth policies. In: Proceedings of the International Conference on Knowledge Engineering and Ontology Development (KEOD), vol. 2, Lisbon, Portugal, 12–14 November, pp. 118–129 (2015)

13. Beneventano, D., Bergamaschi, S., Gagliardelli, L., Po, L.: Driving innovation in youth policies with open data. In: Fred, A., Dietz, J.L.G., Aveiro, D., Liu, K., Filipe, J. (eds.) IC3K 2015. CCIS, vol. 631, pp. 324–344. Springer, Cham (2016). https://doi.org/10.1007/978-3-319-52758-1_18

14. Nesi, P., Bellini, P., Bruno, I.: Graph databases lifecycle methodology and tool to support index/store versioning. In: Guercio, A. (ed.) The 21st International Conference on Distributed Multimedia Systems, Vancouver, Canada, 31 August–2 September, pp. 221–230. Knowledge Systems Institute (2015)

15. Nesi, P., Pantaleo, G., Tenti, M.: Ge(o)lo(cator): geographic information extraction from unstructured text data and web documents. In: 9th International Workshop on Semantic and Social Media Adaptation and Personalization, SMAP, Corfu, Greece, 6–7 November, pp. 60–65. IEEE (2014)

16. Berners-Lee, T.: Linked data (2006). http://www.w3.org/DesignIssues/LinkedData.html. Accessed 30 April 2017

17. Benedetti, F., Bergamaschi, S., Po, L.: Lodex: a tool for visual querying linked open data. In: Proceedings of the ISWC Posters & Demonstrations Track Co-Located with the 14th International Semantic Web Conference (ISWC), Bethlehem, PA, USA, 11 October 2015

18. Benedetti, F., Bergamaschi, S., Po, L.: Online index extraction from linked open data sources. In: Proceedings of the 2nd International Workshop on Linked Data for Information Extraction (LD4IE 2014) Co-Located with the 13th International Semantic Web Conference (ISWC 2014), Riva del Garda, Italy, 20 October 2014, pp. 9–20 (2014)

19. Benedetti, F., Bergamaschi, S., Po, L.: Visual querying LOD sources with lodex. In: Proceedings of the 8th International Conference on Knowledge Capture, K-CAP 2015, Palisades, NY, USA, 7–10 October 2015, pp. 12:1–12:8 (2015)

20. Bellini, P., Nesi, P., Venturi, A.: Linked open graph: browsing multiple SPARQL entry points to build your own LOD views. J. Vis. Lang. Comput. **25**(6), 703–716 (2014)

Accessing the Deep Web with Keywords: A Foundational Approach

Andrea Calì[1,2(✉)] and Martín Ugarte[3]

[1] Department of Computer Science and Information Systems, Birkbeck,
University of London, London, UK
andrea@dcs.bbk.ac.uk
[2] Oxford-Man Institute of Quantitative Finance, University of Oxford, Oxford, UK
[3] Laboratory of Web and Information Technologies,
Université Libre de Bruxelles, Brussels, Belgium
mugartec@ulb.ac.be

Abstract. The Deep Web is constituted by data that are generated dynamically as the result of interactions with Web pages. The problem of accessing Deep Web data presents many challenges: it has been shown that answering even simple queries on such data requires the execution of recursive query plans. There is a gap between the theoretical understanding of this problem and the practical approaches to it. The main reason behind this is that the problem is to be studied by considering the database as part of the input, but queries can be processed by accessing data according to *limitations*, expressed as so-called access patterns. In this paper we embark on the task of closing the above gap by giving a precise definition that reflects the practical nature of accessing Deep Web data sources. In particular, we define the problem of querying Deep Web sources with keywords. We describe two scenarios: in the first, called *unrestricted*, there query answering algorithm has full access to the data; in the second, called *restricted*, the algorithm can access the data only according to the access patterns. We formalise the associated decision problem associated to that of query answering in the Deep Web, explaining its relevance in both the aforementioned scenarios. We then present some complexity results.

1 Introduction

The *Deep Web* (also called *Hidden Web*) [3,6,9] refers to the data content that is created dynamically as the result of interactions with the Web. For example, when we search for a person in a White Pages website, the generated output consists of one or more pages containing the result of a query posed on an underlying database; these pages cannot be indexed by search engines and the underlying database cannot be freely queried by users. When we search in whitepages.com through a form, we are forced to fill in certain fields of the form, for instance the Name field; the result is then structured as a table. A Deep Web source can be naturally modeled as a relational table (or a set of relational tables) that can be queried only according to so-called *access patterns*, each of which enforces

J. Szymański and Y. Velegrakis (Eds.): IKC 2017, LNCS 10546, pp. 177–183, 2018.
https://doi.org/10.1007/978-3-319-74497-1_18

the selection on some of the attributes (i.e. the filling of input fields on a form), which are called *input* attributes. Relational tables accessible through access patterns then are said to have *access limitations*.

Obtaining data dynamically from Deep Web sources is the key problem in the integration of such sources. Interestingly, when Deep Web sources are modelled as relations with access limitations, answering a simple query on such sources may require the evaluation of a *recursive* Datalog query plan [3,7]. In such plans, values obtained as output from one search are used as input for other sources.

In this paper we study the problem of *accessing Deep Web sources via keywords*, that is, given a query, a set of keywords with which to access the sources and a database, computing the answers to the query. Interestingly, the keywords in this context are not used to select the answers or the sources, but to *retrieve* data from the sources. This problem is related to conjunctive query (CQ) answering, an extensively studied topic in the literature [1,3,7]; however, in the case of sources with access limitations a thorough theoretical study of the central problems and their computational complexity is surprisingly still lacking. In this paper we present the keyword querying problem in a formal way, distinguishing two variants of it. We then provide results on the computational complexity of the boolean case of both variants.

2   Preliminaries

We consider the relational setting extended with *access limitations* and *abstract domains*. We assume the reader is familiar with the well-known notions of relations, attributes, variables, constants and ground atoms (a.k.a. facts); and the relational setting in general. For formal definitions we refer the reader to [1].

Access limitations on a relation are constraints imposing that certain attributes must be *selected* (that is, bound to a constant) for the relation to be accessed. More formally, a schema with access limitations is a pair $\langle \mathcal{R}, \Lambda \rangle$, where $\mathcal{R}$ is a relational schema (a set of relations) and Λ is a set of access limitations that specifies, for every attribute of every relational predicate, whether it is an *input* or an *output* attribute; in order to access a relation, all input attributes must be selected[1]. We indicate the access limitations of each relation as a sequence, of 'i' and 'o' symbols written as a superscript in the signature of the relation; an 'i' (resp., 'o') indicates that the corresponding argument is an input (resp., output) argument. A signature has therefore the form r^{Λ_r}, where Λ_r represents the access limitation on r. In our setting (see also [3]) some general domains, called *abstract domains*, are associated to attributes; these attributes are used to distinguish, for instance, strings representing names from strings representing addresses. To avoid notational clutter, we assume that attribute names are assigned so that attributes having the same abstract domain also

---

[1] In general, there could be more than one annotation for each predicate, that is, more than one way of accessing the corresponding relation. However, in this paper we assume there is exactly one access limitation (or pattern) per predicate. Our results can be extended to the general case.

have the same name. The problem that we study in this paper consist of two parts: a database is first accessed through access limitations following the known abstract domains, and the *obtainable* part of the database is then queried by using the most common class of queries, namely *conjunctive queries* (CQs) [1].

In the presence of access limitations on the sources, queries cannot be evaluated as in the traditional case. As we don't have direct access to the database, we need a set I of initial keywords to start *scraping* the database. This has been previously noted in [8], where the authors present an algorithm that extracts all *obtainable* tuples in the answer to the query. This algorithm compiles the evaluation strategy into a suitable Datalog program, which encodes both the access limitations on the sources and the query itself, and is evaluated as follows: starting from a set of initial keywords (that must include those appearing as constants in the query), we access all the relations we can according to the access limitations. With the new facts (if any), we obtain new keywords with which we can repeat the process and access the relations again, until we have no way of making new accesses. The program extracts all facts obtainable while respecting the access limitations, but there may be facts in the sources that cannot be retrieved.

Example 1. Consider the relations $r_1^{ioo}(N, D, C)$ and $r_2^{ioo}(C, S, N)$ depicted in Fig. 2. The tuples in r_1 contain a *Nation*, a typical *Dish* of that nation, and a famous *Chef* that prepares it; the tuples in r_2 contain a *Chef*, the amount of Michelin *Stars* he has obtained and his *Nationality*. The access limitations only allow for searching typical dishes by nation (from r_1), and searching chefs by surname (from r_2). Assume we want to obtain the dishes prepared by chefs with three Michelin stars; this is expressed by the conjunctive query $q(D) \leftarrow r_1(N_1, D, C), r_2(C, 3, N_2)$. However, because of the access limitations, we cannot directly pose this query to the database. Instead, we need to recursively access the database starting from a set of keywords known in advance. For example, assume we know that this database contains information about Italy; we then have available the keyword set $\{Italy\}$. We can thus search r_1 using *Italy*, obtaining the tuple t_1. Now we have the last name of chef Heinz Beck, so we can search r_2 with input *Beck*. This returns s_1, indicating that *Risotto* is a dish prepared by a chef with three Michelin stars (and thus part of our answer). But s_1 also contains the value *Germany*, which we can use as input to query r_1 again; this time we get t_2, which contains the last name of a new chef, *Ducasse*. We can now query r_2 with input *Ducasse*, obtaining tuple s_2 and discovering that *Magenbrot* is also part of the answer. The tuple s_2 also contains a new country, *France*. However, when we query r_1 with *France* we get an empty result, and therefore there are no more tuples we can obtain from the database. Notice that *Onigiri* would also be part of the answer if we were computing the answers without access limitations. In our case we could retrieve this value if *Japan* was one of our initial keywords or it was extracted at some point. The recursive procedure illustrated above is formalised by evaluating the Datalog program depicted in Fig. 1. In this program, relations $\hat{r_1}$ and $\hat{r_2}$

r_1^{ioo}

	N	D	C
t_1	Italy	Risotto	Beck
t_2	Germany	Magenbrot	Ducasse
t_3	Japan	Onigiri	Robuchon

$$\rho_1 : \qquad q(D) \leftarrow \hat{r}_1(N, D, C), r_2(C, 3, N)$$
$$\rho_2 : \hat{r}_1(N, D, C) \leftarrow r_1(N, D, C), dom_N(N)$$
$$\rho_3 : \hat{r}_2(C, S, N) \leftarrow r_2(C, S, N), dom_C(C)$$
$$\rho_4 : \quad dom_C(C) \leftarrow \hat{r}_1(N, D, C)$$
$$\rho_5 : \quad dom_A(N) \leftarrow \hat{r}_2(C, S, N)$$
$$\rho_6 : dom_N(Italy)$$

r_2^{ioo}

	N	S	C
s_1	Beck	3	Germany
s_2	Ducasse	3	France
s_3	Robuchon	3	France

Fig. 1. Datalog program of Example 1.   **Fig. 2.** Database of Example 1.

represent the *obtainable* parts of r_1 and r_2, respectively (assuming we start only from the keyword set $\{Italy\}$). Rule ρ_1 represents the original query (over the *obtainable* versions of r_1 and r_2), rules ρ_2 to ρ_5 encode the recursive access to the sources, and ρ_6 simply *initialises* the constant *Italy* by adding it to the abstract domain of nations. ∎

The previous example shows the typical way in which Deep Web sources are accessed an queried over the web. We now define the notion of answer and the *obtainable* portion of a database under access limitations; such a portion is determined by the initial keywords. Given a CQ q posed over a schema $\mathcal{S} = \langle \mathcal{R}, \Lambda \rangle$, a set of initial keywords $I \subseteq \Delta$, and a database D over schema $\mathcal{R}$, $\rho_{\Lambda,I}(D)$ denotes the set of facts of D that can be recursively obtained under Λ starting from I. The set of answers to q over D with access limitations Λ and initial set of keywords I is denoted by $ans(q, \Lambda, D, I)$ and is defined as the set of answers, in the classic sense, to q over $\rho_{\Lambda,I}(D)$. If q is a Boolean CQ (i.e., with zero-arity head), we write $D \models_{\Lambda,I} q$ when q is true on $\rho_{\Lambda,I}(D)$ (denoted $\rho_{\Lambda,I}(D) \models q$).

3 The Complexity of Querying Under Access Limitations

In this section we study the complexity of answering queries on Deep Web datasets, where data are to be extracted from an initial set of keywords. Surprisingly, the notions of complexity present in the literature do not seem to fully capture the correct difficulty of the problem. To clarify this problem, we present two variants of the Boolean query answering problem (the extension to the non-Boolean case is straightforward).

Definition 1. *Given a database D, a set of initial keywords $I \subseteq \Delta$, a set Λ of access limitations and a BCQ q, the problem of query answering with initial keywords I and query q, on database D and under Λ, is to determine whether $D \models_{\Lambda,I} q$. This is defined in two variants:*

(i) unrestricted *case: this is the problem of determining whether* $D \models_{\Lambda,I} q$, *while having* arbitrary *access to the relations of* D.

(ii) restricted *case: this is the problem of determining whether* $D \models_{\Lambda,I} q$, *while having access to the relations of* D *only according to* Λ.

Notice that the problem in the restricted case is the "classic" case [2,3], where we are computing the answers to a CQ having only limited access to the data, according to Λ. The CQ answering problem in the unrestricted case is also relevant in real-world scenarios. Assume for example that access limitations are enforced by an organisation in order to limit access to data by external users (e.g., those outside the organisation). The organisation has arbitrary access to the data, and it is interested in determining what external users, who probably know certain initial keywords and whose access to the data is limited by Λ, can retrieve from the database. In order to determine this, of course, an algorithm will have the advantage of freely accessing the data, regardless of access limitations.

We need to point out that in the restricted case, if we are to tackle the search problem formally, we need to understand the relations with access limitations as *oracles*; each access (that consists in the processing of an atomic query on a single relation) is a call to an oracle corresponding to the same relation. The execution of such a query takes evidently (at most) linear time in the size of the instance of the relation, therefore the oracle does not really serve to determine a complexity class, as is done, for example, when we have a class $\mathcal{C}_1^{\mathcal{C}_2}$ of problems that can be decided by an algorithm of class $\mathcal{C}_1$ that can call an oracle solving problems in class $\mathcal{C}_2$ (each costing 1, given the nature of the oracle). The oracles in our case do not add computational power; instead they *limit* the access to the data rather than allowing the solution to a problem instance in constant time. In this case, the algorithm cannot receive the instance D as (fully accessible) input; yet we want to measure its complexity considering the size of D. Interestingly, this is why the classical notion of complexity does not capture the actual difficulty of the problem. The following example shows that there are instances in which the two variants of the problem actually present different complexity.

Example 2. Consider the schema $\mathcal{R} = \{r^{i\cdots i}\}$, constituted by a single relation with k input arguments and no output arguments, the single-tuple database $D = \{r(a_1, \ldots, a_k)\}$, the keyword set $I = \{c_1, \ldots, c_m\} \supseteq \{a_1, \ldots, a_k\}$, and the atomic Boolean CQ q defined as $q() \leftarrow r(X_1, \ldots, X_k)$. In the restricted case, to answer q (checking if $r(a_1, \ldots, a_k)$ is in D), one needs to try accessing the relation $r(D)$ with all possible k-tuples of constants of I; in the worst case, this requires m^k accesses to r. On the contrary, in the unrestricted case the query can be answered trivially.   ∎

The above example, which uses very simple CQs (atomic Boolean CQs), shows a case where, if using deterministic algorithms, query answering is easy in the unrestricted case, but at least exponential in the restricted case.

We now briefly discuss a result, stated in previous works [4,5], on CQ answering in our setting. The result states that CQ answering is NP-complete both in the restricted and the unrestricted case. In the light of Example 2, this is somewhat counterintuitive, as the restricted case appears to be computationally more difficult than the unrestricted case. Regarding upper bounds, the most interesting technique is the one used to prove that the problem is in NP in the restricted case: a non-deterministic algorithm is exhibited, whose maximum number of steps, in the worst case, is surprisingly bounded by the number of atoms in the database D. The lower bounds are given instead by the obvious NP lower bound of CQ answering in the case *without* access limitations. However, the lower bound in the restricted case does not constitute a fully satisfactory study of the complexity as it does not make use of the restrictions given by the presence of the oracles; indeed it still remains to *define*: *(1)* what kind of computational model we need to model the oracles; *(2)* what kind of reduction would imply a complexity lower bound in this setting. In addition, it remains to understand whether simpler classes of CQs (e.g. atomic, acyclic or bounded-treewidth CQs) enjoy lower complexity. This will be the subject of future investigation.

4   Discussion

In this paper we have introduced two variants of the problem of querying Deep Web sources with a set of initial keywords, namely the *restricted* and an *unrestricted* case. We have shown that the two variants can differ by an exponential factor in very simple cases. However, the problem of CQ answering with keywords under access limitations has been shown to be NP-complete in both the restricted and unrestricted case. As future work we plan to carry out a formal definition of the associated decision problem for the restricted case, and the characterization of those classes of queries for which the complexity of the two variants differ. For instance, we will investigate whether the NP lower bound holds for atomic queries in the restricted case (which is the case of Example 2), or for other restricted classes of CQs such as acyclic or bounded-treewidth CQs.

Acknowledgments. This work was supported by the EU COST Action IC1302 KEY-STONE. Andrea Calì acknowledges partial support by the EPSRC project "Logic-based Integration and Querying of Unindexed Data" (EP/E010865/1).

References

1. Abiteboul, S., Hull, R., Vianu, V.: Foundations of Databases. Addison-Wesley, Reading (1995)
2. Calì, A., Martinenghi, D.: Conjunctive query containment under access limitations. In: Li, Q., Spaccapietra, S., Yu, E., Olivé, A. (eds.) ER 2008. LNCS, vol. 5231, pp. 326–340. Springer, Heidelberg (2008). https://doi.org/10.1007/978-3-540-87877-3_24
3. Calì, A., Martinenghi, D.: Querying data under access limitations. In: Proceedings of ICDE (2008)
4. Calì, A., Martinenghi, D., Razgon, I., Ugarte, M.: Querying the deep web: back to the foundations. In: Proceedings of AMW (2017). To appear

5. Calì, A., Razgon, I.: Complexity of conjunctive query answering under access limitations (preliminary report). In: Proceedings of SEBD (2014)
6. Chang, K.C.-C., He, B., Zhang, Z.: Toward large scale integration: building a meta-querier over databases on the web. In: Proceedings of CIDR (2005)
7. Li, C.: Computing complete answers to queries in the presence of limited access patterns. Very Large Database J. **12**(3), 211–227 (2003)
8. Li, C., Chang, E.: Query planning with limited source capabilities. In: Proceedings of ICDE (2000)
9. Madhavan, J., Afanasiev, L., Antova, L., Halevy, A.Y.: Harnessing the deep web: present and future. In: Proceedings of CIDR (2009)

The KEYSTONE COST Action

The KEYSTONE IC1302 COST Action

Francesco Guerra[1], Yannis Velegrakis[2(✉)], Jorge Cardoso[3],
and John G. Breslin[4]

[1] Università di Modena e Reggio Emilia, Modena, Italy
`francesco.guerra@unimore.it`
[2] University of Trento, Trento, Italy
`velgias@disi.unitn.eu`
[3] Huawei Research Center, Munich, Germany
`jorge.cardoso@huawei.com`
[4] Insight Centre for Data Analytics, NUI Galway, Galway, Ireland
`john.breslin@nuigalway.ie`

Abstract. As more and more data becomes available on the Web, as
its complexity increases and as the Web's user base shifts towards a
more general non-technical population, keyword searching is becoming
a valuable alternative to traditional SQL queries, mainly due to its simplicity and the lower effort/expertise it requires. Existing approaches suffer from a number of limitations when applied to multi-source scenarios
requiring some form of query planning, without direct access to database
instances, and with frequent updates precluding any effective implementation of data indexes. Typical scenarios include Deep Web databases,
virtual data integration systems and data on the Web. Therefore, building effective keyword searching techniques can have an extensive impact
since it allows non-professional users to access large amounts of information stored in structured repositories through simple keyword-based
query interfaces. This revolutionises the paradigm of searching for data
since users are offered access to structured data in a similar manner to
the one they already use for documents. To build a successful, unified
and effective solution, the action "semantic KEYword-based Search on
sTructured data sOurcEs" (KEYSTONE) promoted synergies across several disciplines, such as semantic data management, the Semantic Web,
information retrieval, artificial intelligence, machine learning, user interaction, interface design, and natural language processing. This paper
describes the main achievements of this COST Action.

1 The Action in a Nutshell

The idea for KEYSTONE (semantic keyword-based search on structured data
sources) as a COST Action was born during a joint research project involving
researchers from the Universities of Modena and Reggio Emilia (Italy), Trento
(Italy) and Zaragoza (Spain). The project was funded by a local foundation and was
established to support research exchanges among international institutions. The
goal of these exchanges was to develop a query language and associated keyword-
based query engine to support users in querying data sources with complex large

© Springer International Publishing AG, part of Springer Nature 2018
J. Szymański and Y. Velegrakis (Eds.): IKC 2017, LNCS 10546, pp. 187–195, 2018.
https://doi.org/10.1007/978-3-319-74497-1_19

schemas. At the end of the project, it was decided to propose a COST action to expand the collaboration into a pan-European network, tap into the background that had been built, and produce additional techniques beyond the state of the art. COST was the right choice for many reasons: (i) It is a *flexible* scheme. It allows researchers to continue the research activities they already have in place, which means that the probabilities of success are significantly higher. (ii) It is *open*: It enables the exchange of methodologies and skills which leads to capability expansion and higher impact; and (iii) It is *oriented towards young researchers*: It has a number of instruments to support early career investigators with participation in research activities, either as trainees, or as activity coordinators.

All of the above reasons made COST the right tool for obtaining significant research experience and management skills. The partners were selected initially based on two criteria. The first was their research area. The areas that were given priority were those related to keyword search, or those that directly or indirectly could be exploited for some contribution towards the advancement of the work on keyword search. The second criterion was the scientific results that each researcher had produced that was related to the topic up until that point in time. The reason for the first criterion was to guarantee the creation of a cohesive network of researchers with common goals and interests. The reason for the second was to achieve the maximum impact and avoid starting from scratch, by building on the state-of-the-art results that had already been achieved. Based on these, researchers from eight European countries were initially selected to participate, and this set was later extended to cover almost every European country, thanks to the active promotion efforts by the participants and the management committee.

KEYSTONE [1, 2] Action was approved at the beginning of 2013. The project kicked off in October 2013 and the official end date was December 2017. The principal target outcome was the coordination of collaboration amongst the fields of semantic data management, the Semantic Web, information retrieval, artificial intelligence, machine learning and natural language processing, to enable research activity and technology transfer in the areas of keyword-based search over structured data sources. The coordination effort aimed to support the development of a search paradigm that provides users with keyword-based searching capabilities for structured data sources as they currently do with documents. Furthermore, it aimed to exploit the structured nature of data sources in defining complex query execution plans by combining partial contributions from different sources.

Alongside these main objectives, the action also aimed towards: (i) promoting the development of novel techniques for keyword-based search over structured data sources; (ii) facilitating the transfer of knowledge and technology to the scientific community and enterprises; and (iii) building a critical mass of research activities and outcomes that would achieve sustainability of the research themes beyond the Action.

The Action Organisation

The Scientific Programme of the Action has been conceived in a manner to achieve the primary and secondary objectives. It consists of three vertical thematic areas, each one covered by a respective working group (Working Groups 1, 2, and 3) and a horizontal activity across the thematic areas that is covered by a fourth working group (Working Group 4).

Working Group 1 is composed of people studying the representation of structured data sources. It investigates possible metadata formats describing data sources and efficient structures for data retrieval from such sources. Working Group 2 works on keyword search techniques. It is the core of the Action since it puts together researchers studying techniques for matching user keywords to database data and metadata structures, and for forming the actual SQL queries that will retrieve the data. Working Group 3 focuses on user interaction and keyword query interpretation. It investigates issues related to the semantic disambiguation of queries based on context and topics related to keyword annotation with respect to some reference ontologies. It also looks at the development of languages for keyword searching and the use of users' feedback in improving the generated results. Finally, Working Group 4 is about research integration, showcases, benchmarks and evaluations, and aims to integrate the activities of the different working groups with the goal of creating a "vademecum" for developing a search engine for structured data sources.

Two Co-Chairs for each Working Group were appointed in the first meeting to guarantee the full involvement of interested researchers in the Action. The Working Group Co-Chairs, alongside the Action Chair, the Scientific Coordinator, the Training Coordinator, the STSM Coordinator and the Dissemination Coordinator, constitute the Executive Scientific Board. This board is in charge of planning and executing the activities approved by the Management Committee of the Action, composed of a maximum of two people per participating country according to COST regulations. The Action had 53 effective members, 36 substitute members and 4 observers, all of them from a total of 31 different countries.

2   The KEYSTONE People

Participation in the Action was open to everyone, but had to be approved by the Management Committee. The network of experts that participated in the various Working Groups were representative of a great number of different fields in all aspects important to the themes of the Action. These experts were renowned researchers working on many related topics that have been supported financially by national governments and the European Commission.

At the end, the Action had involved 238 Working Group Members (177 male, 76.1% – 56 female, 23.9%). These members were distributed across the groups as follows. Note that members could choose to participate in more than one group, according to their interests.

- Working Group 1: 169 Members
- Working Group 2: 170 Members
- Working Group 3: 139 Members
- Working Group 4: 118 Members

90 participants were "early career investigators", i.e. they were within eight years of the date when they obtained their PhD/doctorate.

The geographical distribution of the Working Group Members is not balanced across countries as illustrated in Fig. 1. Spain is the most represented country, with ten other countries having at least ten participants, and the remaining countries having smaller participation. This difference is due to three main reasons: (i) The ability to establish and sustain collaboration from these countries, as it is determined by the support that the country and its infrastructure provides, (ii) the nature of the Action theme, that may not be among the buzzwords of the period in which the Action took place, and (iii) the amount to which each country's research is devoted to these topics (such countries are referred to as Inclusiveness Target Countries – ITC within COST and the European Commission) Around 37% of KEYSTONE participants (88 members) were from these ITC countries.

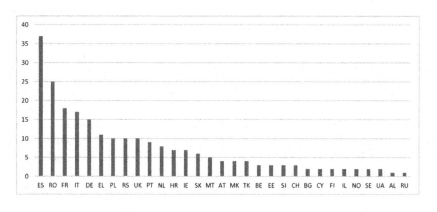

Fig. 1. Geographical distribution of the Working Group Members.

Fig. 2. Working Group Member research keywords.

Fig. 3. Working Group Member research keywords.

In order to obtain a good idea of the actual topics on which Action participants actually work on, over the last five meetings attendees were asked to provide three keywords that they believed best characterized their work. The collected keywords (688 in total) were used to produce the word cloud illustrated in Fig. 2. As the cloud indicates, the most popular keywords were information retrieval, Semantic Web, big data, semantic search and machine learning. Figure 3 presents the same keywords but as a unigram. In this case the terms data, semantic, text, and search are those that can be clearly distinguished.

3   The KEYSTONE Activities

The COST Action's support for networking and coordination activities comes in the form of meetings, short-term scientific missions and training schools.

3.1   Meetings

KEYSTONE organized 10 meetings, with an overall participation of around 500 attendees in total, of which around 350 were financially supported by COST. From the latter, around 47% were from ITCs. In the meetings, there were brainstorming sessions where emergent techniques in keyword search research were collected, analysed, and revised. The sessions were of three types.

- Brain writing
- Round table discussions with academic and industry participants
- Theoretic hackathons

Brain writing is a way to take advantage of group priming effects through writing and reading interaction that reduces barriers with traditional brainstorming due to inhibitions inherent in face-to-face interactions [5]. The participants write down their ideas on a piece of paper, pass them on to a second participant, who reads and further develops them by adding his or her own ideas and comments, and in the sequence passes the paper to a third participant, and so on. The ideas are only passed forward, screened and further developed by different participants, without returning to the original source. Although based on the same principles, group Brain writing has been proven to be more effective than both individual brain writing and traditional brainstorming, specifically when it comes to heterogeneous groups whose members have different levels of knowledge about the issue at hand. KEYSTONE experimented with a mix of brain writing and plenary discussion sessions. In particular, a number of questions are typically defined before the meetings and revised in an initial plenary session. After that the brain writing session starts. After the session, the answers are analysed both in small groups and in plenary sessions. The results of these activities have been materialised as content published on the meeting web pages[1], and a white paper on keyword search in Big Data [3].

Round table discussions and keynotes delivered by various people from industry have been organized in almost all the meetings. The goal of these sessions was to report and analyze some interesting use cases and scenarios. Some examples include the talk delivered by Yahoo's Edgar Meij on "Web-scale semantic search at Yahoo", by Djoerd Hiemstra on "Federated search for real: combining 150 search engines, and counting" in the 1st WG Meeting[2], by Veli Bicer from IBM Ireland on "Handling city data deluge challenges and Applications" at the KEYSTONE Conference 2015[3], Radu Tudoran from the HUAWEI's European Research Centre at the KEYSTONE Conference 2016[4], and Jacek Kawalec from Voicelab at the KEYSTONE Conference 2016[5]). The Action also had calls for discussion sessions on major industrial technology needs (e.g., a panel was held in the Autumn WG Meeting 2014[6] involving four companies, and another session on "Bringing Big Data Analytics to Small & Medium Enterprises" was delivered at the KEYSTONE Conference 2015).

Last but not least, a "theoretical hackathon" was realized in another Working Group Meeting. The attendants were divided into six working groups, and were asked to develop a theoretical proposal for addressing a particular problem. All the solutions were evaluated in a plenary session at the end of the meeting. The topic of the hackathon was proposed by Mauro Dragoni from FBK (Trento, Italy). It consisted of a small dataset containing 331 documents (blog posts) and 35 queries. The documents were enriched with four metadata/semantic layers. Specifically, there was a URI Layer (links to entities detected in the text and mapped to DBpedia entities), a TYPE Layer (conceptual classification of the named entities detected in the text and mapped to both DBpedia and Yago

---

[1] http://www.keystone-cost.eu/keystone/outreach/meetings/.

[2] http://www.keystone-cost.eu/keystone/outreach/meetings/spring-2014-mc-and-wg-meetings/.

[3] http://www.keystone-cost.eu/ikc2015/program.php.

[4] http://www.keystone-cost.eu/ikc2016/program.php.

[5] http://www.keystone-cost.eu/ikc2017/program.php.

[6] http://www.keystone-cost.eu/keystone/outreach/meetings/autumn-2014-mc-and-wg-meetings/.

knowledge bases), a TIME Layer (metadata related to temporal mentions found in the text by using a temporal expression recogniser), and a FRAME Layer (output of an application of semantic role labelling techniques). The final goal of the theoretical hackathon was to develop a functional architecture for a system addressing the problem in hand. In particular, each component of the system had to be described in terms of inputs, outputs, and processes, i.e., algorithms to be implemented. The overall system had to be described in terms of external resources needed (if any), and in terms of the experimental evaluation process that was to be followed alongside the data (datasets, measures, etc.), and format. The results produced by the different groups have been published on the KEYSTONE website[7] and one of them has since been completed, refined and implemented in a paper accepted in the KEYSTONE Conference 2016 [4].

3.2 Short-Term Scientific Missions and Training Schools

Short-term scientific missions are institutional visits aimed at supporting individual mobility, and fostering collaboration between individuals. The Management Committee decided to assign the grants through calls issued periodically during the Action. In four years, KEYSTONE was able to fund 64 missions through 11 calls.

KEYSTONE has also organised three training schools[8], that required an investment of around 70K Euros for supporting the various missions, that was made available to different institutions.

3.3 Dissemination and Scientific Results

KEYSTONE organized a number of dissemination events. In particular, it organized three conferences (IKC2015, IKC2016, and IKC2017). It promoted these conferences via the main mailing list, alongside other specialised channels. Furthermore, the Action proposed the organization of workshops at International Conferences. The PROFILES workshop series (2014–2017) was started within the KEYSTONE Action. These workshops aimed at gathering innovative query and search approaches for large-scale, distributed and heterogeneous linked datasets in line with dedicated approaches to analyze, describe and discover endpoints, as an inherent task of query distribution and dataset recommendation. The PROFILES workshops aimed to become a highly interactive research forum, bringing together researchers and practitioners in the fields of Semantic Web and Linked Data, Databases, Semantic Search, Text Mining, NLP as well as Information Retrieval. Finally, two editions of the SDSW workshop (Surfacing the Deep and the Social Web) was also organised in 2014 and 2015. The Action has also promoted two special issues, one on Keyword Search and Big

---

[7] http://www.keystone-cost.eu/keystone/outreach/meetings/5th-mc-meeting-and-winter-wg-meeting-2016/.

[8] http://www.keystone-cost.eu/keystone/training-schools/.

Data published in the Springer LNCS Transactions on Computational Collective Intelligence (TCCI) Journal[9], and the second as a special issue on Dataset Profiling and Federated Search for Linked Data published with the International Journal on Semantic Web and Information Systems (IJSWIS), 12(3), 2016[10].

COST does not fund research activities, only networking tools. For this reason the results of an Action should not be evaluated based on the scientific products generated by Action Members. Nevertheless, to provide a complete overview of the activities, KEYSTONE Members were very active in publishing articles and papers in international conferences and journals. In the KEYSTONE repository, a set of around 80 papers has been collected, written by at least two people from different countries belonging to the COST Action (53 with an acknowledge to the KEYSTONE Action). Half of them have been authored by people who have met thanks to the Action tools. Finally, 17 applications to international projects, involving at least 2 KEYSTONE Members, have been submitted.

4   Conclusions

The KEYSTONE COST action was completed in December 2017. The Management Committee Members were proud and delighted with the results achieved during the Action. From a networking perspective, the Action organised a large number of events (meetings, training schools, and calls for short-term scientific missions), and a significant number of people were able to participate in these activities. Moreover, new research teams, new connections and new projects were started thanks to the Action. From a scientific perspective, the Action was able to organise a large number of dissemination events, and members were able to publish in important venues. What is interesting to note is that many networks that were created during the Action, became long-term collaborations beyond the end of the Action, which is a strong indication of its success.

Acknowledgements. This paper was supported by COST (European Cooperation in Science and Technology) under Action IC1302 (KEYSTONE), and Science Foundation Ireland under Grant Number SFI/12/RC/2289 (INSIGHT).

References

1. ICT COST Action IC1302. http://www.cost.eu/COST_Actions/ict/IC1302. Accessed 11 Mar 2017
2. KEYSTONE COST Action IC1302. http://www.keystone-cost.eu. Accessed 11 Mar 2017

---

[9] Available at http://link.springer.com/book/10.1007/978-3-662-49521-6 and http://www.springer.com/it/book/9783319592671.

[10] https://www.igi-global.com/journal/international-journal-semantic-web-information/1092.

3. Amaro, R., Breslin, J.G., Cardoso, J., Guerra, F., Trillo-Lado, R., Velegrakis, Y.: KEYSTONE - collecting and generating new ideas. Technical report, KEYSTONE COST Action (2015)
4. Azzopardi, J., Benedetti, F., Guerra, F., Lupu, M.: Back to the sketch-board: integrating keyword search, semantics, and information retrieval. In: Calì, A., Gorgan, D., Ugarte, M. (eds.) KEYSTONE 2016. LNCS, vol. 10151, pp. 49–61. Springer, Cham (2017). https://doi.org/10.1007/978-3-319-53640-8_5
5. Brown, V.R., Paulus, P.B.: Making group brainstorming more effective: recommendations from an associative memory perspective. Curr. Dir. Psychol. Sci. **11**(6), 208–212 (2002)

KEYSTONE WG1: Activities and Results Overview on Representation of Structured Data Sources

Raquel Trillo-Lado[1]([⊠]) and Stefan Dietze[2]

[1] Depto. de Informática e Ingeniería de Sistemas (DIIS) e I3A,
Universidad de Zaragoza, Zaragoza, Spain
raqueltl@unizar.es
[2] L3S Research Center, Appelstrasse 9a, 30167 Hannover, Germany
dietze@l3s.de

Abstract. The main goal of research in the Keystone Action COST IC1302 is to manage *big amounts of heterogeneous data*, particularly *structured data*, in order to provide users (people or software agents) with the data they require in an effective way with the minimum cost. The processes of managing and organizing data to provide users with them in an efficient way also generate new data that can be recollected and exploited to improve the processes; i.e., data about the processes involved can be used as feedback to improve them.

Keystone is organized in 4 working groups: Representation of Structure Data Sources (WG1), Keyword-based Search (WG2), User Interaction and Keyword Query Interpretation (WG3), and Research Integration, Showcases, Benchmarks and Evaluations (WG4). This chapter is focused on the research related to WG1 focusing on profiling, assessment, representation and discovery of structured datasets. The results of WG1 influence WG2 and WG3, whereas WG4 focuses on the integration of the results of all working groups and how to exploit them.

1 Introduction

There exists an increasing amount of data available. Some data are public (for example, on the Web) and everybody can exploit them, while others are accessible only for particular collectives of people under licenses that constrain their exploitation and exploration (for example, the clinical history of patients in hospitals, industrial patents, etc.). Moreover, in the last decade there has been an increment of the amount of structured data sources available, due to multiple reasons such as:

- the development of Information and Communication Technologies (ICT) which provide an infrastructure to digitalized, process and consume data;
- the popularization of the Linked Data Web and the Internet of Things, which foster a change of behavior on people and many companies and administrations, who decided to publish structured data (some of them coming from different types of sensors) on the Web; and

J. Szymański and Y. Velegrakis (Eds.): IKC 2017, LNCS 10546, pp. 196–214, 2018.
https://doi.org/10.1007/978-3-319-74497-1_20

– new politics fostered by different organizations and governments (for example, the Organization for Economic Cooperation and Development -OECD-declared that all publicly funded data should be available for everybody).

The main goal of research in the Keystone Action COST IC1302 is to manage *big amounts of heterogeneous data*, especially *structured data*, in order to provide users (people or software agents) with the data they require in an effective way with the minimum cost. Keystone is organized in 4 working groups: Representation of Structure Data Sources (WG1), Keyword-based Search (WG2), User Interaction and Keyword Query Interpretation (WG3), and Research Integration, Showcases, Benchmarks and Evaluations (WG4) as shown in Fig. 1. This chapter is focused on the research related to WG1, whose results influence WG2 and WG3, whereas WG4 focuses on the integration of the results of all working groups and how to exploit them.

Independently of the kind of data considered, the consumption or reuse of structured data (taking into account its licenses and legislation) is limited yet. Thus, in the Web of Linked Data, most users only consume and reuse well-known general-purpose reference data sources, such as WikiData and DBpedia, despite the fact that there exist other domain-specific data sources that could be more appropriate for their purposes. We consider that the causes of this behavior are the difficulties to locate, identify and exploit suitable data sources due to:

– *Noise and inconsistencies appear in the generation, transfer and transformation of data.* Thus, the longer the transfer chain and the more transformations, the more noise and inconsistencies are introduced.
– *A big amount of technologies to store and index structured data sources have appear recently.* There exist multiple technologies, such as MongoDB, Cassandra, traditional relational databases, graph databases and different RDF stores, to store and index structured data sources. So, there is a big amount

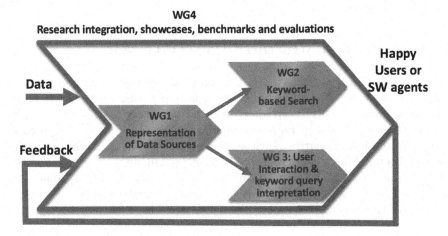

Fig. 1. Working groups of the Keystone Action COST IC-1302.

Fig. 2. Pipeline considered to publish or select a specific data source.

of interesting alternatives and it is difficult to decide which one is the most appropriate in a specific context, as there are not consensus guidelines and/or standards to allow users to select the most appropriate technologies for particular contexts.

- *The lack of knowledge and tools with reliable information about the nature of distributed third-party datasets.* For instance with respect to their quality, dynamics, temporal coverage or the addressed domains.
- *The lack of knowledge and tools to locate the data sources that are interesting for users with an specific purpose in an efficient way*; ideally, in an totally automatic way even when the users do not ask for it explicitly (i.e., based on a pull-based approach).

So, in this chapter, the research of different research groups and authors involved in Keystone WG1 is organized in the areas or categories of the pipeline (or data source value chain) in Fig. 2: Generation of Structured Data (WG1.A); Storing and Indexing of Structured Data (WG1.B); Characterization, Integration and Federation of Data Sources (WG1.C); and Selection and Retrieval of Data Sources (WG1.D).

Moreover, information about the different research groups that contribute to the research on which Keystone WG1 is focused, is also provided in Sect. 6 and the list of the authors that contributed to the elaboration of this survey chapter is provided in Sect. 7.

2   Generation of Structured Data (WG1.A)

The first question that arose when discussions about the generation of structured data took place in Keystone Working Group 1 was: *where do structured data come from?*, i.e., *who or what generates structured data?* The received feedback was organized in four overlapping groups: (1) from unstructured or semi-structured data sources (such as documents written in natural language and traditional HTML web pages), (2) from human users in a collaborative way, (3) from sensors and Internet of Things (IoT) devices, and (4) from other structured data sources. Moreover, discussions about how to publish or generate structured data are also relevant at this point (see Sect. 2.5).

2.1 From Unstructured or Semi-structured Data Sources

Since its creation in 2001, Wikipedia has become one of the most important sources of reliable information on the Web. Thus, currently, there are more than 280 active versions of Wikipedia in different languages. Wikipedia articles are typically split into two parts: (1) a body of unstructured text with details on the article subject and (2) an optional semistructured box usually called *infobox*. A considerable number of projects have exploited infoboxes in order to create structured data, such as Google's Knowledge Graph, Microsoft's Satori, and DBpedia [4] (the most famous one nowadays). More recently, in 2012, Wikimedia Deutschland proposed the Wikidata project [55], whose main goal is providing high-quality structured data acquired and maintained collaboratively to be directly used by Wikipedia to enrich its contents. DBpedia and Wikidata have become two important structured data sources in the current Linked Data Web. Thus, according to [42], DBpedia is the second node with more incoming links on the Linked Data Web, whereas Wikidata has been continuously increasing its popularity since its creation [56]. So, a great amount of data sources refer to them. A comparison between DBpedia and Wikidata and an analysis of their evolution are also done [23] by considering different criteria, metrics and frameworks focused on the quality of structured data sources [25,40,58]. There also exist recent works based on a wide set of techniques (text mining and ontology alignment, entity linking [21], etc.) such as [31], whose main purpose is the discovery of relationships among the elements of wikis written in different natural languages.

A great effort has been also made to develop techniques to extract structured data from texts and documents. So, techniques, tools and frameworks to perform extraction of data from the Web and texts have been developed. Some examples of this tools are: DBpediaSpotlight[1], Babelfy[2], different Temporal Taggers (e.g., SUTime[3] and HeidelTime[4]), Stanford Name Entity Recognition (NER)[5] and *Part of speech (POS)* tagging systems. On the other hand, there also exist other digital resources with a great potential from which structured data can also be extracted, such as images, video, multidimensional arrays containing for example environmental data, data streams coming from sensors with a certain frequency, etc. Some works around these topics are [20,54]. The former work presents a tool to create structured data sources about meteorological issues, while the latter one is focused on revealing new information about a virus by using *Information Extraction (IE)* techniques combined with existing genome sequenced data. However, there are not widely standard methods or techniques to answer the following questions: what features should be considered for images, video, and streaming data from sensors?, how a unique identifier for all data of these kinds of data sources should be built?, should this kind of data be associated to a

---

[1] https://github.com/dbpedia-spotlight/dbpedia-spotlight.
[2] http://babelfy.org/.
[3] https://nlp.stanford.edu/software/sutime.shtml.
[4] http://heideltime.ifi.uni-heidelberg.de/heideltime.
[5] https://stanfordnlp.github.io/CoreNLP/.

geographical position?, which granularity should be considered (country, GPS coordinates, region, ...)?, etc.

2.2   From Human Users in a Collaborative Way

In the context of Knowledge Representation and Artificial Intelligence, structured data sources are usually called *Knowledge Bases*. Thus, a *Knowledge Base* is considered a store of information or data that is available to draw on, or the underlying set of facts and rules of a certain domain stored in a specific format. Therefore, creating/generating a structured data source is quite similar to creating a Knowledge Base in these contexts.

Some authors considered that a Knowledge Base (KB) is composed of two main elements [37]: (1) a set of ontologies that establish the model of the data that the KB contains (this set of ontologies is also known as TBox or Terminological Box), and (2) data or instances that represent facts of the domain modeled by the TBox (this set of data or instances is also known as ABox or Assertional Box). There is a certain agreement of the definition of ontology; thus, the most popular definition of ontology is "explicit specification of a conceptualization" [35]. However, there exist different approaches to create ontologies. Some groups and tools use bottom-up approaches starting from folksonomies [57], while other methodologies such as NeON [53] follow a top-down approach that considers as starting point the knowledge of domain experts. On the other hand, up to our knowledge, there is no widely-adopted tool or technique to populate a KB, i.e., there does not exist a well-known technique or tool to create data of the ABox component. Nevertheless, some Extraction-Transformation and Load (ETL) systems have been adapted to populate a specific KB in certain domains. Besides, there are some emerging tools oriented to non-technical users that suggest attributes/properties and values to be filled by users to populate a KB in a collaborative way [49]. Moreover, adapting recommender system techniques, such as collaborative recommender techniques, content-based recommender techniques, knowledge-based recommender techniques, context aware recommender techniques and so on [51], could be also a possibility to be explored. The main challenge of using Recommender Systems in this context is how to evaluate their performance, as there are not standard benchmarks or datasets. So, a recent framework to generate synthetic data for the evaluation of context-aware recommendations systems was created [16]. On the other hand, recent studies focused on analyzing how the data sources evolve along the time, in particular on how the evolution of the editions of data performed collaboratively is [50].

Despite the fact that there is neither a widely-adopted methodology to create the TBox of a KB nor a widely-adopted system to populate the KB (to insert/update and delete data in the ABox component), there exists a widely adopted set of standard languages to create KB and ontologies. The most popular languages to create ontologies are: RDFS [11] and OWL [34], standardized by the World Wide Web Consortium (W3C), while the most popular language to populate ontologies is RDF [32].

2.3 From Sensors and IoT Devices

With the popularization of the Internet of Thing, multiple devices provide digital data coming from different types of sensors (temperature, location, humidity, etc.) for different purposes: remote control, automatic control, monitoring areas, etc. Independently of the type of sensor and the purpose of obtaining those data, different issues have arisen:

- Which devices should process the data? where the data process should be performed? in the sensors themselves?, in the infrastructure used to create the sensor network?, in servers where all data are collected and grouped? Different research groups have focused on solving these questions and new trends such as *Fog Computing* or *Edge Computing* extend the Cloud Computing paradigm to the edge of the network [52].
- When data should be transmitted from the sensors to the network? each certain time or period or when a relevant change happens (changes of values bigger than a certain threshold). The proposal in [38] considers only the transmission of certain values and a function to predict the new values, and when the trend of the sequence of values changes, a new transmission of values and prediction functions is performed. Other works follow a pull approach, i.e., consulting the current values of the sensors when they are required instead of generating and transmitting data from the sensors all the time (push approach).
- Which type of data should be provided to the consumers: raw data or smart data? The purpose of smart data is avoiding overload of raw data that are difficult to process and digest by final users; on the other hand when smart data are provided, usually several filters to simplified the output are applied and some filters could remove relevant raw data for the final user.

Another important issue that arises in the discussions about the totally connected world is how to exploit structured data by taking into account privacy and security issues. Moreover, industries demand methods to anonymize personal data in order to exploit them while guaranteeing the protection of their clients and workers and dealing with the right to forgetfulness in an appropriate way. So, guidelines, techniques and tools that deal with these issues from an interdisciplinary point of view are required. Frameworks and directives about security and/or safety issues usually consider the following dimensions of security represented as a triangle (as when priority to one of them is given, the other ones usually become weaker points): *Availability*, *Confidentiality* and *Integrity* of data. Besides, some frameworks consider other sub-dimensions of *Integrity* such as *Authenticity* and *Traceability* (or the provenance of data, where recent relevant works have been published [39,45]). Finally, we would like to remark that works related to the recent *block-chains* are also emerging to take into account security issues in environments with sensors [41].

Finally, notice that nowadays a great amount of data are also generated by the execution of different processes. This data are usually stored in logs of different type with a specific structure. Therefore, they could by analyze to extract knowledge about the processes executed and evaluate their performance. These issues are study on a recent research area called Process Mining [1].

2.4 From Other Structured Data Sources

Nowadays, there exist a great number of *secondary data sources*, that obtain their contents from one or several different data sources, in contrast to *primary data sources*, that create their own contents from scratch. For example, the content of *Data-ware houses* for analytical purposes is usually generated from transactional systems, along the time. In this context, tools to facilitate: (a) the extraction of the data from the original systems, (b) the transformation of the data to integrate and clean it, and (c) loading the transformed data in the destiny systems have been popularized. Some examples of popular *Extraction Transformation and Load (ETL)* systems are Rapid Miner[6], Talend[7] and Pentaho[8]. All these tools provide mechanisms to deal with data curation. Nevertheless, this is a topic where there exist some open research issues such as *Entity De-duplication, Entity Disambiguation* and dealing with *multilingual aspects*.

Standards to translated relational data bases into semantic data sources based on RDF such as Direct Mapping [3] and R2RML [22] have also become popular in recent years. However, their use have not been widely adopted yet. When this translation is performed, there are two alternatives options: (1) materializing the RDF data by storing the same data in two different storage (one representation based on a relational approach, and another based on an RDF approach) and (2) using wrappers to create an virtual RDF model maintaining the original relational data base. The first option requires to deal with the problem of data redundancy (the same data stored by using two different models and structures), while the second option usually requires more processing time. A more complex scenario arise when dealing with heterogeneous data sources, that use different models with different semantics, is required.

2.5 Methodologies, Standards and Good Practices to Publish and Consume Structured Data

The main principles to publish Linked Data were established by Tim Berners-Lee et al. in 2006[9]. This proposal is based on: (1) use URIs as names for things/resources, (2) use HTTP dereference URIs so that people can look up data about the resources that they represent by means of a browser, (3) include links to other URIs in order to discover more things. These principles were refined later by Bizer et al. [8]. Besides, the releasing of DBpedia caused the creation of new RDF-based data sources on the Web, as it showed the required steps to develop and implement a *linked data source*. After that, a standard formal language to query that kind of data sources was required. So, in 2008, the

---

[6] https://rapidminer.com.

[7] https://www.talend.com.

[8] www.pentaho.com.

[9] https://www.w3.org/DesignIssues/LinkedData.html.

Protocol and RDF Query Language (SPARQL) was released as W3C a Recommendation [28]. Later, in 2013, this standard was updated [33]. Moreover, web services, *called SPARQL endpoints*, that allow to submit SPARQL queries to RDF data sources were also standardized. Unfortunately, a high percentage of users is not able to express their information needs in a SPARQL query as it requires to know the following elements: (1) the syntax of SPARQL in order to build a syntactically correct query, and (2) the underlying data structure of the source, i.e., how the data are organized (its schema or intension) and its semantics, in order to build a semantically correct query and to express the information need properly.

In order to easy the automatic interpretation and process of the available content of the web pages, i.e., to made them understandable for machines and not only for humans (that can read them), semantic annotations were created. A semantic annotation is an annotation embedded in the HTML source of a web pages that makes explicit the semantic meaning of a certain content (for example, a sequence of characters) for a machine. The standard language to make semantic annotations is the W3C Recommendation RDFa (RDF annotation). This language was release as Recommendation in 2012 [43], and later updated in 2015 [44]. Despite the fact that there exist a great amount of semantically annotated and linked data on the Web, most of its current content of the Web is not annotated. On the other hand, during the last decade, initiatives promoted by the main search engine companies (Google, Yandex, Bing, etc.) have created standard vocabularies (ontologies) to annotate the web content (Schema.org [36] has been one of these successful initiatives). Moreover, these companies promote the use of annotation by ranked annotated web pages on the first positions of the pages of results of the searches performed by their users.

In conclusion, currently, there exist two main ways of consuming Linked Data Web: (1) crawling web pages with semantic annotations (such as RDFa annotations) periodically in order to discover new data, and (2) querying SPARQL endpoints either to find out their structure or to obtain specific data.

3   Storing and Indexing of Structured Data (WG1.B)

In 1970, Edgar F. Codd defined the foundations of the relational database model to structure data within a database. This model has been widely used and considered so far, and its implementations satisfy the properties ACID (Atomicity, Consistency, Isolation and Durability). At the same time as the foundations of the relational model were being defined, Donald D. Chamberlin and Raymond F. Boyce, developed a language called Specifying Queries As Relational Expressions (SQUARE) to query databases based on that model. The evolution of SQUARE was later, in 1974, called Structured English Query Language (SEQUEL). SEQUEL was oriented to non-experts users because it specified "what" data to retrieve instead of "how" to retrieve them (i.e., it was a declarative language instead of a procedurallanguage). SEQUEL was renamed and standardized as the widely adopted Structured Query Language (SQL) in the middle of the 80's and became the most used language to query data sources in the 80's and the 90's decade. Thus, although other types of models (e.g., deductive, pure object oriented, etc.) were proposed, they did not achieve commercial success.

With the explosion of the Web in the middle of 90's decade, the use of databases oriented to manage text documents increased. Moreover, currently there exist a wide range of different types of data sources with different purposes based on different models which are generally classify NoSQL databases or Not only SQL databases. The most popular ones are the following ones:

1. graph-oriented databases (where the Triple Stores for managing RDF fit),
2. multivalued databases,
3. object-oriented databases,
4. columnar databases,
5. key-value databases, and
6. multi-model databases.

Most of these new types of models focused on satisfying a different set of properties from ACID properties. Thus, the NoSQL databases focus on the Basically Availability, Soft-State, Eventually Consistent (BASE) properties [10] emerged when *Consistency, Availability and Partition-Tolerance (CAP)* theorem became popular around 2000 [9]. Moreover, notice that the storage of these data sources can be distributed on a network. On the other hand, federation of independent data sources is commonly required to tackled complex problems; for example, in order to create pollutant dispersions models for an city is required to obtain data from meteorological models, traffic models, geographical information systems, and the geometry of the buildings of the city.

Regarding the structures and indexes to store the structured data sources, the most popular ones are the following ones:

1. balance trees and B+ trees for relational databases,
2. inverted indexes for databases oriented to store documents, and
3. different formats based on text files for RDF such as RDF Turtle [24], RDF N-Triple [5], RDF/XML, RDF/JSON, etc.

Moreover, several Keystone members has proposed different structures to index and store RDF in a binary way. The most popular approaches proposed are: Head Dictionary Triple (HDT) [29], HDT-MR (based on Map-Reduce) [30], RDFCSA (a compact RDF store based on compressed Suffix Arrays, a well-known self-index) [13] and K2-Triples (a compressed vertical partitioning for RDF) [2]. Moreover, works about versioning RDF, i.e., the evolution of an RDF data source along time have also been proposed. Some relevant works are: compressed kd-tree for temporal-graphs [18], compressed suffix-array from temporal-graphs [12] and RDF-Archive [19].

Finally, notice that indexes or structures to improve the access or storage of structure data sources can be classified by considering the following categories: (1) *In Memory Structures* vs *In Disk Structures*; (2) *Compact Structures* vs

Structures Over Plain Data (generally text); and (3) *Self-indexing Structures* where the index and the data are kept in a unique in-memory data structure that allows indexed searches and to recover the original data.

4 Characterization, Integration and Federation of Data Sources (WG1.C)

At this point the main questions about characterization, integration and federation of data sources discussed in the context of the Semantic Web by Keystone Working Group 1 were: *which meta-data should be considered to describe a (RDF) data source?*, *how to evaluate the quality of a data source?* and *how to integrate/federate heterogeneous data sources?*.

With respect to the first question, notice that, currently, there exist multiple standards languages and initiatives to describe the content of a data source, such as: RDFS [11], OWL [34], VoID[10] and DCAT[11]. Nevertheless, recently, some Keystone members have been working on a survey to provide a comprehensive overview of the RDF dataset profiling features, methods, tools and vocabularies [7]. With respect to the second question, a great amount of work have been done recently. Some works focus on defining methodologies and metrics grouped in dimensions to study the quality of the data sources such as [58]; while others focused of creating methods and tools to perform that evaluation efficiently. Some recent tools are: qSKOS[12], Skosify[13], Luzzu [25] and PoolParty[14]. Finally, with respect to the third question, some systems developed by Keystone members in order to integrate/federate heterogeneous data sources are briefly described in the following:

- *MOMIS* [14]. It is an open data tool, developed by the University of Modena and Reggio Emilia and the Enterprise DataRiver, to perform data integration from heterogeneous static data sources.
- *SOS-SM* [47,48]. It is a framework, developed by the University of Santiago de Compostela, whose aim is the semantic mediation between environmental observation datasets through OGC Sensor Observations Service interfaces. The framework combines a mediator/wrapper architecture with a Local As View approach for data integration, supported by a global model based on the Semantic Sensor Network ontology proposed by the W3C. General purpose wrappers were also developed to incorporate vector-based datasets recorded in spatial relational databases and raster-based datasets accessed through UNIDATA NETCDF Subset services.

There also exist multiple initiatives and projects to exploit open data in the context of smart cities [46]. However, up to our knowledge, most of them are

---

[10] https://www.w3.org/TR/void/.

[11] https://www.w3.org/TR/vocab-dcat.

[12] https://github.com/cmader/qSKOS.

[13] https://github.com/NatLibFi/Skosify.

[14] https://www.poolparty.biz/.

focused on specific domains such as transportation, pollution, energy, point of interests for tourists, etc. On the other hand, KnowledgeManagement4City [6] is an ontology oriented to model smart city services. This ontology provides a unified view that facilitates the creation of any service for the city, as all services are managed in an uniform way.

5   Selection and Retrieval of Data Sources (WG1.D)

At this point two main questions were discussed by Keystone Working Group 1 were: *how to discover or recommend structure data sources?* and *how to discover equivalent concepts, properties and instances from two different data sources?*. With respect to the first question, different research groups involved in the WG1 of Keystone Action COST IC1302 have published recent works about recommendation. Some representatives examples are: [15,17]. On the other hand, with respect to the second question, some relevant research papers have been also recently published [26,27].

6   Composition of Working Group 1

According to the information in the website of the Keystone Action COST IC1302 (http://www.keystone-cost.eu/), the Working Group 1 is composed of 162 members (41 females and 121 males) belonging to 28 research groups (see Tables 1 and 2). For more detail about the host countries of the different researchers involved in the working group see Table 3. Most of members of the working group are currently active in research areas related to the Working Group 1 of Keystone (Representation of Structured Data Sources). In more detail, the distribution of people involved who have provided feedback for this chapter, by considering their host countries, is shown in Table 4.

When the papers recollected to analyze the research results of the Keystone WG 1 are clustered by considering the research groups to which their authors belong, clusters showing collaborations on topics related to WG1 among the research groups participating in this package are created (see Figs. 3 and 4). Notice that the research groups that have published more joint papers with authors from other research groups are those groups whose researchers have been involved the leadership of the WG 1 (the leaders of the WG1 belong to the research groups represented by DE1 and ES4) or the network (the chair of the Action belongs to the research group IT1, while the scientific coordinator of the action belongs to the research group represented by IT2).

Finally, research groups were also categorized by considering the research topics of the papers that they provided and the steps of the data value chain defined in this chapter (WG1.A, WG1.B, WG1.C and WG1.D). Moreover, the category other was also considered (Fig. 5).

Table 1. Research groups in Keystone Working Group 1 per country (part 1 of 2).

Country	Name of the research group and number of researchers
Albania (AL)	Computer Engineering Department Epoka University in Tirane (1 researcher)
Austria (AT)	Vienna University of Economics and Business (1 researcher)
	Information and Software Engineering Group (IFS) Institute of Software Technology and Interactive Systems (ISIS) TU Wien (1 researcher)
Belgium (BE)	None research group
Bulgaria (BG)	Bulgarian Academy of Sciences in Sofia (1 researcher)
Croatia (HR)	None research group
Cyprus (CY)	None research group
Estonia (EE)	School of Information Technologies. Dept. of Software Science. Tallinn University of Technologies (1 researcher)
Finland (FI)	School of Information Technologies. Dept. of Software Science of Tallinn University of Technologies (1 researcher)
France (FR)	University Claude Bernard Lyon (1 researcher)
	CNRS - Centre national de la recherche scientifique (1 researcher)
Germany (DE)	L3S Research Center of the Leibniz University Hannover (2 researchers)
	Hannover University of Applied Sciences and Arts (2 researchers)
Greece (GR)	Department of Computer Science and Biomedical Informatics School of Sciences, University of Thessaly (1 researcher)
	Computer Science Department, University of Crete (1 researcher)
	Software Technology and Network Applications Laboratory Department of Electronic and Computer Engineering Technical University of Crete (1 researcher)
	Institute for the Management of Information Systems Research and Innovation Center ATHENA in Athens (1 researcher)
	Knowledge and Uncertainty Research Laboratory (RAB Lab) Department of Informatics and Telecommunications University of Peloponnese (1 researcher)
Ireland (FI)	Insight Center for Data Analytics National University of Ireland -NUIGalway- (1 researcher)
Italy (IT)	Databases (DBGroup), University of Modena and Reggio Emilia (2 researchers)
	Data Management Group Dept. of Information Engineering and Computer Science University of Trento (1 researcher)
	Process and Data Intelligence (PDI), Information Technology Center Fondazione Bruno Kessler (1 researcher)
	Department of Computer Science and Engineering University of Bologna (1 researcher)
Macedonia (MK)	None research group
Malta (MT)	None research group
Netherlands (NL)	None research group
New Zealand (TK)	None research group
Norway (NO)	None research group
Poland (PL)	None research group
Portugal (PT)	None research group
Romania (RO)	Faculty of Automatic Control and Computers Computer Science Department University Politehnica of Bucharest (1 researcher)
Serbia (RS)	None research group
Slovenia (SI)	None research group
Slovakia (SK)	None research group

Table 2. Research groups in Keystone Working Group 1 per country (part 2 of 2).

Country	Name of the research group and number of researchers
Spain (SP)	DataWeb Group, Depto. of Computer Science University of Valladolid, Segovia (1 researcher)
	Databases Laboratory (LBD). Computer Science and Technology Faculty University of A Coruña (5 researchers)
	Databases Laboratory (LBD) Computer Graphics and Data Engineering (COGRADE) Singular Information Technologies Research Center (CiTIUS) University of Santiago de Compostela (1 researcher)
	Computer Science and Software Engineering Department (DIIS) University of Zaragoza (5 researchers)
	Aragon Institute of Engineering Research (I3A) University of Zaragoza (2 researchers)
	Khaos Research, Depto. of Computer Languages and Computing Sciences University of Malaga (3 researchers)
	ETSE Telecomunicación, University of Vigo (1 researcher)
	Barcelona Supercomputing Center (1 researcher)
Sweden (SE)	None research group
Switzerland (CH)	University of Geneva, Faculty of economics and social sciences Department Hautes études commerciales (1 researcher)
Ukraine (UA)	None research group
United Kingdom (UK)	None research group

Table 3. Number of researchers in Keystone Working Group 1 per country.

Country	N° people	Country	N° people	Country	N° people
Albania (AL)	1	Austria (AT)	2	Belgium (BE)	3
Bulgaria (BG)	3	Croatia (HR)	4	Cyprus (CY)	1
Estonia (EE)	1	Finland (FI)	2	France (FR)	10
Germany (DE)	12	Greece (GR)	8	Ireland (FI)	5
Italy (IT)	13	Macedonia (MK)	1	Malta (MT)	4
Netherlands (NL)	5	New Zealand (TK)	2	Norway (NO)	None
Poland (PL)	2	Portugal (PT)	5	Romania (RO)	23
Serbia (RS)	7	Slovenia (SI)	2	Slovakia (SK)	3
Spain (SP)	27	Sweden (SE)	7	Switzerland (CH)	2
Ukraine (UA)	2	United Kingdom (UK)	5		

Table 4. Number of researchers per country who provided feedback to create this chapter.

Country	N° people	Country	N° people	Country	N° people
Albania (AL)	None	Austria (AT)	2	Belgium (BE)	None
Bulgaria (BG)	1	Croatia (HR)	None	Cyprus (CY)	None
Estonia (EE)	1	Finland (FI)	1	France (FR)	2
Germany (DE)	2	Greece (GR)	5	Ireland (FI)	1
Italy (IT)	5	Macedonia (MK)	None	Malta (MT)	None
Netherlands (NL)	None	New Zealand (TK)	None	Norway (NO)	None
Poland (PL)	None	Portugal (PT)	None	Romania (RO)	1
Serbia (RS)	None	Slovenia (SI)	None	Slovakia (SK)	None
Spain (SP)	12	Sweden (SE)	None	Switzerland (CH)	2
Ukraine (UA)	None	United Kingdom (UK)	None		

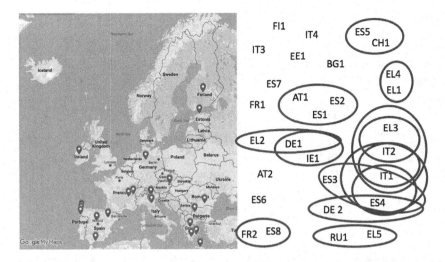

Fig. 3. Research groups clustered by considering joint papers related to WG1 in the last 4 year.

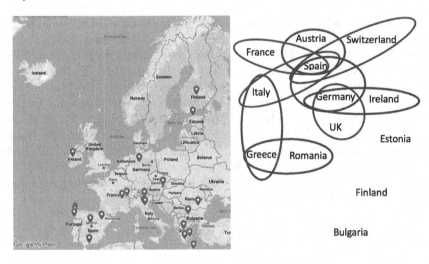

Fig. 4. Countries of the researchers from WG1 clustered by considering joint papers related to topics of WG1.

7   Researchers Contributing to This Survey

We sincerely thank every member of the working group for the work done along the last four years. We specially thank those members that help us to analyze the state of the art of research related to Keystone WG1 and provided us with references to their research papers. These researchers are the following ones (in alphabetic order by surname): Prof. José F. Aldana, Prof. Nieves R. Brisaboa, Dr. Ioannis Anagnostopoulos, Dr. Ilaria Bartolini, Dr. Fernando Bobillo,

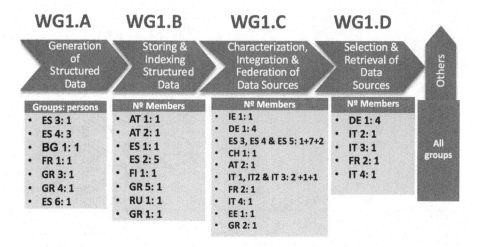

Fig. 5. Research groups of Keystone Action COST IC-1302 categorized according to the data value chain defined in this chapter.

Dr. John Breslin, Dr. Ana Cerdeira Pena, Dr. Elena Demidova, Dr. Stefan Dietze, Dr. Mauro Dragoni, D. Dudić, Dr. Pablo Fafalios, Prof. Gilles Falquet, Prof. Antonio Fariña Martínez, Dr. Javier D. Fernández, Catarina Ferreira da Silva, Dr. Francesco Guerra, Dr. Ramón Hermoso, Dr. Claudia Ifrim, Dr. Sergio Ilarri, Dr. Ekaterini Ioannou, Dr. Javier Lacasta, Dr. Susana Ladra, Dr. Martín López Nores, Dr. Mihai Lupu, Dr. Miguel A. Martínez, Dr. Javier Nogueras, Dr. Enn Õunapuu, V. Pajić, Dr. José Ramón Paramá Gabía, Dr. Laura Po, Prof. José Ramón Ríos Viqueira, Dr. Ma del Mar Roldán, Dr. Tarcísio Souza, Dr. Yannis Stavrakas, Dr. Velislava Stoykova, Prof. Vagan Terziyan, Dr. Raquel Trillo Lado, Dr. Genoveva Vargas, Prof. Yannis Velegrakis, and Dr. Manolis Wallace. Thus, feedback to create this chapter has been received from 12 different countries (see more details in Table 4).

References

1. van der Aalst, W.M.P.: Process Mining - Data Science in Action, 2nd edn. Springer, Heidelberg (2016). https://doi.org/10.1007/978-3-662-49851-4
2. Álvarez-García, S., Brisaboa, N.R., Fernández, J.D., Martínez-Prieto, M.A., Navarro, G.: Compressed vertical partitioning for efficient RDF managbreakement. Knowl. Inf. Syst. **44**(2), 439–474 (2015). https://doi.org/10.1007/s10115-014-0770-y
3. Arenas, M., Bertails, A., Prud'hommeaux, E., Sequeda, J.: A direct mapping of relational data to RDF (2012). http://www.w3.org/TR/2012/REC-rdb-direct-mapping-20120927/
4. Auer, S., Bizer, C., Kobilarov, G., Lehmann, J., Cyganiak, R., Ives, Z.: DBpedia: a nucleus for a web of open data. In: Aberer, K., et al. (eds.) ASWC/ISWC 2007. LNCS, vol. 4825, pp. 722–735. Springer, Heidelberg (2007). https://doi.org/10.1007/978-3-540-76298-0_52. http://dl.acm.org/citation.cfm?id=1785162.1785216

5. Beckett, D.: RDF 1.1 n-triples, a line-based syntax for an RDF graph, W3C recommendation, 25 February 2014
6. Bellini, P., Benigni, M., Billero, R., Nesi, P., Rauch, N.: Km4city ontology building vs data harvesting and cleaning for smart-city services. J. Vis. Lang. Comput. **25**(6), 827–839 (2014)
7. Ben Ellefi, M., Bellahsene, Z., John, B., Demidova, E., Dietze, S., Szymanski, J., Todorov, K.: RDF dataset profiling - a survey of features, methods, vocabularies and applications. Semantic Web J. (2017). http://www.semantic-web-journal. net/content/rdf-dataset-profiling-survey-features-methods-vocabularies-and-applications. Accepted in August 2017 (to appear)
8. Bizer, C., Heath, T., Berners-Lee, T.: Linked data - the story so far. Int. J. Semantic Web Inf. Syst. **5**(3), 1–22 (2009)
9. Brewer, E.: Invited keynote on 19th ACM Symposium on Principles of Distributed Computing (PODC) (2000)
10. Brewer, E.: Pushing the cap: strategies for consistency and availability. Comput. **45**(2), 23–29 (2012). https://doi.org/10.1109/MC.2012.37
11. Brickley, D., Guha, R.: RDF schema 1.1, W3C recommendation, 25 February 2014. https://www.w3.org/TR/rdf-schema/
12. Brisaboa, N.R., Caro, D., Fariña, A., Rodríguez, M.A.: A compressed suffix-array strategy for temporal-graph indexing. In: de Moura, E., Crochemore, M. (eds.) SPIRE 2014. LNCS, vol. 8799, pp. 77–88. Springer, Cham (2014). https://doi.org/ 10.1007/978-3-319-11918-2_8
13. Brisaboa, N.R., Cerdeira-Pena, A., Fariña, A., Navarro, G.: A compact RDF store using suffix arrays. In: Iliopoulos, C., Puglisi, S., Yilmaz, E. (eds.) SPIRE 2015. LNCS, vol. 9309, pp. 103–115. Springer, Cham (2015). https://doi.org/10.1007/ 978-3-319-23826-5_11
14. Cabri, G., Guerra, F., Vincini, M., Bergamaschi, S., Leonardi, L., Zambonelli, F.: Momis: exploiting agents to support information integration. Int. J. Cooperative Inf. Syst. **11**(3), 293–314 (2002)
15. Cadegnani, S., Guerra, F., Ilarri, S., del Carmen Rodríguez-Hernández, M., Lado, R.T., Velegrakis, Y., Amaro, R.: Exploiting linguistic analysis on URLs for recommending web pages: a comparative study. Trans. Comput. Collect. Intell. **26**, 26–45 (2017)
16. del Carmen Rodríguez-Hernández, M., Ilarri, S., Hermoso, R., Lado, R.T.: DataGenCARS: a generator of synthetic data for the evaluation of context-aware recommendation systems. Pervasive Mob. Comput. **38**, 516–541 (2017). https://doi. org/10.1016/j.pmcj.2016.09.020
17. del Carmen Rodríguez-Hernández, M., Ilarri, S., Lado, R.T., Guerra, F.: Towards keyword-based pull recommendation systems. In: ICEIS, vol. 1, pp. 207–214. SciTePress (2016)
18. Caro, D., Rodríguez, M.A., Brisaboa, N.R., Fariña, A.: Compressed k^d-tree for temporal graphs. Knowl. Inf. Syst. **49**(2), 553–595 (2016). https://doi.org/10.1007/ s10115-015-0908-6
19. Cerdeira-Pena, A., Fariña, A., Fernández, J.D., Martínez-Prieto, M.A.: Self-indexing RDF archives. In: Bilgin, A., Marcellin, M.W., Serra-Sagristà, J., Storer, J.A. (eds.) 2016 Data Compression Conference, DCC 2016, Snowbird, UT, USA, 30 March–1 April 2016, pp. 526–535. IEEE (2016). https://doi.org/10.1109/DCC. 2016.40
20. Dudic, D., Zlatanovic, I., Gligorević, K., Urosevic, T.: Solar: a software tool for meteorological data processing. Agri. Eng. **39**(4), 51–61 (2014). ISSN 0554-5587

21. Dai, H.-J., Wu, C.-Y., Tzong-Han, R., Hsu, T.W.-L.: From entity recognition to entity linking: a survey of advanced entity linking techniques (2013)
22. Das, S., Sundara, S., Cyganiak, R.: R2RML: RDB to RDF mapping language (2012). http://www.w3.org/TR/2012/REC-rdb-direct-mapping-20120927/
23. Abián, D., Guerra, F., Guerra, F., Martinez-Romanos, J., Trillo-Lado, R.: Wikidata and DBpedia: a comparative study. In: Proceedings of the 3rd International Keystone Conference (2017)
24. Beckett, D., Berners-Lee, T., Prud'hommeaux, E., Carothers, G., Machina, L.: RDF 1.1 turtle, terse RDF triple language, W3C recommendation, 25 February 2014
25. Debattista, J., Auer, S., Lange, C.: Luzzu: a methodology and framework for linked data quality assessment. J. Data Inf. Qual. **8**(1), 4:1–4:32 (2016). https://doi.org/10.1145/2992786
26. Ben Ellefi, M., Bellahsene, Z., Dietze, S., Todorov, K.: Beyond established knowledge graphs-recommending web datasets for data linking. In: Bozzon, A., Cudre-Maroux, P., Pautasso, C. (eds.) ICWE 2016. LNCS, vol. 9671, pp. 262–279. Springer, Cham (2016). https://doi.org/10.1007/978-3-319-38791-8_15
27. Ben Ellefi, M., Bellahsene, Z., Dietze, S., Todorov, K.: Dataset recommendation for data linking: an intensional approach. In: Sack, H., Blomqvist, E., d'Aquin, M., Ghidini, C., Ponzetto, S.P., Lange, C. (eds.) ESWC 2016. LNCS, vol. 9678, pp. 36–51. Springer, Cham (2016). https://doi.org/10.1007/978-3-319-34129-3_3
28. Prud'hommeaux, E., Seaborne, A.: SPARQL Query Language for RDF, W3C Recommendation, 15 January 2008. https://www.w3.org/TR/rdf-sparql-query/
29. Fernández, J.D., Martínez-Prieto, M.A., Gutiérrez, C., Polleres, A., Arias, M.: Binary RDF representation for publication and exchange (HDT). J. Web Sem. **19**, 22–41 (2013). https://doi.org/10.1016/j.websem.2013.01.002
30. Giménez-García, J.M., Fernández, J.D., Martínez-Prieto, M.A.: HDT-MR: a scalable solution for RDF compression with HDT and MapReduce. In: Gandon, F., Sabou, M., Sack, H., d'Amato, C., Cudré-Mauroux, P., Zimmermann, A. (eds.) ESWC 2015. LNCS, vol. 9088, pp. 253–268. Springer, Cham (2015). https://doi.org/10.1007/978-3-319-18818-8_16
31. Gottschalk, S., Demidova, E.: Multiwiki: interlingual text passage alignment in Wikipedia. ACM Trans. Web **11**(1), 6:1–6:30 (2017)
32. Klyne, G., Carroll, J.J., McBride, B.: RDF 1.1 concepts and abstract syntax, W3C recommendation, 25 February 2014. https://www.w3.org/TR/rdf11-concepts/
33. The W3C SPARQL Working Group: SPARQL 1.1 W3C recommendation, 21 March 2013. https://www.w3.org/TR/sparql11-overview/
34. W3C OWL Working Group: OWL 2 web ontology language document overview, 2nd edn., W3C Recommendation, 11 December 2012. https://www.w3.org/TR/owl2-overview/
35. Gruber, T.R.: A translation approach to portable ontology specifications. Knowl. Acquis. **5**(2), 199–220 (1993). https://doi.org/10.1006/knac.1993.1008
36. Guha, R.V., Brickley, D., MacBeth, S.: Schema.org: evolution of structured data on the web. Queue **13**(9), 1010–1037 (2015). http://doi.acm.org/10.1145/2857274.2857276
37. Hernández, I.R.: Development of a system to populate Knowledge Bases on the Web of Data, Final Project for the Computer Science Degree. University of Zaragoza (2016)

38. Ilarri, S., Wolfson, O., Mena, E., Illarramendi, A., Sistla, A.P.: A query processor for prediction-based monitoring of data streams. In: Kersten, M.L., Novikov, B., Teubner, J., Polutin, V., Manegold, S. (eds.) Proceedings of the 12th International Conference on Extending Database Technology, EDBT 2009, Saint Petersburg, Russia, 24–26 March 2009, International Conference Proceeding Series, vol. 360, pp. 415–426. ACM (2009). https://doi.org/10.1145/1516360.1516409

39. Karsai, L., Fekete, A., Kay, J., Missier, P.: Clustering provenance facilitating provenance exploration through data abstraction. In: Binnig, C., Fekete, A., Nandi, A. (eds.) Proceedings of the Workshop on Human-In-the-Loop Data Analytics, HILDA@SIGMOD 2016, San Francisco, CA, USA, 26 June–1 July 2016, p. 6. ACM (2016). https://doi.org/10.1145/2939502.2939508

40. Kontokostas, D., Westphal, P., Auer, S., Hellmann, S., Lehmann, J., Cornelissen, R., Zaveri, A.: Test-driven evaluation of linked data quality. In: Proceedings of the 23rd International Conference on World Wide Web, WWW 2014, pp. 747–758. International World Wide Web Conferences (2014). http://svn.aksw.org/papers/2014/WWW_Databugger/public.pdf

41. Kosba, A.E., Miller, A., Shi, E., Wen, Z., Papamanthou, C.: Hawk: the blockchain model of cryptography and privacy-preserving smart contracts. IACR Cryptology ePrint Archive 2015, 675 (2015). http://dblp.uni-trier.de/db/journals/iacr/iacr2015.html#KosbaMSWP15

42. Lehmann, J., Isele, R., Jakob, M., Jentzsch, A., Kontokostas, D., Mendes, P.N., Hellmann, S., Morsey, M., van Kleef, P., Auer, S., Bizer, C.: DBpedia - a large-scale, multilingual knowledge base extracted from Wikipedia. Sem. Web J. 6(2), 167–195 (2015). http://jens-lehmann.org/files/2015/swj_dbpedia.pdf

43. Sporny, M., Digital Bazaar, Inc.: RDFa lite 1.1, W3C recommendation 7 June 2012. https://www.w3.org/TR/2012/REC-rdfa-lite-20120607/

44. Sporny, M., Digital Bazaar, Inc.: RDFa lite 1.1, 2nd edn., W3C recommendation, 17 March 2015. https://www.w3.org/TR/2015/REC-rdfa-core-20150317/

45. Oliveira, W., Missier, P., Ocaña, K., de Oliveira, D., Braganholo, V.: Analyzing provenance across heterogeneous provenance graphs. In: Mattoso, M., Glavic, B. (eds.) IPAW 2016. LNCS, vol. 9672, pp. 57–70. Springer, Cham (2016). https://doi.org/10.1007/978-3-319-40593-3_5

46. Nesi, P., Po, L., Viqueira, J.R.R., Trillo-Lado, R.: An integrated smart city platform. In: Proceedings of the 3rd International Keystone Conference (2017)

47. Regueiro, M.A., Viqueira, J.R.R., Stasch, C., Taboada, J.A.: Sensor observation service semantic mediation: generic wrappers for in-situ and remote devices. In: Comyn-Wattiau, I., Tanaka, K., Song, I.-Y., Yamamoto, S., Saeki, M. (eds.) ER 2016. LNCS, vol. 9974, pp. 269–276. Springer, Cham (2016). https://doi.org/10.1007/978-3-319-46397-1_21

48. Regueiro, M.A., Viqueira, J.R.R., Stasch, C., Taboada, J.A.: Semantic mediation of observation datasets through sensor observation services. Future Gener. Comp. Syst. 67, 47–56 (2017)

49. Rodriguez-Hernandez, I., Trillo-Lado, R., Yus, R.: WikInfoboxer: a tool to create Wikipedia infoboxes using DBpedia. In: XXI Jornadas de Ingeniería del Software y Bases de Datos (JISBD 2016), Demo track, Salamanca (Spain), 4 p., September 2016

50. Sarasua, C., Checco, A., Demartini, G., Difallah, D.E., Feldman, M., Pintscher, L.: Editing behavior over time power vs. Standard Wikidata editors at Wikidatacon (2017). https://www.slideshare.net/cristinasarasua/editing-behavior-over-time-power-vs-standard-wikidata-editors-81276124

51. Smith, B., Linden, G.: Two decades of recommender systems at Amazon.com. IEEE Internet Comput. **21**(3), 12–18 (2017)
52. Stojmenovic, I., Wen, S.: The fog computing paradigm: scenarios and security issues. In: Proceedings of the 2014 Federated Conference on Computer Science and Information Systems, Warsaw, Poland, 7–10 September 2014, pp. 1–8 (2014). https://doi.org/10.15439/2014F503
53. Suárez-Figueroa, M.C., Gómez-Pérez, A., Fernández-López, M.: The NeOn methodology for ontology engineering. In: Suárez-Figueroa, M., Gómez-Pérez, A., Motta, E., Gangemi, A. (eds.) Ontology Engineering in a Networked World. Springer, Heidelberg (2012). http://oa.upm.es/21469/
54. Pajic, V., Banovic, M.B.B., Dudic, D.: Mining PMMoV genotype-pathotype association rules from public databases. In: Proceedings of International Conference Belgrade Bioinformatics (BelBI), Belgrade, Serbia (2016)
55. Vrandecic, D.: Wikidata: a new platform for collaborative data collection. In: Mille, A., Gandon, F.L., Misselis, J., Rabinovich, M., Staab, S. (eds.) WWW (Companion Volume), pp. 1063–1064. ACM (2012)
56. Vrandečić, D., Krötzsch, M.: Wikidata: a free collaborative knowledgebase. Commun. ACM **57**(10), 78–85 (2014). http://doi.acm.org/10.1145/2629489
57. Wal, T.V.: Folksonomy coinage and definition (2007). http://vanderwal.net/folksonomy.html
58. Zaveri, A., Rula, A., Maurino, A., Pietrobon, R., Lehmann, J., Auer, S.: Quality assessment for Linked Data: a survey. Semant. Web J. (2015). http://www.semantic-web-journal.net/content/quality-assessment-linked-data-survey

KEYSTONE WG2: Activities and Results Overview on Keyword Search

Julian Szymański[1(✉)] and Elena Demidova[2]

[1] Department of Computer Systems Architecture, Faculty of Electronic Telecommunications and Informatics, Gdańsk University of Technology, Gdańsk, Poland
julian.szymanski@eti.pg.gda.pl
[2] L3S Research Center, Leibniz Universität Hannover, Hannover, Germany
demidova@L3S.de

Abstract. In this chapter we summarize activities and results achieved by the Keyword Search Working Group (WG2) of the KEYSTONE Cost Action IC1302. We present the goals of the WG2, its main activities in course of the action and provide a summary of the selected publications related to the WG2 goals and co-authored by WG2 members. We conclude with a summary of open research directions in the area of keyword search for structured data.

1 WG2 - Keyword Search - Objectives

The amount of structured data published on the Web, including entity-centric Web Data, Linked Open Data cloud (LOD)[1] and Knowledge Graphs is constantly growing. These data comes from various sources and domains and has a potential to foster creation of new services and businesses for political, social and commercial activities. In this context, it becomes crucial to enable end users to easily retrieve relevant data from heterogeneous distributed structured sources.

One of the most flexible techniques enabling novice users to access structured data is keyword search. Currently, semantic keyword search over structured sources such as Web Data, LOD cloud, Knowledge Graphs, relational databases and other kinds of structured sources faces severe limitations. This includes insufficient dataset profiling techniques, such as systematic assessment of dataset characteristics [1], ambiguity of keyword queries, scalability problems, as well as lack of query routing techniques that take into account both, query semantics and structured dataset profiles.

Keyword search pipelines over structured data, such as those addressed by WG2, typically include several building blocks, each bringing in its own challenges, namely:

1. Data preprocessing and indexing,
2. Query understanding and interpretation,

---

[1] LOD cloud diagram: http://lod-cloud.net/.

© Springer International Publishing AG, part of Springer Nature 2018
J. Szymański and Y. Velegrakis (Eds.): IKC 2017, LNCS 10546, pp. 215–223, 2018.
https://doi.org/10.1007/978-3-319-74497-1_21

3. Federated search,
4. Retrieval models and ranking, and
5. Integration and fusion of search results.

During the COST Action IC1302 (October 2013 - October 2017) 68 members[2] joined the Keyword Search Working Group (WG2) and collaborated on the topics related to keyword search on structured data. These collaborations included a range of activities, including joint research activities as well as dissemination and communication events. Together, we aimed at the development of novel methods that address research challenges along all the components of the keyword search pipeline and enable effective and efficient keyword search over structured data sources. In the following we provide a more detailed overview of these activities in Sect. 2, refer to selected research contributions of the WG2 members in Sect. 3 and summarize future research directions in Sect. 4.

2   Dissemination and Communication Activities

During the KEYSTONE COST Action we conducted a number of dissemination and communication activities. These activities included regular Working Group meetings and organization of workshops on the topics related to dataset profiling and federated search at the key venues in the field of Semantic Web such as the Extended Semantic Web Conference (ESWC) in 2014 - 2016 and the International Semantic Web Conference (ISWC) in 2017. Furthermore, we organized a special issue of the IJSWIS in 2016 and conducted a survey closely related to the WG2 topics accepted for publication in the Semantic Web Journal in 2017. Several of these activities were carried out in close collaboration with the WG1 Working Group "Representation of structured data sources" of the KEYSTONE Cost Action. In particular our activities included:

- Organization of several Working Group meetings that aimed at defining research agenda and establishing collaborations within the network. These meeting took place as follows:
  - 24-25 March 2014, Leiden, (NL).
  - 25 May 2014, Hersonissos, Crete, (GR).
  - 17-18 October 2014, Riva del Garda, Trento, (IT).
  - 10-11 May 2015, Kosice, (SK).
  - 22-23 February 2016, Marseille, (FR).
  - 20-21 February 2017, Belgrade, (RS).
- Co-organization of the PROFILES workshop series on Dataset PROFIling and fEderated Search for Web Data (in collaboration with WG1):
  - PROFILES 2014 workshop at the 11th Extended Semantic Web Conference (ESWC 2014), May 26, 2014, Anissaras, Crete, Greece [2].
  - PROFILES 2015 workshop at the 12th Extended Semantic Web Conference (ESWC 2015), June 1, 2015, Portoroz, Slovenia [3].

---

[2] http://www.keystone-cost.eu/keystone/work-group/wg2/ 68 members.

- PROFILES 2016 workshop at the 13th Extended Semantic Web Conference (ESWC 2016), May 30, 2016, Anissaras, Crete, Greece [4].
- PROFILES 2017 workshop at the 16th International Semantic Web Conference (ISWC 2017), October 22, 2017, Vienna, Austria [5].

The PROFILES workshops series initiated and co-organized by the KEYSTONE COST Action starting from 2014 gathered novel works from the fields of semantic query interpretation and federated search for entity-centric Web Data, dataset selection and discovery as well as automated profiling of datasets using scalable data assessment and profiling techniques. We aimed at promoting research on approaches to analyze, describe and discover data sources - including but not limited to SPARQL endpoints - as a facilitator for applications and tasks such as query distribution, semantic search, entity retrieval and recommendation.

- A Special Issue on Dataset Profiling and Federated Search for Linked Data, published in The International Journal on Semantic Web and Information Systems (IJSWIS) 12 (3), 2016 [6]. In this special issue we included articles performing text analysis and dataset catalog creation. Furthermore, several important aspects of dataset selection were addressed, including their evolution, connectivity, scalable discovery and quality [6].
- A survey on RDF Dataset Profiling - a Survey of Features, Methods, Vocabularies and Applications [1]. In this survey, we provided a first comprehensive overview of the RDF dataset profiling features, methods, tools and vocabularies. We organized these building blocks of dataset profiling in a taxonomy and illustrated the links between the dataset profiling and feature extraction approaches and several application domains. This survey aimed towards data practitioners, data providers and scientists, spanning a large range of communities and drawing from different fields such as dataset profiling, assessment, summarization and characterization. Ultimately, this work intended to facilitate the reader to identify the relevant features for building a dataset profile for intended applications together with the methods and tools capable of extracting these features from the datasets as well as vocabularies to describe the extracted features and make them available.

3 Selected Publications Related to the WG2 Objectives

Figure 1 presents a typical keyword search pipeline. In this section, we briefly summarize selected contributions of WG2 according to the pipeline components.

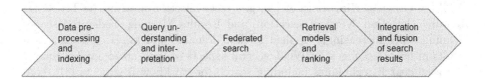

Fig. 1. Keyword search pipeline.

3.1   Data Preprocessing and Indexing

Preprocessing and indexing are the key building blocks to facilitate keyword search. This step becomes particularly challenging in the presence of multilingual context, as well as in large-scale, noisy, domain-specific and non-textual datasets. WG2 contributions that address these challenges include analysis of multilingual entity and event-centric context in [7–10] as well as language-specific fact extraction [11]. The methods for efficient access to large-scale data include efficient URL-based indexing in [12] and extraction of topically coherent interlinked subcollections from the Web [13,14] and Web archives [15,16]. Furthermore, a range of classification and annotation techniques were proposed in [17–20]. This is complemented with techniques for building domain-specific language-resources, e.g. gazetteers in the nutrition domain [21].

3.2   Query Understanding and Interpretation

Query understanding and interpretation over structured data is a challenging task due to the query ambiguity and a large number of possible interpretations. This task becomes even more difficult in presence of non-textual data, e.g. multimedia or sensor data, as well as within complex domains such as scientific literature in life sciences. In WG2 we addressed certain aspects of query understanding and interpretation in these settings. The proposed methods included combining user and database perspective for keyword query interpretation over structured data [22], interactive approaches to query interpretation using ontologies [23,24], combination of semantic and machine learning techniques for query interpretation [25] and network analysis [26]. Furthermore, specialized domains such as multimedia retrieval in digital libraries [27] as well as techniques for retrieval of specific text passages in life sciences [28] were addressed.

3.3   Federated Search

One of the key challenges in the context of federated search is the lack of reusable datasets and benchmarks for evaluation of federated search results within particular domains. The task of evaluation of federated search results is partially supported by the Text Retrieval Conferences (TREC) within the Federated Web Search Track, where federated search over unstructured data is addressed [29]. The tasks covered by this track include Resource Selection (i.e. selection of the suitable search engine for the query), Vertical selection (i.e. classification of the query in the correct domain) and Results Merging (i.e. the combination of the results of several search engines into a single ranked list). In this context, "FedWeb Greatest Hits" dataset [30] is a test-collection used in the TREC for Resource Selection, Vertical selection, and Results Merging. Federated search techniques are increasingly applied to new domains and kinds of data, which results in new challenges. In WG2, several aspects of such novel applications of federated search techniques including search for workflow fragments [31], context extraction from datasets [32] and semantic mediation for geospatial data [33] were considered.

3.4 Retrieval Models and Ranking

In the context of WG2, a wide variety of retrieval models and ranking algorithms was considered. This includes machine learning approaches for ranking such as learning to rank models [34], approaches to retrieval from small text collections using latent semantic analysis and relevance feedback [35], ontology-based approaches to Information Retrieval [36], entity retrieval for structured data [37] and selectivity-based keyword extraction methods [38]. Furthermore, recommendations approaches developed for specific domains included recommendations of multimedia visiting paths in cultural heritage applications [39] as well as collaborative and content-based recommendation approaches in scientific digital libraries [40].

3.5 Integration and Fusion of Search Results

Search result integration and fusion play an important role to provide a comprehensive overview of information retrieved from different sources. One particular approach to integration and fusion search results considered in WG2 addresses unsupervised search results clustering using document titles and snippets [41]. Further related approaches to data integration and fusion considered in WG2 include crowd sourcing-based improvement of data quality through mapping verification using games of purpose [42, 43], fusion of entity-centric Web Markup [44] and mediation between heterogeneous environmental observation datasets [45].

4 Future Research Directions

Keyword-based search is an established paradigm for Information Retrieval, where keyword queries are matched with unstructured documents. When applied to structured data, Information Retrieval methods require significant adaptation, which has been the subject of extensive studies over the past years in a number of communities including Information Retrieval, Databases, Semantic Web, Web and NLP.

With the four V's of Big Data, namely Volume, Variety, Velocity and Veracity new challenges arise in the field. Big structured data, e.g. Web Data, Linked Data and Knowledge Graphs, require development of methods that: (1) significantly improve scalability and efficiency of indexing and search to address an increased Volume, (2) enhance actuality of data within index structures to cope with the Velocity aspects, (3) account for an increased Variety of data with advanced integration and fusion as well as (4) address the Veracity dimension e.g. with quality analysis and provenance verification.

Further important challenges are related to keyword search in specialized domains containing large-scale, multilingual, scientific (e.g. in the life sciences domain) or non-textual data (e.g. multimedia, spatio-temporal and sensor data). Research directions in these domains can include e.g. domain-specific semantic data representation to enable application of search techniques and adequate presentation of domain-specific, multilingual or non-textual search results.

Finally, semantic dataset descriptions i.e. dataset profiles [1] become increasingly important in the context of federated query and search in particular in the emerging application areas. Generation of dataset profiles and, even more importantly, their tight integration with federated search and query approaches is an important direction for further research.

Acknowledgements. This chapter was supported by COST (European Cooperation in Science and Technology) under Action IC1302 (KEYSTONE).

References

1. Ben Ellefi, M., Bellahsene, Z., Breslin, J., Demidova, E., Dietze, S., Szymanski, J., Todorov, K.: RDF dataset profiling - a survey of features, methods, vocabularies and applications. Semant. Web J. (2017)
2. Demidova, E., Dietze, S., Szymanski, J., Breslin, J.G. (eds.): Proceedings of the 1st International Workshop on Dataset PROFIling & fEderated Search for Linked Data, co-located with the 11th Extended Semantic Web Conference, PROFILES@ESWC 2014, Anissaras, Crete, Greece, 26 May 2014, vol. 1151. CEUR Workshop Proceedings, CEUR-WS.org (2014)
3. Berendt, B., Dragan, L., Hollink, L., Luczak-Rösch, M., Demidova, E., Dietze, S., Szymanski, J., Breslin, J.G. (eds.): Joint Proceedings of the 5th International Workshop on Using the Web in the Age of Data (USEWOD 2015) and the 2nd International Workshop on Dataset PROFIling and fEderated Search for Linked Data (PROFILES 2015), co-located with the 12th European Semantic Web Conference (ESWC 2015), Portorož, Slovenia, 31 May–1 June 2015, vol. 1362. CEUR Workshop Proceedings, CEUR-WS.org (2015)
4. Demidova, E., Dietze, S., Szymanski, J., Breslin, J.G. (eds.): Proceedings of the 3rd International Workshop on Dataset PROFIling and fEderated Search for Linked Data (PROFILES 2016), co-located with the 13th ESWC 2016 Conference, Anissaras, Greece, 30 May 2016. vol. 1597. CEUR Workshop Proceedings. CEUR-WS.org (2016)
5. Demidova, E., Dietze, S., Szymanski, J., Breslin, J.G. (eds.): Proceedings of the 4th International Workshop on Dataset PROFIling and fEderated Search for Web Data (PROFILES 2017) co-located with The 16th International Semantic Web Conference (ISWC 2017), Vienna, Austria, 22 October 2017, vol. 1927. CEUR Workshop Proceedings, CEUR-WS.org (2017)
6. Demidova, E., Dietze, S., Szymanski, J., Breslin, J. (eds.): Special issue on dataset profiling and federated search for linked data. Int. J. Semant. Web Inf. Syst. (IJSWIS), **12** (2016)
7. Gottschalk, S., Demidova, E.: MultiWiki: interlingual text passage alignment in Wikipedia. TWEB **11**, 6:1–6:30 (2017)
8. Zhou, Y., Demidova, E., Cristea, A.I.: What's new? Analysing language-specific Wikipedia entity contexts to support entity-centric news retrieval. In: Nguyen, N.T., Kowalczyk, R., Pinto, A.M., Cardoso, J. (eds.) Transactions on Computational Collective Intelligence XXVI. LNCS, vol. 10190, pp. 210–231. Springer, Cham (2017). https://doi.org/10.1007/978-3-319-59268-8_10
9. Zhou, Y., Demidova, E., Cristea, A.I.: Who likes me more?: analysing entity-centric language-specific bias in multilingual Wikipedia. In: The 31st Annual ACM Symposium on Applied Computing, Pisa, Italy, 4–8 April 2016, pp. 750–757 (2016)

10. Zhou, Y., Demidova, E., Cristea, A.I.: Analysing entity context in multilingual wikipedia to support entity-centric retrieval applications. In: Semantic Keyword-Based Search on Structured Data Sources - First COST Action IC1302 International KEYSTONE Conference, IKC 2015, Coimbra, Portugal, 8-9 September 2015, pp. 197–208 (2015). Revised Selected Papers

11. Boiński, T., Chojnowski, A.: Towards facts extraction from text in Polish language. In: 2017 IEEE International Conference on Innovations in Intelligent SysTems and Applications (INISTA), pp. 13–17. IEEE (2017)

12. Souza, T., Demidova, E., Risse, T., Holzmann, H., Gossen, G., Szymanski, J.: Semantic URL analytics to support efficient annotation of large scale Web archives. In: Cardoso, J., Guerra, F., Houben, G.-J., Pinto, A.M., Velegrakis, Y. (eds.) KEYSTONE 2015. LNCS, vol. 9398, pp. 153–166. Springer, Cham (2015). https://doi.org/10.1007/978-3-319-27932-9_14

13. Gossen, G., Demidova, E., Risse, T.: iCrawl: improving the freshness of Web collections by integrating social Web and focused Web crawling. In: The 15th ACM/IEEE-CE Joint Conference on Digital Libraries, Knoxville, TN, USA, 21–25 June 2015, pp. 75–84 (2015)

14. Demidova, E., Barbieri, N., Dietze, S., Funk, A., Holzmann, H., Maynard, D., Papailiou, N., Peters, W., Risse, T., Spiliotopoulos, D.: Analysing and enriching focused semantic Web archives for parliament applications. Future Internet 6, 433–456 (2014)

15. Gossen, G., Demidova, E., Risse, T.: Extracting event-centric document collections from large-scale Web archives. In: The 21st International Conference on Theory and Practice of Digital Libraries, TPDL 2017, Thessaloniki, Greece, pp. 116–127 (2017)

16. Gossen, G., Demidova, E., Risse, T.: Analyzing Web archives through topic and event focused sub-collections. In: The 8th ACM Conference on Web Science, WebSci 2016, Hannover, Germany, 22–25 May 2016, pp. 291–295 (2016)

17. Szymanski, J., Rzeniewicz, J.: Identification of category associations using a multilabel classifier. Expert Syst. Appl. 61, 327–342 (2016)

18. Szymanski, J.: Comparative analysis of text representation methods using classification. Cybern. Syst. 45, 180–199 (2014)

19. Draszawka, K., Szymański, J., Guerra, F.: Improving css-KNN classification performance by shifts in training data. In: Cardoso, J., Guerra, F., Houben, G.-J., Pinto, A.M., Velegrakis, Y. (eds.) KEYSTONE 2015. LNCS, vol. 9398, pp. 51–63. Springer, Cham (2015). https://doi.org/10.1007/978-3-319-27932-9_5

20. Virik, M., Simko, M., Bieliková, M.: Blog style classification: refining affective blogs. Comput. Inform. 35, 1027–1049 (2016)

21. Tagarev, A., Toloşi, L., Alexiev, V.: Domain-specific modeling: towards a food and drink gazetteer. In: Cardoso, J., Guerra, F., Houben, G.-J., Pinto, A.M., Velegrakis, Y. (eds.) KEYSTONE 2015. LNCS, vol. 9398, pp. 182–196. Springer, Cham (2015). https://doi.org/10.1007/978-3-319-27932-9_16

22. Bergamaschi, S., Guerra, F., Interlandi, M., Lado, R.T., Velegrakis, Y.: Combining user and database perspective for solving keyword queries over relational databases. Inf. Syst. 55, 1–19 (2016)

23. Demidova, E., Zhou, X., Nejdl, W.: Efficient query construction for large scale data. In: The 36th International ACM SIGIR conference on research and development in Information Retrieval, SIGIR 2013, Dublin, Ireland, 28 July–01 August 2013, pp. 573–582 (2013)

24. Demidova, E., Oelze, I., Nejdl, W.: Aligning freebase with the YAGO ontology. In: 22nd ACM International Conference on Information and Knowledge Management, CIKM 2013, San Francisco, CA, USA, pp. 579–588 (2013)
25. Bergamaschi, S., Guerra, F., Interlandi, M., Lado, R.T., Velegrakis, Y.: QUEST: a keyword search system for relational data based on semantic and machine learning techniques. PVLDB **6**, 1222–1225 (2013)
26. Bernabei, C., Guerra, F., Lado, R.T.: Keyword search in structured data and network analysis: a preliminary experiment over DBLP. In: 10th International Workshop on Semantic and Social Media Adaptation and Personalization, SMAP 2015, Trento, Italy, 5–6 November 2015, pp. 1–6 (2015)
27. Bartolini, I., Patella, M.: Multimedia queries in digital libraries. In: Colace, F., De Santo, M., Moscato, V., Picariello, A., Schreiber, F.A., Tanca, L. (eds.) Data Management in Pervasive Systems. DSA, pp. 311–325. Springer, Cham (2015). https://doi.org/10.1007/978-3-319-20062-0_15
28. Aydin, F., Husunbeyi, Z.M., Ozgur, A.: Automatic query generation using word embeddings for retrieving passages describing experimental methods. Database **2017** (2017)
29. Demeester, T., Trieschnigg, D., Nguyen, D., Zhou, K., Hiemstra, D.: Overview of the TREC 2014 federated Web search track. In: The 23rd Text Retrieval Conference (TREC) (2014)
30. Demeester, T., Trieschnigg, D., Nguyen, D., Hiemstra, D., Zhou, K.: FedWeb greatest hits: presenting the new test collection for federated Web search. In: Proceedings of the 24th International Conference on World Wide Web (WWW), pp. 27–28 (2015)
31. Belhajjame, K., Grigori, D., Harmassi, M., Ben Yahia, M.: Keyword-based search of workflow fragments and their composition. In: Nguyen, N.T., Kowalczyk, R., Pinto, A.M., Cardoso, J. (eds.) Transactions on Computational Collective Intelligence XXVI. LNCS, vol. 10190, pp. 67–90. Springer, Cham (2017). https://doi.org/10.1007/978-3-319-59268-8_4
32. Kapitsaki, G.M., Kalaitzidou, G., Mettouris, C., Achilleos, A.P., Papadopoulos, G.A.: Identifying context information in datasets. In: Christiansen, H., Stojanovic, I., Papadopoulos, G.A. (eds.) CONTEXT 2015. LNCS (LNAI), vol. 9405, pp. 214–225. Springer, Cham (2015). https://doi.org/10.1007/978-3-319-25591-0_16
33. Regueiro, M.A., Viqueira, J.R., Stasch, C., Taboada, J.A.: Semantic mediation of observation datasets through sensor observation services. Future Gener. Comput. Syst. **67**, 47–56 (2017)
34. Tax, N., Bockting, S., Hiemstra, D.: A cross-benchmark comparison of 87 learning to rank methods. Inf. Proc. Manage. **51**, 757–772 (2015)
35. Layfield, C., Azzopardi, J., Staff, C.: Experiments with document retrieval from small text collections using latent semantic analysis or term similarity with query coordination and automatic relevance feedback. In: Calì, A., Gorgan, D., Ugarte, M. (eds.) KEYSTONE 2016. LNCS, vol. 10151, pp. 25–36. Springer, Cham (2017). https://doi.org/10.1007/978-3-319-53640-8_3
36. Meštrović, A., Calì, A.: An ontology-based approach to information retrieval. In: Calì, A., Gorgan, D., Ugarte, M. (eds.) KEYSTONE 2016. LNCS, vol. 10151, pp. 150–156. Springer, Cham (2017). https://doi.org/10.1007/978-3-319-53640-8_13
37. Fetahu, B., Gadiraju, U., Dietze, S.: Improving entity retrieval on structured data. In: Arenas, M., et al. (eds.) ISWC 2015. LNCS, vol. 9366, pp. 474–491. Springer, Cham (2015). https://doi.org/10.1007/978-3-319-25007-6_28

38. Beliga, S., Meštrović, A., Martinčić-Ipšić, S.: Selectivity-based keyword extraction method. Int. J. Semant. Web Inf. Syst. (IJSWIS) **12**, 1–26 (2016)
39. Bartolini, I., Moscato, V., Pensa, R.G., Penta, A., Picariello, A., Sansone, C., Sapino, M.L.: Recommending multimedia visiting paths in cultural heritage applications. Multimedia Tools Appl. **75**, 3813–3842 (2016)
40. Azzopardi, J., Ivanovic, D., Kapitsaki, G.: Comparison of collaborative and content-based automatic recommendation approaches in a digital library of serbian PhD dissertations. In: Calì, A., Gorgan, D., Ugarte, M. (eds.) KEYSTONE 2016. LNCS, vol. 10151, pp. 100–111. Springer, Cham (2017). https://doi.org/10.1007/978-3-319-53640-8_9
41. Staff, C., Azzopardi, J., Layfield, C., Mercieca, D.: Search results clustering without external resources. In: 2015 26th International Workshop on Database and Expert Systems Applications (DEXA), pp. 276–280. IEEE (2015)
42. Boiński, T.: Game with a purpose for verification of mappings between Wikipedia and Wordnet. In: Calì, A., Gorgan, D., Ugarte, M. (eds.) KEYSTONE 2016. LNCS, vol. 10151, pp. 159–170. Springer, Cham (2017). https://doi.org/10.1007/978-3-319-53640-8_14
43. Jagoda, J., Boiński, T.: Assessing word difficulty for quiz-like game. In: The International Keystone Conference, IKC 2017 (2017)
44. Dietze, S.: Retrieval, crawling and fusion of entity-centric data on the Web. In: Calì, A., Gorgan, D., Ugarte, M. (eds.) KEYSTONE 2016. LNCS, vol. 10151, pp. 3–16. Springer, Cham (2017). https://doi.org/10.1007/978-3-319-53640-8_1
45. Regueiro, M.A., Viqueira, J.R.R., Stasch, C., Taboada, J.A.: Semantic mediation of observation datasets through sensor observation services. Future Gener. Comp. Syst. **67**, 47–56 (2017)

KEYSTONE WG3: Activities and Results Overview on User Interaction

Omar Boucelma[✉][iD]

Aix-Marseille University, CNRS, ENSAM, Toulon University,
LSIS UMR 7296, 13397 Marseille, France
omar.boucelma@univ-amu.fr

1 WG3 Objectives

User Interaction WG investigates issues related to the semantic disambiguation of the queries based on the context and on the keyword annotations with respect to some reference ontologies, the development of languages for keyword searching and the use of users' feedbacks for improving results. Moreover, the WG studies techniques for identifying the "scope" of a keyword query, i.e. determining what are the data source elements to be returned to the user and in which form (e.g., in a graphical way).

WG3 is composed of 50 members who conduct research in various fields. At the Keystone winter 2017 meeting[1], WG3 participants enumerate three main research topics categorized as follows:

1. Information Retrieval/Natural Language Processing
   - Natural language disambiguation
   - Named entity recognition
   - Keyword query cleaning
   - Semantic relatedness
   - Exploratory Search
2. Databases
   - Keyword search over Relational Data/Linked Data
   - Examplar query
   - Query augmentation
3. Machine Learning/Information Extraction
   - Query disambiguation
   - Document annotation

In the sequel we highlight some of WG3 publications.

---

[1] http://www.keystone-cost.eu/keystone/6th-mc-meeting-and-winter-2017-wg-meeting/.

© Springer International Publishing AG, part of Springer Nature 2018
J. Szymański and Y. Velegrakis (Eds.): IKC 2017, LNCS 10546, pp. 224–229, 2018.
https://doi.org/10.1007/978-3-319-74497-1_22

2   Review of Selected Papers

2.1   Improving Document Retrieval in Large Domain Specific Textual Databases Using Lexical Resources

2.2   Selectivity-Based Keyword Extraction Method

In [4] authors propose a novel Selectivity-Based Keyword Extraction (SBKE) method, which extracts keywords from the source text represented as a network. The node selectivity value is calculated from a weighted network as the average weight distributed on the links of a single node and is used in the procedure of keyword candidate ranking and extraction. Authors show that selectivity-based keyword extraction slightly outperforms an extraction based on the standard centrality measures: in/out-degree, betweenness and closeness. Therefore, they include selectivity and its modification - generalized selectivity as node central-ity measures in the SBKE method. Selectivity-based extraction does not require linguistic knowledge as it is derived purely from statistical and structural infor-mation of the network. The experimental results point out that selectivity-based keyword extraction has a great potential for the collection-oriented keyword extraction task.

In [9], large collections of textual documents represent an example of big data that requires the solution of three basic problems: the representation of documents, the representation of information needs and the matching of the two representations. This paper outlines the introduction of document indexing as a possible solution to document representation. Documents within a large textual database developed for geological projects in the Republic of Serbia for many years were indexed using methods developed within digital humanities: bag-of-words and named entity recognition. Documents in this geological database are described by a summary report, and other data, such as title, domain, keywords, abstract, and geographical location. These metadata were used for generating a bag of words for each document with the aid of morphological dictionaries and transducers. Named entities within metadata were also recognized with the help of a rule-based system. Both the bag of words and the metadata were then used for pre-indexing each document. A combination of several tf_idf based measures was applied for selecting and ranking of retrieval results of indexed documents for a specific query and the results were compared with the initial retrieval system that was already in place. In general, a significant improvement has been achieved according to the standard information retrieval performance measures, where the InQuery method performed the best.

2.3   Uncertainty Detection in Natural Language

Designing approaches able to automatically detect uncertain expressions within natural language is central to design efficient models based on text analysis, in particular in domains such as question-answering, approximate reasoning, knowledge-based population. In [6], authors, first, review several contributions and classifications defining the concept of uncertainty expressions in natural language, and the related detection methods that have been proposed so far. Then, they introduce a new supervised and generic approach for detecting uncertainty. The approach is based on the statistical analysis of multiple lexical and syntactic features used to characterize sentences through vector-based representations that can be analyzed by proven classification methods. The global performance of the approach is demonstrated and discussed with regard to various dimensions of uncertainty and text specificities.

2.4 Disambiguation of User Sentiment

In [1], usage of an opinion process mining method ABSA (Aspect Based Sentiment Analysis) is described. In ABSA, texts are analyzed to extract the sentiments that their authors express towards certain features and characteristics of particular entities, such as products or persons. Key role in the effectiveness of this process plays the accurate and complete identification of the entities' discussed aspects within the text, as well as of the evaluation expressions that accompany these aspects. Nevertheless, what entities may be considered as aspects and what evaluation expressions may characterize them, depends largely on the domain at hand. With that in mind, in this paper we propose an approach for representing and populating semantic lexicons that contain domain-specific aspect-evaluation-polarity relations and, as such, can be (re-)used towards more effective ABSA in concrete domains and scenarios.

2.5 Collective Intelligence for Exploratory Keyword Search

In [10], authors address an exploratory search challenge by presenting a new (structure-driven) collaborative filtering technique. The aim is to increase search effectiveness by predicting implicit seeker's intents at an early stage of the search process. This is achieved by uncovering behavioral patterns within large datasets of preserved collective search experience. Authors apply a specific tree-based data structure called a TB (There-and-Back) structure for compact storage of search history in the form of merged query trails' sequences of queries approaching iteratively a seeker's goal. The organization of TB-structures allows inferring new implicit trails for the prediction of a seeker's intents. Experiments that have been conducted demonstrate both: the storage compactness and inference potential of the proposed structure.

2.6 Exploiting Linguistic Analysis on URLs for Recommending Web Pages: A Comparative Study

In this paper, [5], authors analyze and compare three different approaches to leverage information embedded in the structure of web sites and the logs of their web servers to improve the effectiveness of web page recommendation. They propose to exploit the context of the users' navigations. These approaches do not require either information about the personal preferences of the users to be stored and processed, or complex structures to be created and maintained. The paper also reports some comparative experiments using a real-world website to analyze the performance of the proposed approaches.

2.7 Semantic Description of Liver Computerized Tomography Images

Semantic representations and querying are critical in interpretation of data, which is otherwise very difficult (if not impossible) to develop 'natural' and subjective (i.e. tailored to the users' needs/foci) user interfaces and to have an intuition about the results of any analysis and/or processing. Medicine is a special domain where such a semantic representation is a keystone in developing computerized methods due to the critical (and required) human component in all decision making processes.

The paper [7] is focused on demonstrating how an ontology can indeed be beneficial for such semantic processing. Authors developed ONLIRA (Ontology of the Liver for Radiology) and used it (as a sample application) to search for similar radiology reports. Then they studied the performance of searching the ontology-based radiology reports in comparison to searching free text reports using NLP techniques.

Experiments have been conducted on the basis of 30 radiology reports of different patients written in natural language and converted into ONLIRA instances. To highlight differences between two search/retrieval approaches (Keyword based vs. Semantic), five queries expressed in both (Description Logic) DL query and keywords, have been tested. To establish a gold standard, two board certified radiologists manually evaluated each query to decide which reports should be retrieved. Both approaches have been evaluated against the gold standard by comparing their precision and recall.

2.8 Keyword-Based Search of Workflow Fragments and Their Composition

Workflow specification, in science as in business, can be a difficult task, since it requires a deep knowledge of the domain to be able to model the chaining of the steps that compose the process of interest, as well as awareness of the computational tools, e.g., services, that can be utilized to enact such steps. To assist designers in this task, authors in [3], propose a methodology and an associated mechanisms for the specifications of scientific workflows by reusing workflow fragments. In particular, they show how semantic keyword search can be utilized to effectively identify the workflow fragments that are relevant for the composition of new workflow. They describe a methodology that consists in exploiting existing workflow specifications that are stored and shared in repositories, to identify workflow fragments that can be re-utilized and re-purposed by designers when specifying new workflows. Specifically, they present a method for identifying fragments that are frequently used across workflows in existing repositories, and therefore are likely to incarnate patterns that can be reused in new workflows. They describe a keyword-based search method for identifying the fragments that are relevant for the needs of a given workflow designer. They present an algorithm for composing the retrieved fragments with the initial (incomplete) workflow that the user designed, based on compatibility rules that have been identified, and showcase how the algorithm operates using an example from eScience.

2.9 Discovery and Recommendation of Web Services

A web services recommendation system is described in [8]. The salient idea of the paper is to go beyond traditional matchmaking techniques in taking leverage of the available information on objects (services and users) for structuring the ecosystem of web services as a heterogeneous multigraph where nodes (services and users) are connected by labeled edges having different semantics, i.e., similarity, popularity, follow and track relations, etc. A service may be recommended to a given user either as a response to his/her request or based on his/her profile. The contribution of this work is twofold: (i) the design of a multigraph model where intra-services, intra-users and inter services/users links are exhibited; (ii) a novel recommendation approach based multigraph search is proposed. A prototype has been implemented on top of a Neo4j graph database, enabling both keyword-based queries and graph analytics.

3   Conclusion

The first conclusion to draw is related to the COST EU instrument. Thanks to the flexibility and the bottom-up research approach promoted by this instrument, researchers from different countries and different disciplines had the opportunity to share their know-how.

From the research perspective, while Human-Computer Speech (HCI) is gaining momentum as a technique of computer interaction, we still need to get access to large unstructured datasets in order extract relevant information from them. As illustrated in [2], combining HCI with keyword-search is probably the next challenge to achieve.

References

1. Alexopoulos, P., Wallace, M.: Creating domain-specific semantic lexicons for aspect-based sentiment analysis. In: 10th International Workshop on Semantic and Social Media Adaptation and Personalization, SMAP 2015, Trento, Italy, 5–6 November 2015, pp. 1–6 (2015). https://doi.org/10.1109/SMAP.2015.7370083
2. Audhkhasi, K., Rosenberg, A., Sethy, A., Ramabhadran, B., Kingsbury, B.: End-to-end ASR-free keyword search from speech. In: 2017 IEEE International Conference on Acoustics, Speech and Signal Processing, ICASSP 2017, New Orleans, LA, USA, 5–9 March 2017, pp. 4840–4844 (2017). https://doi.org/10.1109/ICASSP.2017.7953076

3. Belhajjame, K., Grigori, D., Harmassi, M., Yahia, M.B.: Keyword-based search of workflow fragments and their composition. Trans. Comput. Collect. Intell. **26**, 67–90 (2017). https://doi.org/10.1007/978-3-319-59268-8_4

4. Beliga, S., Meštrović, A., Martinčić-Ipšić, S.: Selectivity-based keyword extraction method. Int. J. Semantic Web Inf. Syst. (IJSWIS) **12**(3), 1–26 (2016)

5. Cadegnani, S., Guerra, F., Ilarri, S., del Carmen Rodríguez-Hernández, M., Lado, R.T., Velegrakis, Y., Amaro, R.: Exploiting linguistic analysis on urls for recommending web pages: a comparative study. Trans. Comput. Collect. Intell. **26**, 26–45 (2017). https://doi.org/10.1007/978-3-319-59268-8_2

6. Jean, P., Harispe, S., Ranwez, S., Bellot, P., Montmain, J.: Uncertainty detection in natural language: a probabilistic model. In: Proceedings of the 6th International Conference on Web Intelligence, Mining and Semantics, WIMS 2016, Nîmes, France, 13–15 June 2016, pp. 10:1–10:10 (2016). https://doi.org/10.1145/2912845.2912873

7. Kökciyan, N., Türkay, R., Üsküdarli, S., Yolum, P., Bakir, B., Acar, B.: Semantic description of liver CT images: an ontological approach. IEEE J. Biomed. Health Inform. **18**(4), 1363–1369 (2014). https://doi.org/10.1109/JBHI.2014.2298880

8. Slaimi, F., Sellami, S., Boucelma, O., Ben, H.A.: A multigraph approach for web services recommendation. In: Debruyne, C., Panetto, H., Meersman, R., Dillon, T., Kühn, E., O'Sullivan, D., Ardagna, C.A. (eds.) OTM 2016. LNCS, vol. 10033, pp. 282–299. Springer, Cham (2016). https://doi.org/10.1007/978-3-319-48472-3_16

9. Stanković, R., Krstev, C., Obradović, I., Kitanović, O.: Improving document retrieval in large domain specific textual databases using lexical resources. Trans. Comput. Collect. Intell. **26**, 162–185 (2017). https://doi.org/10.1007/978-3-319-59268-8_8

10. Terziyan, V., Golovianko, M., Cochez, M.: TB-structure: collective intelligence for exploratory keyword search. In: Calì, A., Gorgan, D., Ugarte, M. (eds.) KEYSTONE 2016. LNCS, vol. 10151, pp. 171–178. Springer, Cham (2017). https://doi.org/10.1007/978-3-319-53640-8_15

KEYSTONE Activities and Results Overview on Training Schools

Charlie Abela[1], Antonio Fariña[2], Mihai Lupu[3], Raquel Trillo-Lado[4], and José R. R. Viqueira[5(✉)]

[1] University of Malta, Msida, Malta
charlie.abela@um.edu.mt
[2] Database Laboratory, University of A Coruña, A Coruña, Spain
fari@udc.es
[3] Information and Software Engineering Group, Vienna University of Technology, Vienna, Austria
mihai.lupu@tuwien.ac.at
[4] Department of Computer Science and Systems Engineering, I3A, University of Zaragoza, Zaragoza, Spain
raqueltl@unizar.es
[5] Centro Singular de Investigación en Tecnoloxías da Información, Universidade de Santiago de Compostela, Santiago de Compostela, Spain
jrr.viqueira@usc.es

Abstract. This chapter reports on the results and provides a brief overview of the topics addressed by the 25 lectures and 8 industrial talks given in the three Training Schools organized in the scope of the KEYSTONE (Semantic KEYword-based Search on sTructured data sOurcEs) COST action IC1302.

Keywords: Information retrieval · Linked data · Big data Keyword-based search

1 Introduction

One of the deliverables of the KEYSTONE (Semantic KEYword-based Search on sTructured data sOurcEs) COST action IC1302 was an annual training school. The aim of these training schools was to provide academic and professional training to students who are in the last stages of their research education, i.e., Early Career Investigators (ECI), PhD Students and even post-graduate and graduate students.

This chapter reports on the results of the three Training Schools organized in the scope of the KEYSTONE COST action, by summarizing their numbers and describing their activities.

This article is based upon work from the COST Action KEYSTONE IC1302, supported by COST (European Cooperation in Science and Technology).

J. Szymański and Y. Velegrakis (Eds.): IKC 2017, LNCS 10546, pp. 230–238, 2018.
https://doi.org/10.1007/978-3-319-74497-1_23

The 1st KEYSTONE Training School [1] was held over five days, between the 20th and 24th of July 2015, in the Faculty of ICT, University of Malta, Malta and it was organized by Charlie Abela (Coordinator), Joel Azzopardi, Joseph Bonello and Jean Paul Ebejer. It consisted of 7 lectures given by 7 distinguished academics from 6 different countries. Besides, two experts from the industry complemented the training with relevant talks. The training school attracted 32 students from over 20 EU countries. The COST action granted 20 students to attend the school.

The 2nd KEYSTONE Training School [3] was held in Centro Singular de Investigación en Tecnoloxías da Información (CiTIUS) of the Universidade de Santiago de Compostela (USC), Santiago de Compostela, Spain, over five days, between the 18th and 22th of July 2016. It was organized by José R.R. Viqueira (Coordinator), Antonio Fariña and Raquel Trillo. It consisted of a keynote and 7 lectures given by 8 distinguished academics from 6 different countries. As in the previous school, two industrial talks were also given. The training school attracted 36 participants from 13 different countries. The COST action granted 24 students out of 40 received applications.

The 3rd KEYSTONE Training School [2] was held over 5 days, between the 21st and 25th of August 2017 in the Institute for Software Technology and Interactive Systems, TU Wien, Austria. It was organized by Mihai Lupu (Coordinator), Allan Hanbury and Fajar J. Ekaputra. It consisted of 15 lectures (between 1 and 4.5 h) given by 13 distinguished academics from 6 different countries. It included 4 industry lectures, presented by two multinational corporations (Siemens and T-Mobile) and two Austrian mid-size enterprises (Semantic Web Company and Catalyst). It attracted 35 participants from 14 countries and 21 grants were given out of 38 received applications.

The lectures of the three schools reviewed topics in three main research areas, namely, Information Retrieval (IR), Linked Data (LD) and Big Data. The lectures were complemented by a set of hands-on sessions and activities. Besides, during the final days of each school, a data hackathon was organized and students were asked to solve a number of practical problems using the knowledge and insights they had acquired, as well as leveraging their own background expertise and experience. To support these activities, Microsoft Azure educator and student passes were provided by Microsoft. Finally, thanks to the sponsors of each school, awards were assigned to the three best performing teams in each hackathon.

The remainder of this chapter is organized as follows. Section 2 provides a brief overview of the topics addressed by the 25 lectures and 8 industrial talks. The hackathon organized in each school is briefly described in Sect. 3 and, finally, Sect. 4 concludes the chapter.

2   Lectures

The lectures of the three schools reviewed many interesting topics of three main research areas related to the KEYSTONE COST action, i.e., Information

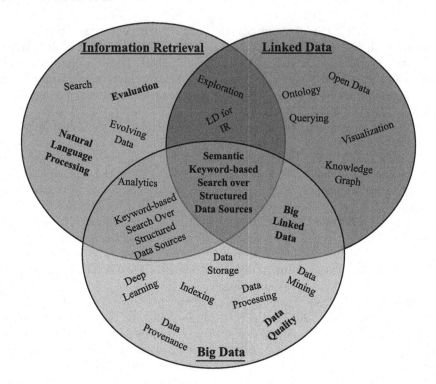

Fig. 1. Graphical representation of topics in the training schools.

Retrieval (IR), Linked Data (LD) and Big Data, as it is graphically depicted in Fig. 1. As representative examples, various tutorials covered different aspects of Natural Language Processing (NLP), IR Evaluation, Data Quality, Big Linked Data and Semantic Keyword-based Search over Structured Data Sources. Brief descriptions of each tutorial are next given in the following subsections.

2.1 Linked Data

The resolution of semantic conflicts is a key issue to achieve real semantic keyword-based search. Semantic Web and Linked Data are therefore key research areas for the KEYSTONE action.

Dr. Elmar Kiesling[1] gave an introductory tutorial [2] to the topic of Linked Data. The tutorial started with a brief look back at the history of Linked Data and the Semantic Web. Then it continued with a discussion on the key principles, concepts, core standards and protocols. Finally, it finished with a hands-on experience in querying and processing Linked Data.

---

[1] Vienna University of Technology (TU Wien), Vienna, Austria.

A keynote on Linked Open Data [3] was given by Prof. Asunción Gómez-Prez[2], where challenges related to Linked Data were explored and relevant opportunities for new research were presented.

Two tutorials covering the exploration, querying, and visualization of Linked Open Data sources [2,3] were given by Dr. Laura Po[3]. In these tutorials, the major challenges that should be addressed by exploration tools were initially discussed, and based on that, various tools developed by the Semantic Web community were presented. One of the tutorials included also a hands-on session.

Finally, related to the above, Prof. Heiko Paulheim[4] gave a keynote [2] on knowledge graphs on the Web. Some of the most prominent knowledge graphs, such as DBpedia, YAGO, and Wikidata were introduced and efforts to improve their coverage and quality were also described. In addition, new resources such as WebIsA were also presented.

2.2 Information Retrieval

Information Retrieval (IR) is the area were keyword-based search was first attempted. Thus, many researchers involved in the KEYSTONE action come from this area. Various tutorials presented important topics inside IR.

Search, Exploration, and Analytics of Evolving Data [1] were reviewed by Dr. Nattiya Kanhabua[5]. The tutorial showed the impact upon various components of IR systems of temporal web dynamics, by reviewing time-aware IR approaches.

The topic of IR evaluation was covered by two different tutorials. First, Dr. Mihai Lupu[6] gave an introductory tutorial to IR evaluation [3]. The lecture covered fundamental issues of this topic, but beyond that, it touched upon other aspects of Information Access Evaluation, by putting the work in relationship with database systems evaluation. Related to the above, the use of collective intelligence to crowdsource groundtruth for large scale IR evaluation [3] was introduced by Dr. Sergej Zerr[7].

Finally, Dr. Mauro Dragoni[8] gave two tutorials that showed the use of linked data resources to improve information retrieval effectiveness. In particular, his first tutorial introduced the use of ontologies in IR [1], whereas the second tutorial presented solutions for aggregating multiple dimensions through multi-criteria analysis to compute document relevance [3].

2.3 Natural Language Processing

Natural Language Processing (NLP) is a key area in IR, and therefore also of major importance for Keyword-based Search over Structured Data Sources.

---

[2] Universidad Politécnica de Madrid (UPM), Spain.
[3] University of Modena and Reggio Emilia (UNIMORE), Italy.
[4] University of Mannheim, Germany.
[5] L3S Research Center, University of Hannover, Germany.
[6] Vienna University of Technology (TU WIEN), Vienna, Austria.
[7] University of Southampton, United Kingdom.
[8] Fondazione Bruno Kessler, Trento, Italy.

Various tutorials reviewed topics such as text representation, information extraction, statistical semantics, and semantic annotation and expansion.

Prof. Julian Szymanski[9] gave a tutorial on text representation for data mining, where basic approaches for text categorization using supervised and unsupervised methods were provided, a method for dimensionality reduction was introduced and various proposed approaches were demonstrated by their application to Wikipedia articles [1].

An introduction to the topic of Information Extraction [2] was given by Dr. Elena Demidova.[10] The tutorial provided an overview of the basic blocks of Information Extraction, including methods for named entity extraction and linking, temporal extraction, relation extraction, and open Information Extraction.

Semantic annotation and expansion for keyword queries [3] was reviewed by Prof. Ranka Stankovic[11]. The tutorial presented different approaches for query expansion using ontologies and a keyword-based semantic retrieval approach.

Finally, Navid Rekabsaz[12] gave a tutorial on statistical semantics with dense vectors [2], where heuristics and various methods for creating word representations were reviewed.

2.4 Big Data and Big Linked Data

Big Data aims at the proper analysis of data for decision making where one or various of the three following aspects are involved: (i) *large volume of data*, i.e., datasets that range from Tera to Petabytes; (ii) *high velocity of processing*, i.e., data streams that must be processed in real time; or (iii) *much variety*, i.e., heterogeneous datasets that might include non structured text, multimedia, and sensor data. Keyword-based search is an appropriate user interface for the discovery of datasets affected by the three above aspects. Various tutorials reviewed different topics related to Big Data and Big Linked Data.

An introduction to Big data storage and analytics, including network science and graph stores [3] was given by Prof. Genoveva Vargas-Solar[13]. The lecture addressed different techniques for analysing and visualizing big data collections, including a vision of the analytics process as a complex and greedy task and visualization as out of the box solutions that can help to analyse, and interpret big data collections.

Prof. Stephane Marchand-Maillet[14] gave a tutorial on large scale and high dimensional issues in data indexing, processing and mining [1]. The lecture presented reference-based indexing using pivots or permutations to access big datasets dealing with high-dimensional sparse space issues.

---

[9] University of Gdańk, Gdańsk, Poland.
[10] L3S Research Center, Leibniz Universität Hannover, Germany.
[11] University of Belgrade, Serbia.
[12] Vienna University of Technology (TU WIEN), Vienna, Austria.
[13] Centre national de la recherche scientifique (CNRS), France.
[14] University of Geneva, Switzerland.

Prof. Vagan Terziyan[15] gave a systematic, structured, and multidisciplinary view to Deep Learning for Cognitive Computing [2]. The course described challenges and opportunities within Cognitive Computing, summarized relationships with other scientific domains, introduced the major related service providers, gave an introduction on major theories, methods and algorithms and provided a friendly introduction to Deep Learning.

Data quality issues were covered by two different lectures. Dr. Paolo Missier[16] gave a tutorial on Provenance and Quality [1]. The lecture started with an introduction to data provenance, including the essential elements of W3C PROV recommendation for provenance modeling. Next, recent contributions that connect data provenance and quality were reviewed. Finally, it presented speculative questions related to keyword search to motivate future research needs.

A tutorial on Scalable Linked Big Data Quality Assessment [2] was given by Dr. Jeremy Debattista[17], where state-of-the-art linked data quality frameworks were presented and relevant W3C Data Quality vocabulary was introduced. Linked Data Quality metrics and relevant probabilistic techniques for their computation were also presented.

The access to Big Data sources with Linked Data technologies (Big Linked Data) was addressed by three lectures. In particular, a tutorial on Technologies for Big Linked Data [2] was given by Prof. Sherif Sakr[18]. The lecture provided a review of the new generation of big data processing systems and their applications to the linked data domain. It also highlighted current open research challenges and discussed promising future research directions.

Finally, two tutorials with relevant hands-on sessions on the management of compressed Big Linked semantic data [1,2] were given by Prof. Antonio Farina[19], Prof. Miguel A. Martinez-Prieto[20], and Dr. Javier D. Fernández[21]. The lectures introduced fundamental concepts of Compact Data Structures and RDF self-indexes to analyze RDF data compression based on the elimination of two different types of syntactic redundancy. The *HDT* compact data structure and binary serialization format was described and its main characteristics analyzed, together with its application in different linked data projects. Finally, the tutorials presented also different modeling strategies and compact self-indexes, such as *RDF-CSA* and *K2-triples*, to cope with RDF versions.

---

[15] University of Jyväskylä, Finland.
[16] Newcastle University, United Kingdom.
[17] Fraunhofer IAIS and Univ. of Bonn, Germany.
[18] King Saud bin Abdulaziz University for Health Sciences and University of New South Wales, Sydney, Australia.
[19] Universidade da Coruña, Spain.
[20] University of Valladolid, Spain.
[21] Wirtschaftsuniversität Wien (WU), Austria.

2.5   Semantic Keyword-Based Search over Structured Data Sources

Three lectures were given exactly in the topic of the KEYSTONE COST action. Dr. Elena Demidova[22] gave a tutorial on Interactive keyword-based access to large-scale structured datasets [3]. The lecture started with an introduction to keyword-based access to structured data, showing the trade-off between usability and expressiveness. It continued with issues related to the preparation of the data for keyword-based access, giving special attention to indexing and it finished with a presentation of methods for interactive query construction, i.e., the generation of structured queries from user keywords.

Two lectures were given on different applications of semantic keyword-based search over structured data sources. Dr. Mauro Dragoni[23] gave a tutorial on Semantic Keyword Search Within the Medical Domain [2]. The lecture introduced the concept of Ontology and analyzed the use of semantic-based retrieval approaches by comparing them with classic ones. Then, it provided guidelines for the construction of semantic-based retrieval solutions and presented the medical domain as a suitable use case for these solutions.

Finally, a lecture on Semantic Keyword-based Search on GeoSpatial Data Sources [2] was given by Prof. José R.R. Viqueira[24]. The tutorial provided an introduction to the representation and management of geospatial data, as prior knowledge to cover both Geographic Information Retrieval and GeoSpatial Semantic Web technologies. The lecture finished with four examples of related challenging problems.

2.6   Industrial Talks

The industry had also a very important role in the KEYSTONE Training Schools and a prove of that are the eight talks given in different topics by representatives of distinct companies.

Dr. John Abela, Lecturer at the University of Malta and Chief Technical Officer of Ascent Software Ltd., presented a number of case studies that his company was involved in [1]. These case studies included examples from foreign exchange markets, telecommunications, and astrophysics.

Dr. Reinhold Karner, serial entrepreneur, spoke about emerging markets for big data [1]. He focused on Economy 4.0, outlining those aspects that are revolutionizing the global economy, including urbanization, technology, demographics, and globalization.

Dr. José Manuel González Chenlo, from Hewlett Packard Enterprise, presented a number of case studies, that included examples of how to use Elastic Search on information systems in fields related to health information systems and medical history management [3].

---

[22] University of Southampton, United Kingdom.
[23] Fondazione Bruno Kessler, Trento, Italy.
[24] Universidade de Santiago de Compostela, Spain.

Dr. Miguel Luaces, associate professor of the University of A Coruña and member of the enterprise Enxenio S.L., spoke about emerging markets for software development and new ways to tackle the design, development, deployment, and maintenance of software systems [3].

Dr. Andreas Falkner, from Siemens, gave a talk on Linking Product Configuration and Data Analytics at Siemens Corporate Technology [2].

Tomas Knap, from Semantic Web Company, gave a talk on RDF Data Processing and Integration Tasks in PoolParty UnifiedViews [2]. UnifiedViews (http://unifiedviews.eu), has become a widely used and accepted solution for management of RDF data processing and integration tasks. Besides, PoolParty (https://www.poolparty.biz/) is a world-class semantic technology suite for organizing, enriching, and searching knowledge, which is available on the market for more than 7 years.

Martin Weber, from Catalyst, gave a talk on Data Science in Action: How we accelerate business with AI [2]. He showed how different Artificial Intelligence mechanisms can be combined to deliver seamless customer experience at scale.

Finally, Dr. Wasif Masood, from T-Mobile, gave a talk on Large scale customer experience management [2], where he showed that customer experience management is a use case for the application of cluster computing to massively distributed data. He gave insights about customer experiences in telecom domain and how big data is contributing/influencing it.

3   Hackathon

An important part of each of the three KEYSTONE Training Schools consisted of a practical hands-on exercise in the form of a day-and-a-half programming hackathon. Participants were asked to form groups of two or three participants, and a series of tasks were presented to them to solve. In total, there were between seven and nine groups who participated in the data hackathons in the different schools.

The topics of the hackathons varied in the different schools and ranged from searches of specific genes and DNA/protein sequences across the human genome [1], to the searching of DBpedia and GeoNames [3] and to resolving keyword-search over medical domain documents by using specific ontologies [2].

The participants were free to choose the operating system, the programming language, and the techniques to use to implement their solutions. Microsoft Azure accounts were distributed to each team. Mentoring and support from a team of lecturers was available for the groups in order to help them to address issues from both an academic as well as technical perspective.

At the end of the hackathon, each team had to demonstrate their solutions to four judges and deliver a lightning short presentation in front of the other teams describing the techniques they employed in their solutions. Awards were assigned to the three best performing teams.

4   Conclusion

The attendees were issued with attendance certificates for the events. Their feedback was very positive and strongly indicated that the schools were up to their expectations both content wise as well as from an organizational perspective. The events were successful also due to the team effort involved, which included the COST program, the lecturers who provided their expertise for the lectures and the practical sessions, the local organizers, and the sponsors who contributed to the awards and the organization of the events. All materials are provided openly on the websites of the three training schools, available from the URLs provided in the References section below.

References

1. Abela, C., Azzopardi, J., Bonello, J., Ebejer, J.P.: 1st KEYSTONE training school: keyword search over big data. http://keystone.opendatamalta.org. Accessed 04 Nov 2017
2. Lupu, M., Hanbury, A., Ekaputra, F.J.: 3rd KEYSTONE Training School: Keyword search in Big Linked Data. https://www.ifs.tuwien.ac.at/keystone.school/. Accessed 04 Nov 2017
3. Viqueira, J.R., Lado, R.T., Farina, A.: 2nd KEYSTONE Training School: Keyword search in Big Linked Data. https://eventos.citius.usc.es/keystone.school. Accessed 04 Nov 2017

KEYSTONE Activities and Results Overview on Enabling Mobility & Fostering Collaborations Through STSM

Abdulhussain E. Mahdi[✉]

Keystone STSM Chair, Department of Electronic and Computer Engineering,
University of Limerick, Limerick, Ireland
Hussain.Mahdi@ul.ie

Abstract. This article gives an overview of the research mobility, connectivity and collaboration activities facilitated by the Keystone Cost Action IC1302 in the context of its Short-Term Scientific Missions (STSMs). It provides data and figures regarding all funded STSMs over the term of the action in terms of the funding mechanism used, distribution among members, and participating personnel and institutions, along of with summaries of associated research projects.

Keywords: Mobility and connectivity · COST action · STSM

1 Introduction - COST Short Term Scientific Missions (STSMs)

Driven by its mission of increasing scientific collaboration in Europe and making it more competitive, COST supports a wide range of networking tools, such as workshops, conferences, training schools, and short-term scientific missions (STSMs). Among these activities, the STSMs are based on a concept of particular interest to young scientists by allowing them to learn from an institution or laboratory in another COST country [1, 2]. The missions are inter-laboratory exchange visits aimed at strengthening the existing COST Actions by allowing scientists to go to an institution or laboratory in another COST country, or in an approved Near Neighbour Country[1] (NNC) or International Partners Countries[2] (IPC) to foster collaboration, to learn a new technique or to perform experiments using instruments, resources and/or methodologies not available in the home institution/laboratory [1].

Keystone Action utilised STSMs to effectively foster collaboration among its 31 member countries. As reported by many other COST Actions [2], Keystone STSMs have proved to be one of the most effective networking instruments. This article provides an overview of the STSM activities of Keystone Action over its four-year duration.

---

[1] See: http://www.cost.eu/about_cost/strategy/international_cooperation/nnc.

[2] See: http://www.cost.eu/about_cost/strategy/international_cooperation/ipc.

© Springer International Publishing AG, part of Springer Nature 2018
J. Szymański and Y. Velegrakis (Eds.): IKC 2017, LNCS 10546, pp. 239–259, 2018.
https://doi.org/10.1007/978-3-319-74497-1_24

2   Keystone STSM Activities in Figures

Keystone Action funded 64 STSMs over its four-year duration, with the total awarded funding accounting for just over 18% of the Action's overall expenditure. The application process was facilitated via 12 regularly scheduled calls for applications with an average of three calls per calendar year [3]. Table 1 gives details of all STSM calls and number of successful applications.

Table 1. Keystone STSM call schedule and number of approved and funded missions

Year	Call	Application deadline	# of Approved STSMs
2014	1st	28th Feb 2014	2
	2nd	1st May 2014	7
	3rd	15th June 2014	3
2015	1st	30th Jan 2015	7
	2nd	15th March 2015	3
	3rd	30th April 2015	4
2016	1st	29th Feb 2016	8
	2nd	8th May 2016	11
	3rd	17th Sept 2016	6
2017	1st	2nd March 2017	7
	2nd	1st June 2017	5
	3rd (ITC Target)	2th Sept 2017	1

With regards to participation, 90% of the Action's member countries availed at least once from these missions as an applicant or host country. Figure 1a and b show the overall distribution of awarded STSMs among Keystone participating countries.

In awarding the STSM funding, Keystone management committee sought to achieve a gender balance among awardees in each of the above calls whenever possible. Overall, 32% of STSM awardees were females with rest of the awards going to male applicants – see Fig. 2. The Action also gave priority in awarding STSM funding to young scientists (ECI – Early Career Investigators) from all participating countries, with 37.1% of funded STSMs awarded to ECI applicants as shown in Fig. 3.

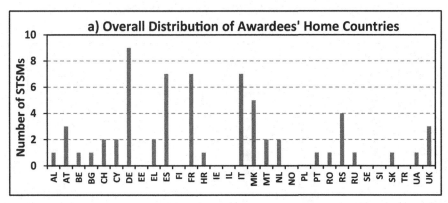

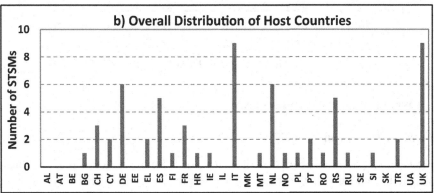

Fig. 1. Distribution of funded STSMs among (a) Home counties and (b) Host countries

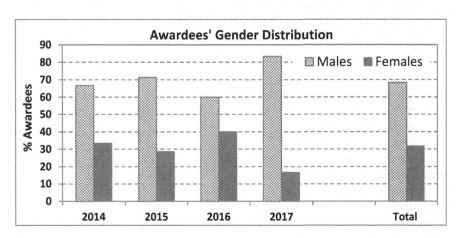

Fig. 2. STSM gender distribution

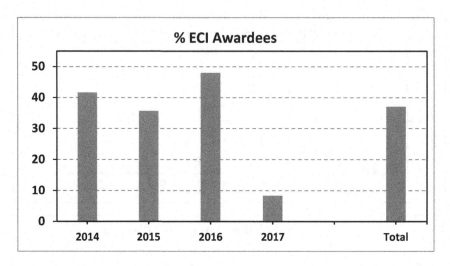

Fig. 3. STSM ECI awardees

3   Overview of Keystone STSMs

3.1   Main Themes and Topics

As stated in its published objectives, the main goal of Keystone Action is to coordinate collaboration among its members to enable research activity and technology transfer in the area of keyword-based search over structured data sources [4]. Therefore, all funded STSMs embraced the overarching themes of keyword-based search and structured data, with the particular subjects covering the following topics:

– structured data sources
– keyword based search
– summarisation approach
– embedded markup
– biomedical ontology-based search
– deep web
– open world assumption
– search recommendation systems
– formal concept analysis
– meteorological events
– complex event processing
– case similarity & relevance analysis
– quantitative data
– linked data resources

Figure 4 shows a quick word-cloud of the main keywords related to the titles and subjects of all Keystone funded STSMs.

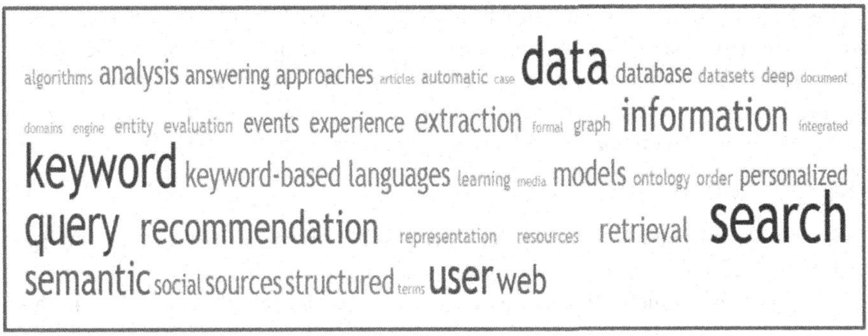

algorithms analysis answering approaches articles automatic case **data** database datasets deep document domains engine entity evaluation events experience extraction formal graph **information** integrated **keyword** keyword-based languages learning media models ontology order personalized **query** recommendation representation resources retrieval **search** semantic social sources structured terms **user** web

Fig. 4. Word-cloud of keystone's STSM keywords

3.2 Summaries of Keystone STSMs

This section lists the titles of all Keystone funded STSMs, along with the names of researchers involved and a summary description of each.

• Improvement of Automatic Formalization Processes for thesauri

– **Visiting Researcher:** Javier Lacasta, IAAA, Universidad de Zaragoza, Spain
– **Host:** Gilles Falquet, Universite de Geneve, Geneve, Switzerland

This STSM dealt with the problem of formalizing knowledge models through automatic alignment between these models and formal ontologies, via: (a) Study of alignment approaches between knowledge models such as thesauri and ontologies; and (b) Use of these approaches to construct an automatic formalization process that improves the definition of concepts and relations in knowledge models for information retrieval; analysis of the performance of these formalized models for information retrieval and comparison with the original ones.

• Exploratory- and Keyword- Based Design of Data-Intensive Scientific Workflows

– **Visiting Researcher:** Khalid Belhajjame, Université Paris-Dauphine, Paris, France
– **Host:** Alessandro Bozzon, Delft University of Technology, Delft, Netherlands

This STSM focused on how exploratory techniques together with keyword based search algorithms can be used to drive the specification of data intensive scientific workflows. The STSM involved: (a) Requirements analysis for a key-word and exploratory design of data intensive scientific workflows. Document requirements and opportunities, and evaluate candidate techniques and tools for use in the implementation; (b) Framework design to specify how existing exploratory and

• Extraction and Representation of Place Names for the Reconstruction of Itineraries from Texts

– **Visiting Researcher:** Ludovic Moncla, Université de Pau et des Pays de l'Adour, France
– **Host:** Javier Nogueras Iso, IAAA Research Group, University of Zaragoza, Spain

This STSM dealt with the extraction and representation of place names for the reconstruction of itineraries from textual sources. In particular, it focused on the problem of toponym resolution in the case of processing texts which describe trip itineraries (e.g. hiking descriptions) in small areas where fine-grain toponyms are not usually found in well-known toponym databases such as Geonames or Open Street Maps.

- Keyword Search on Graph Data

- **Visiting Researcher:** Paolo Missier, Newcastle University, Newcastle upon Tyne, UK
- **Host:** Francesco Guerra, University of Modena and Reggio Emilia,Modena, Italy

The focus of this STSM in on the study of keyword search over non-relational data, and in particular graph data. This is motivated by the growing importance of a specific type of graph, namely graphs that represent data provenance. For research data in particular, this highly structured form of metadata represents evidence of sound experimental data production and enables its validation. The problem of translating keyword-based search to relational queries has been investigated over the years, however, extensions to non-relational data and graph data models in particular has not received the same attention.

- Semantic Classification of Liver Radiological Reports

- **Visiting Researcher:** María del Mar Roldán-García, Universidad de Malaga, Malaga, Spain
- **Host:** Burak Acar, Boğaziçi University, Turkey

The aim of this STSM is to combine the VAVLab word about ONLIRA and its use for query processing and case similarity/relevance analysis of liver cases with the KHAOS experience about semantic web technologies and the development of biomedical ontologies based on SNOMED CT and ICD10.

- Keyword-based Search over Structured Data Sources

- **Visiting Researcher:** Nattiya Kanhabua, Universität Hannover, Hannover, Germany
- **Host:** Kjetil Nørvåg, Norwegian University of Science and Technology, Norway

This STSM aimed to conduct research collaboration with the host and PhD students under his supervision, within the context of three projects she is involved in: ForgetIT, ALEXANDRIA and TIMETool. For ForgetIT, her research goal is to develop approaches and technologies for intelligent preservation management that keeps the archived information concise, relevant and digestible by managed forgetting and contextualized remembering.

- Keyword Search on Relational Data in the Deep Web

- **Visiting Researcher:** Andrea Cali, University of London, Birkbeck College, London, UK
- **Host:** Riccardo Torlone, Università Roma Tre, Italy

The goal of this mission is to devise novel techniques for keyword search on relational data in the Deep Web, where. Querying Deep Web data requires specific techniques. One of the major problems here is the extraction of the schemata of Deep Web sources. Since keyword search on databases frees us from having to know the schema of the data, the Deep Web scenario is particularly suitable for it. Work focused on the study of query answering algorithm and their complexity, under the limitations implied by source restrictions, and in the presence of integrity constraints.

- From Recommender Systems to Personalized Academic Search Engines

- **Visiting Researcher:** Stefan Langer, Otto-von-Guericke Universität Magdeburg, Germany
- **Host:** Georgia Kapitsaki, University of Cyprus, Cyprus

This STSM is related to the applicant's PhD research on a recommender system which explores how user models can be most effectively created based on the data of Docear's users. The aim is on extending this work to personalized academic search engines by integrating a personalized academic search engine to Docear. The mission focuses on the question whether the user modelling algorithms of the recommender system could be utilized for instance to suggest search terms to the users.

- Context Information Extraction from Social Media Structured Sources

- **Visiting Researcher:** Georgia Kapitsaki, University of Cyprus, Aglantzia, Cyprus
- **Host:** Geert-Jan Houben, Delft University of Technology, Netherlands

Context-aware applications are relevant both for web and mobile environments and can exploit information available in different web resources (e.g., web services, social media, microblogs). The focus of this STSM is on structured sources available in social media in order to extract context-relevant information. Specifically, the extraction of context-relevant data from user models/profiles in social media is the main objective of the STSM along with the former formulation of social media-based user context metamodel.

- Semantic and Crowdsourced Keyword-based Search

- **Visiting Researcher:** Marco Brambilla, Politecnico di Milano, Milano, Italy
- **Host:** Khalid Belhajjame, Université Dauphine Paris, France

This STSM is related to keyword-based search over structured and rich data sources. In particular, it brought together the complementary expertise of the two groups on semantic modelling and querying of data, together with crowdsourcing, media analysis, and structured web content, at the purpose of working together on an initial publication and then continue the collaboration in the long term. The main focus is in integration of crowd sourcing practices in keyword based search and classification of rich, structured web content.

- Keyword Based Search Foundations

- **Visiting Researcher**: Jorge Cardoso, University of Coimbra, Coimbra, Portugal
- **Host:** Francesco Guerra, Universita' di Modena e Reggio Emilia, Italy

The aim of this STSM is to elaborate a scientific document delineating the research paths to explore during the full length of the KEYSTONE Cost Action. The scientific document to write will identify how recent research findings can contribute to the development of new keyword-based search mechanisms and which fields/approaches should be explored. The document to write will extend the KEYSTONE proposal with the results obtained from the meetings held in the first year.

- Improving Users' Search Behaviour

  - **Visiting Researcher:** Claudia Hauff, Delft University of Technology, Delft, NL
  - **Host:** Fabio Crestani, University of Lugano, Lugano, Switzerland

Users of search systems are often not able to create queries that allow systems to return the documents that are most suitable to the users. If search systems are able to teach users of how to improve their querying, by providing examples of better queries, one bottleneck in the user-system search interaction process could be removed. A prerequisite for this setup is to find means of improving a user`s given query in a way that is not artificial. This research visit was geared towards kick-starting the collaboration on this research work between KEYSTONE partners in Lugano and Delft.

- Query Recommendation and As-You-Type Search in Social Media

  - **Visiting Researcher:** Bogdan Cautis, University of Paris-Sud 11 (I.U.T. Orsay), France
  - **Host:** Hossein Vahabi, Yahoo Labs Barcelona, Spain

The focus of this STSM is social-aware query paradigms. Providing the most accurate answers or query suggestions, while the user is typing her query, almost instantaneously, can be extremely beneficial. This as-you-type search problem is challenging, as answers pertain to a query interpretation by which the last term in the query sequence can match keyword prefixes. Moreover, as it is necessary to serve fast the top-k results matching the query in its current form, we need solutions with an anytime behaviour.

- Keyword-based Search and Keyword Interpretation in Recommendations Systems

  - **Visiting Researcher**: María del Carmen Hernández, Unversity of Zaragoza, Zaragoza, Spain
  - **Host**: Francesco Guerra, University of Modena and Reggio Emilia, Italy

The focus of this STSM is context-based recommendations and keyword-based search in mobile environments, with the specific goal of studying keyword-based mechanisms to express the necessity of information of the user, and techniques to enrich the information about items recommended by using external data sources, as well as strategies to obtain quantitative ratings from textual opinions, and to find relevant opinions for a potential item to recommend.

- Aggregated Search on the Web of Data

  - **Visiting Researcher:** Khalid Belhajjame, Université Paris Dauphine, Paris, France
  - **Host:** Norman W. Paton, University of Manchester, UK

This STSM focused on solution for exploring and searching over the Web of Data. Typically, data publishers provide SPARQL endpoints that can be used to query their datasets. While useful, this approach fell short in meeting the needs of users who wish to issue their search over a number of datasets, as opposed to a single dataset (endpoint). To address this problem, a handful of researchers have investigated federated search. Work examines these techniques with the long standing data integration field in databases.

- LearnWeb EXPLORER – Guided Search for Linked Data Resources

- **Visiting Researcher**: Ivana Marenzi, L3S Research Center, Germany
- **Host:** Yannis Velegrakis, University of Trento, Trento, Italy

This STSM involved joint research on the problem of guided search, in the context of linked data resources. Target users are non-expert users who have only a vague idea of which resources are available to fulfil their information needs. We involved investigating an approach which guides these users through an iterative and interactive querying process to better understand their information need and through this process provide them with resources from the linked data cloud which best fulfil their information need.

- Semantic Representation of Liver Patients Radiological Reports

- **Visiting Researcher:** Maria del Mar R. Garcia, University of Málaga, Malaga, Spain
- **Host:** Burak Acar, Bogazici University, Turkey

The theme of this STSM is combining the VAVLab work on ONLIRA and its use for query processing and case similarity/relevance analysis of liver cases with the KHAOS experience in semantic web technologies and the development of biomedical ontologies based on SNOMED CT and ICD10. The focus is on developing a new ontology (LiCO), based on ONLIRA, to include information about Liver Patients, such as laboratory results, previous diagnosis, physical examination, etc., populating this ontology with RDF data from CaReRa and building a semantic classification systems using DBOWL.

- Experimenting ML Techniques in Keyword Search for Structured Databases

- **Visiting Researcher**: Francesco Guerra, University of Modena and Reggio Emilia, Modena, Italy
- **Host:** Julian Szymanski, Gdansk University of Technology, Poland

This STSM has three purposes: (a) Machine Learning and Keyword Search: source selection; (b) Information Retrieval, Machine Learning and Keyword Search; and (c) Data Science in Action: a short course about practical Data Science techniques will be delivered to the PhD students and the students of the Artificial Intelligence Course at the University of Gdansk.

- Semantic Expansion of Keyword Queries in Resource Sharing Websites

- **Visiting Researcher:** Sergio Oramas, Universitat Pompeu Fabra, Barcelona, Spain
- **Host:** Michael P O'Mahony, University College Dublin, Ireland

This STSM focused on creating a methodology for semantic annotation and expansion of keyword queries, and the use of the extended query for searching through the structured data source provided by the tagging ontology of Freesound. The main idea is to apply Entity Linking and Word Sense Disambiguation to the keyword query, and expand it using WordNet and DBpedia.

- QyX: QuerY-driven eXample-based Discovery of Dataspace Mappings

  - **Visiting Researcher:** Federica Mandreoli, Università di Modena e Reggio Emilia, Italy
  - **Host:** George H. L. Fletcher, Eindhoven University of Technology, Eindhoven, Netherlands

The main aim of this STSM is to exploit the queries issued by users to discover mappings on-the-fly that can be used to answer such queries satisfactorily. For this study, "answering a query satisfactorily" means defining any predicates mentioned in the body of the query which aren't present in query and that yield to a query answer the user is satisfied with. In other words, discover a possible set of mappings necessary to define all such predicates.

- Consideration of Semantics in the Analysis of Citations

  - **Visiting Researcher:** Manolis Wallace, University of the Peloponnese, Tripolis, Greece
  - **Host:** Yannis Velegrakis, University of Trento, Trento, Italy

This STSM focused on: (1) Semantics in citation analysis: the STSM brought the two collaborators to work together towards achieving the goal of deep semantic analysis of citation networks; (2) Research laboratory set up: applicant is in the process of setting up the environment required to efficiently perform research at a high level in the fields of semantics and uncertainty. The STSM allowed the applicant to discuss the pains, risks and challenges of the laboratory startup process and gain from the experience of the dbTrento group.

- Keywords Across Domains

  - **Visiting** Researcher: Mihai Lupu, Vienna University of Technology, Vienna, Austria
  - **Host:** Gabriella Pasi, Universita di Milano Bicocca, Milan, Italy

This STSM helped establishing interaction paths between the information retrieval group at the Vienna University of Technology and at the University of Milano Bicocca covering three of the four WG of Keystone: Keyword Search, User Interaction and keyword query interpretation, and Research integrations, showcases, benchmarks and evaluations. Specifically, Concretely, the STSM explored two keyword-related domains: image tags and nano-publications for scientific articles.

- Performance Evaluation of Algorithms for Keyword Search in Social Media Data

  - **Visiting Researcher:** Atanas Hristov, University of Inform Science & Techn, Ohrid, Macedonia
  - **Host:** Iva Nikolova, Technical University of Sofia, Sofia, Bulgaria

This STSM aimed to investigate the efficiency of the algorithms that perform keyword search in social media data. The main focus was to evaluate the three major challenges of keyword search in structured and semi-structured data. The first challenge is to determinate what is the semantics of keyword search in structured data. The second challenge is to determinate what constitutes a good answer. The last challenge is to determinate how to perform keyword search efficiently.

- Experimenting in Techniques and Approaches in Search on Structured Georeferenced Bibliographic Data Sources

- **Visiting Researcher:** Dragan Ivanović, University of Novi Sad, Novi Sad, Serbia
- **Host:** Marjan Čeh, University of Ljubljana, Slovenia

The aim of this STSM is to research literature about using NLP techniques in order to find out toponyms from the text in order to enable automatic georeferencing of publications; create a strategy for using the similar or the same system to georeference theses and dissertations defended at the University of Novi Sad; and research using Google Maps JavaScript API for automatic georeferencing keywords from a query in order to enable keywords-based search on georeferenced publications.

- Evaluating Semantic Search - Improving Crowdsourcing through Malicious Activity Detection

- **Visiting Researcher:** Ujwal Gadiraju, L3S Research Center, Hannover, Germany
- **Host:** Gianluca Demartini, University of Sheffield, Sheffield, UK

This STSM focused on the problem of quality and reliability of about crowdsourced data and results, given that crowdsourcing microtasks are often plagued by malicious activity that is prevalent in the crowd, as previous work by the proposers had shown. Proposed visit explored proposing solutions to this problem through the automatic detection of malicious workers at scale.

- Complex Event Processing for Recommendation in Keyword-based Search

- **Visiting Researcher:** Ramon H. Traba, University of Zaragoza, Zaragoza, Spain
- **Host:** Jurgen Dunkel, University of Applied Sciences and Arts, Hannover

This STSM focused on studying how recommendation processes for keyword-based search can be enhanced by taking into account events occurring in the environment. With this in mind the applicant sought a host institution with a known expertise in complex event processing, which may definitely help him achieve an interesting new direction on his research lines.

- Information Retrieval: Extending the Theory of Accessibility Measures

- **Visiting Researcher:** Aldo Lipani, Inst of Software Techn & Interactive Systems, Vienna, Austria
- **Host:** Evangelos Kanoulas, University of Amsterdam, Netherlands

The STSM focused on extending the retrievability theory on keywords based domains including keyword query distributions in order to better approximate the users behaviour when searching on a search engines in specific domains.

- Towards Better Vector Representations for Biomedical corpus-based Lexical Semantic Relatedness Measures

  - **Visiting Researcher:** Maciej Rybinski, Universidad de Málaga, Málaga, Spain
  - **Host:** Palmira Marrafa, University of Lisbon, Lisboa, Portugal

This STSM focused on evaluating the possibilities of enhancing distributional semantic relatedness approximation methods with more sophisticated vector representation models. The work carried out was divided between the literature studies and exploratory experiments with various modelling techniques. Work also outlined the follow-up stage of the work, which would be carried out after the conclusion of the STSM.

- Interactive Language Learning: Recommending Keywords with POS Tagged Multilingual Word Graphs

  - **Visiting Researcher:** Benjamin Bergner, Otto-von-Guericke-University, Germany
  - **Host:** Alexandre Miguel Pinto, University of Coimbra, Portugal

This STSM focused on replacing the learner's daily reading of mother tongue articles with equally interesting articles in the target language. He therefore chooses domains/categories of interest. Users are then able to select an article within the domain. Before reading, the user will be motivated to translate system chosen 'important' words that are needed to understand the article primarily. Already translated words are visualized and can collaboratively be used to aid other users.

- Ontology-based Information Retrieval: A Graph Based Approach

  - **Visiting Researcher:** Ana Mestrovic, University of Rijeka, Rijeka, Croatia
  - **Host:** Andrea Calì, University of London, Birkbeck College, UK

This STSM focused on devising a novel technique, or better a framework, for Information Retrieval with the aid of a domain ontology, with inspiration from the ideas discussed at the KEYSTONE WG meeting in Marseille. The main idea behind the research is to make use of an ontological layer so as to improve IR. In particular, the ontological layer will allow to carry out IR by using a subset of the words (a sort of base), with all other words expressed as a function of the base words.

- Searching Big Data Under Open World Assumption

  - **Visiting Researcher:** Mariia Golovianko, Kharkiv National University of Radioelectronics, Ukraine
  - **Host:** Vagan Terziyan, University of Jyväskylä, Jyväskylä, Finland

The aim of this STSM is to study and develop the techniques for query answering in Big Data under Open World Assumption. The specific objectives are: - Invention of the possibilities for improvement of existent techniques of Big Data querying; - Enhancement of current search techniques with semantic methods and models based on Open World Assumption; - Investigation on funding possibilities and research project submission; - Research paper draft for further publication.

- Defining Research Framework for Automatic Recommendation of New PHD Publications and Personalization of Ranking Search Results

- **Visiting Researcher:** Joel Azzopardi, University of Malta, Msida, Malta
- **Host:** Dragan Ivanović, University of Novi Sad, Novi Sad, Serbia

The aim of this STSM is to extend the features of the PHD UNS digital library by developing a personalized recommendation system for the users of this library. Work involved: 1. Reviewing literature on information retrieval, and adaptive hypermedia systems; 2. Designing a solution on the basis of the techniques and approaches reviewed; 3. Initial implementation of the recommendation solution as designed in 2; 4. Preparing an evaluation plan for the developed recommendation system.

- Query Answering in Evolving Datasets

- **Visiting Researcher:** Paolo Sottovia, University of Trento, Trento, Italy
- **Host:** Wolfgang Nejdl, L3S - Research Center, Hannover, Germany

This STSM focused on a new technique for entity linkage, introducing a new temporal model based on probabilistic methods which, combined with an innovative decision strategy, is able to handle this new concept of entity evolution at large scale. From the result given by temporal entity linkage we want to exploit the evolution of the entities into the query answering process. This techniques is going to improve the keyword search since the answer will not be generated from an exact match with the input query keywords to the database terms, but also by an expansion with the temporal evolution of the involved database terms.

- Efficient Ground Truth Generation with Crowdsourcing Competitions

- **Visiting Researcher:** Markus Rokicki, L3S Research Center, Hannover, Germany
- **Host:** Sergej Zerr, University of Southampton, Southampton, UK

This STSM aimed to prepare an extensive experimental evaluation of the ability of the crowd to provide real valued judgments in our framework. The visit focused on modelling input presented to and expected from crowd workers, and designing the feedback that is presented to the worker. This is based either on existing gold standard data or on agreement between workers. Work also involved exploring implementation of experiments, addressing design decisions with respect to the user interface, as well as anticipated implementation challenges.

- Multi-objective Optimization for Feature Selection in Text Classification Problems

- **Visiting Researcher:** Atanas Hristov, University for Inform Science & Techn, Ohrid, Macedonia
- **Host:** Georgios Petrou, Neapolis University, Cyprus

This STSM focused on reviewing, identifying and analysing the general problems and modern trends in the area of multi-objective optimization and text classification problems with special focus on high performance algorithms, tools and application for this purpose.

- Semantics Analysis in Citations Data

  - **Visiting Researcher:** Xenia Koulouri, University of the Peloponnese, Tripolis, Greece
  - **Host:** Florin Pop, University Politehnica of Bucharest, Romania

The purpose of this STSM is to work together and combine the theory of the applicant with the relevant software of hosts. First, the applicant conducted a presentation of her work to hosts. The visit concluded with a tour of the POLITEHNIKA University of Bucharest and the area of research laboratory, providing the applicant with experience of how a research laboratory works.

- Graph-based Visualization of Query Results Set Based on Methods from Formal Concept Analysis

  - **Visiting Researcher:** Peter Butka, Technical University of Kosice, Kosice, Slovakia
  - **Host:** Andreas Nürnberger, Otto-von-Guericke-University, Magdeburg, Germany

This STSM focused on structured visualization of query results set from web engines based on the methods from the area of Formal Concept Analysis (FCA). These methods are used for creation of concept-based hierarchies for organization and exploration of data sets defined by object-attribute data tables. The main idea is to extract input characteristics for application of FCA-based methods from query results set acquired from web engine and visualize this set within graph-based search visualization tool.

- Personalization of Search on a Digital Library of PhD Dissertations by Re-ranking Search Results Based on Automatic User Personalization and Recommendation

  - **Visiting Researcher:** Dragan Ivanović, University of Novi Sad, Novi Sad, Serbia
  - **Host:** Joel Azzopardi, University of Malta, Msida, Malta

The STSM focused on extending the features of the PHD UNS digital library by researching and implementing personalization of search results, using automatic recommendation software component that was developed as a result of the research performed within a previous Keystone STSM. This component is considered as a "black box" whereby the inputs are the user and a series of dissertations and the output is a list of recommendation scores for the list of recommendations.

- Temporal Entity-Centric Information Propagation in Multilingual Texts

  - **Visiting Researcher**: Simon Gottschalk, L3S Research Centre, Hannover, Germany
  - **Host:** Elena Demidova, University of Southampton, UK

This STSM facilitated joint research on the problem of information propagation across languages that becomes evident in the evolving descriptions of entities. Work focused on the evolution of entities through the cross-lingual information propagation by an extensive automated comparison of Wikipedia articles using means like translation, interlingual entity disambiguation and time expression alignment.

- Keyword-based Search in Non-structured Data sources of Relevant Meteorological Events

  - **Visiting Researcher:** Dario Stojanovski, Ss. Cyril & Methodius University, Macedonia
  - **Host:** Jose Viqueira, Universidade de Santiago de Compostela, Spain

  The main focus of this STSM was researching keyword-based search in non-structured data sources and matching relevant meteorological events from both structured environmental and non-structured textual data sources. One potential use case is tracking relevant news articles to relevant meteorological events, such as severe weather conditions. Retrieving relevant documents to given query keywords is a well-researched area, however matching them to environmental datasets is not.

- Reputation Propagation in Twitter

  - **Visiting Researcher:** Anastasia Giachanou, Università della Svizzera italiana, Lugano, Switzerland
  - **Host:** Julio Gonzalo, National University of Distance Education (UNED), Madrid, Spain

  This STSM focused on advancing research on reputation monitoring by addressing the problem of reputation propagation in Twitter. These are tweets that are relevant to an entity, contain opinion that can have an effect on the entity's reputation, and which will be retweeted. Work involved proposing & developing a method that uses a set of different features (sentiment, content, Twitter-specific) with the aim to address the problem of reputation propagation.

- Context Enrichment of User Recommendations

  - **Visiting Researcher:** Georgia Kapitsaki, University of Cyprus, Nicosia, Cyprus
  - **Host:** Dragan Ivanovic, University of Novi Sad, Novi Sad, Serbia

  The goals of this STSM are: (1) To investigate whether the user profile data be used to help in transformation of keyword based query to a structured query; (2) To create a relevant user meta-model for capturing required information in order to assist in the above and be applicable in different cases; and (3) To implement and evaluate tools for the acquisition of user information that can be used to build a user profile and enrich the search process.

- Clustering Similar Events Across Languages Using Simple Event Ontology Population

  - **Visiting Researcher:** Liubov Kovriguina, ITMO University, Saint-Petersburg, Russia
  - **Host:** Elena Demidova, University of Southampton, UK

This STSM focused on development of methods and algorithms enabling extraction and clustering of equivalent and related events in the news articles across languages. This task is challenging for: (1) There is a methodological problem of the event definition, with a variety of definitions proposed in the literature; (2) There is a question of which events should be considered as equivalent or related, and which kind of event relations are the most meaningful for a given application. Therefore, it is necessary to define formal criteria for the event notion and relatedness in the application context.

- Reinforcement of Keyword Based Search Over Urban Social Data Sources with Quantitative Data from Call Data Records for Point of interest Recommendation

  - **Visiting Researcher:** Alessandro Bozzon, Delft University of Technology, Delft, NL
  - **Host:** Marco Brambilla, Politecnico di Milano, 20133 Milano, Italy

This STSM focused on the extensions of keyword-based search over social network content integrated with data produced by mobile phone operators - so called call data records [CDR] - for point of interest recommendation purposes. The theme of the STSM lies within the road map of the KeyStone action, and is strongly linked to keyword search of structured datasets.

- Reinforcement of Keyword Based Search Over Social Network Content with Quantitative Data from Location-based IoT

  - **Visiting Researcher:** Marco Brambilla, Politecnico di Milano, 20133 Milano, Italy
  - **Host:** Alessandro Bozzon, Delft University of Technology, Netherlands

This STSM focused on the possible extensions of keyword-based search over social network content integrated with IoT sensors spread around in the physical world. Work involved the definition of a joint research vision and path, as well as an initial joint work on a small initial publication which will guide the subsequent joint research collaboration in the long term.

- A Novel Summarisation Approach from Embedded Markup on the Web

  - **Visiting Researcher:** Davide Taibi, National Research Council of Italy, Palermo, Italy
  - **Host:** Stefan Dietze, L3S - Research Center, Hannover, Germany

This STSM focused on investigating an approach for retrieving and analysing entity summaries from embedded markup, as well as the coverage and complementarity of retrieved facts, compared to existing knowledge graphs. This work falls in the framework of previous collaborations between the two research centres.

- Cross-lingual Extraction and Aligning of Keywords and Key-phrases from Monolingual and Multilingual Textual Resources

  - **Visiting Researcher:** Olivera Kitanovic, University of Belgrade, Belgrade, Serbia
  - **Host:** Sanda Martincic-Ipsic, University of Rijeka, Rijeka, Croatia

The aim of this STSM is the extraction of keywords and key-phrases from documents in Serbian and Croatian language, their use for query expansion in both languages and comparison of the obtained results. The idea for research is inspired by the KEYSTONE Conference paper under title "Network-Enabled Keyword Extraction for Under-Resourced Languages" [Slobodan Beliga et al.]. Extraction of the keywords will be based on the Selectivity-Based Keyword Extraction (SBKE) method.

- Interlingual Information Extraction in Temporal Web Collections

- **Visiting Researcher:** Elena Demidova, L3S Research Center, Hannover, Germany
- **Host:** Dmitry Mouromtsev, ITMO University, Saint-Petersburg, Russia

The goal of this STSM is to initiate a joint grant application between the L3S Research Centre and the ISST Laboratory in the area of multilingual Information Extraction for the joint funding program of the DFG (German Research Foundation) and Russian Foundation for Basic Research - RFBR.

- Search Optimization on Semantic Keyword-based Search Engine over Structured Data

- **Visiting Researcher:** Elton Domnori, Epoka University, Tirane, Albania
- **Host:** Carmen Elvira, University of Zaragoza, Zaragoza, Spain

Keymantic is a search engine over relational database that uses semantic analysis over the database schema to generate the response for the user. The system's input is a set of keywords and generates a ranked set of database queries to retrieve the data. A modified version of the Hungarian algorithm has been used in order to retrieve the top-k results. The algorithm used is not optimal and presents some side-effects such as generating the same response in different iterations. This STSM focused on overcoming this obstacle with the support of the experts in the field.

- Use of Semantic Technologies for Improvement of Sharing and Reusing Educational Resources and Data

- **Visiting Researcher:** Ranka Stankovic, University of Belgrade, Serbia
- **Host:** Stefan Dietze, L3S Research Center, Hannover, Germany

The focus of this STSM is the use of LRMI terms on the Web by assessing LRMI-based statements extracted from datasets, since the LRMI initiative has provided a set of vocabulary terms, now part of the schema.org vocabulary, to enable the markup of resources of educational value. Qualitative study of LRMI usage on the Web was done on a large dataset which is available for three different years in L3S.

- Analysing Wikidata Edits Over Time

- **Visiting Researcher:** Cristina Sarasua, University Koblenz-Landau, Koblenz, Germany
- **Host:** Gianluca Demartini, University of Sheffield, Sheffield, UK

The goal of this STSM is to analyse Wikidata edits in order to identify factors that influence the productivity of users, the quality of edits and the quality of items descriptions. The structured nature of the data makes it possible to study the exact pieces of information that humans work on, as well as the actions they perform on them.

- Investigation of Multi-Lingual Search Using LSA

  - **Visiting Researcher:** Colin Layfield, University of Malta, Msida, Malta
  - **Host:** Dragon Ivanovich, University of Nova Sad, Serbia

This STSM focused on the investigation of the suitability of Latent Semantic Analysis (LSA) applied towards a corpus of academic documents in more than one language for search/Information Retrieval purposes. It involved an investigation as to the suitability of the application of LSA with a semantic space comprised of multiple languages. The target languages is a minimum of two of the following: Serbian, Croatian, Montenegrin or Bosnian.

- Working With AIS Data

  - **Visiting Researcher:** Claudia Ifrim, Politehnica University Of Bucharest, Romania
  - **Host:** Manolis Wallace, University of the Peloponnese, Tripolis, Greece

This STSM focused on organizing future collaboration between the two collaborators on the theme "Working with AIS data" and meeting in person members of the Knowledge and Uncertainty Research Laboratory at University of the Peloponnese. The goal is to write a paper for the coming Keystone conference.

- Curating Data Analysis Workflows for Better Workflow Discovery

  - **Visiting Researcher:** Khalid Belhajjame, Université Paris Dauphine, Paris, France
  - **Host:** Luciano Gerber, Manchester Metropolitan University, UK

This STSM focused on examining problems that have to do with the curation of workflow-based data transformation and analyses with the objective to improve their search and ultimately reuse and reproducibility.

- Dynamic Optimisation of Keyword Searches in the Deep Web

  - **Visiting Researcher:** Martín Ugarte, Université Libre de Bruxelles, Bruxelles, Belgium
  - **Host:** Andrea Calí, Birkbeck University of London, UK

The objective of this STSM was to connect the fields of dynamic query evaluation and keyword queries in the Deep Web.

- Natural Language Processing Keyword Search for Related Languages

  - **Visiting Researcher:** Velislava Stoykova, Institute for Bulgarian Language, Sofia, Bulgaria
  - **Host:** Ranka Stankovic, University of Belgrade, Belgrade, Serbia

This STSM focused on the topic of "Natural Language Processing Keyword Search for Related Languages" is in the scope of the KEYSTONE Action and aimed to summarize the research experience of both University of Belgrade and Bulgarian Academy of

Science, Institute for Bulgarian Language in searching massive amount of lexical data to extract types of semantic relations by using keywords.

- Keyword Search Over People With Expertise

- **Visiting Researcher:** Yannis Velegrakis, University of Trento, Trento, Italy
- **Host:** Bogdan Cautis, University of Paris Sud, Orsay, France

This STSM focused on the study of the problem of expert finding under keyword queries, looking particularly at the problem identifying a set of persons from a database of persons that is no larger than k and their characteristics satisfy some generic properties as a whole. This kind of queries find many applications in real time scenarios where a group of people needs to get selected for a task.

- Keyword Search over the Web of Things

- **Visiting Researcher:** Omar Boucelma, AIX Marseille Universite, Marseille, France
- **Host:** Francesco Guerra, University of Modena and Reggio Emilia, Modena, Italy

The focus of this STSM was to explore a useful combination of keyword-based search mechanisms with a Semantic WoT framework in order to enable the development of intelligent applications such as recommendation of things of interest or advanced data analytics.

- Detecting Fake News: Web Data Analysis for Fact Verification

- **Visiting Researcher:** Konstantin Todorov, LIRMM, Montpellier, France
- **Host:** Stefan Dietze, L3S Research Centre, Hannover, Germany

This STSM focused on the dataset recommendation problem, by addressing a number of open issues, such as the elaboration of a reliable ground truth for the recommendation task, based on parts of the LOD by using crowdsourcing techniques, as well the consideration of the population of schema elements in the profile generation. The visit also helped the preparation of a proposal for a joint call of the French National Research Agency (ANR) and the German Research Foundation (DFG).

- Analysis and Study of Mobile Keyword-Based Search

- **Visiting Researcher:** Mohammad Nejadi, Università della Svizzera italiana, Lugano, Switzerland
- **Host:** Josiane Mothe, Toulouse Institute of Computer Science Research (IRIT), France

This STSM focused on designing a number of representative mobile search tasks to use in a simulated experimentation enabling us to study user behaviour under different circumstances for various tasks. The goal is to investigate how different relevance criteria contribute to the user's information seeking behaviours and satisfaction, and enable the design of a more effective keyword-based mobile search system with an adaptive method of combining different relevance criteria.

- Search As Learning: Experiments with Keyword-based Search in Large Scale Online Learning

  - **Visiting Researcher:** Leif Azzopardi, University of Glasgow, UK
  - **Host:** Claudia Hauff, Delft University of Technology, Delft, Netherlands

  DelftX delivers MOOCs to hundreds of thousands of students - a key challenge faced is to personalize the experience and ensure that students find relevant answers and information regarding the course material. Each MOOC provides lectures, notes, videos, Q&As, discussions, various data, and other related resources - yet the search functionality is limited. This STSM focused on implementing various keyword based approaches to improve student's access to information and help enhance their learning experience.

- Keyword Search on Big Data

  - **Visiting Researcher:** Nikolche Spasevski, St Kliment Ohridski University, Biota, Macedonia
  - **Host:** Ioannis Doxiadis, National and Kapodistrian University of Athens, Greece

  Keyword search over graph-like databases offers an alternative way to access and use semi-structured data that neither requires mastery of a query language, nor deep knowledge of the database's potentially quite complex schema. This STSM facilitated a discussion of the problems, challenges and opportunities for improving the exploration of graph-like databases. The focus was on building systems to resolve these two problems: keyword search in big graphs and team formation in social networks.

- Learning Effective Semantic Word Representation Models for IR

  - **Visiting Researcher:** Navid Rekabsaz, TU Wien, Vienna Austria
  - **Host:** Carsten Eickhoff, Swiss Federal Ins of Tech, Zurich, Switzerland

  This STSM is related to PhD of the applicant and focused on learning effective semantic word representation models as well as exploiting these models more effectively in information retrieval tasks. The visit focused on exploiting the possibilities provided by the neural network and deep learning methods. While learning semantic representations has been extensively studied in the NLP domain, this focus is on learning representations tailored for IR tasks.

- Parallel Multi-objective Optimization for Keyword Search

  - **Visiting Researcher:** Atanas Hristov, Univ. of Inform. Science & Techn., Ohrid, Macedonia
  - **Host:** Aleksandar Ribakj, University of Novi Sad, Novi Sad, Serbia

  This STSM focused on multiobjective optimization as applied for feature selection in text classification problems where the desired classification should simultaneously satisfy several, usually contradictory, criteria. The parallel multiobjective optimization algorithms to be considered by exploring the simultaneous execution of evolutionary algorithms using different subpopulations and analyzing the issues of granularity, communication, and strategies included in the algorithm to bind the space of solutions explored by each subpopulation/island to avoid overlapping of these searching.

References

1. COST: COST Action Networking Tools (2017). http://www.cost.eu/COST_Actions/networking. Accessed 26 Sept 2017
2. COST: Short-Term Missions, Long-Lasting Results (2017). http://www.cost.eu/media/cost_stories/Short-Term-Scientific-Missions. Accessed 26 Sept 2017
3. Keystone COST Action IC 1302, STSM Calls (2014). http://www.keystone-cost.eu/keystone/outreach/short-term-scientific-missions-stsms/stsm-call-2017/. Accessed 26 Sept 2017
4. Keystone COST Action IC 1302, Keystone Objectives (2014). http://www.keystone-cost.eu/keystone/home-page/objectives/. Accessed 26 Sept 2017

Author Index

Printed in the United States
By Bookmasters